Date Due

MAR 27 1996		
MAY 26 2009		

The Guarded Gate

THE GUARDED GATE

The Reality of
American Refugee Policy

**Norman L. Zucker and
Naomi Flink Zucker**

HARCOURT BRACE JOVANOVICH, PUBLISHERS

San Diego New York London

Requests for permission to make copies of any part of the work should be
mailed to:
Permissions, Harcourt Brace Jovanovich, Publishers, Orlando, Florida 32887.

Excerpt from *Call It Sleep* by Henry Roth, copyright © 1934, 1962 by Henry
Roth. Permission granted by Roslyn Targ Literary Agency, Inc., New York.

Excerpt from *In Search of Refuge* by Yvonne Dilling with Ingrid Rogers is
reprinted with permission, copyright © 1984 by Herald Press, Scottdale, PA
15683.

Library of Congress Cataloging-in-Publication Data
Zucker, Norman L.
  The guarded gate.
  Bibliography: p.
  Includes index.
    1. Refugees—Government policy—United States—History.
I. Zucker, Naomi Flink.   II. Title.
JV6601.R4Z83   1987   353.0081'7   87-8594
ISBN 0-15-137575-5

Designed by Francesca M. Smith

Printed in the United States of America

First edition

A B C D E

FOR THE MEMORY OF
Salomon J. Flink

Contents

Graph and Tables

Foreword

Refugees are one of the most serious problems of our time. Millions of people throughout the world are forced to move against their will. Some are uprooted as a result of deliberate government policy. Others are displaced by intolerable conditions of insecurity and poverty. Almost all of them are suffering severe hardships.

The United States has traditionally responded to the plight of refugees with a special rhetoric of welcome. America perceives itself as a nation of immigrants and refugees and as a country where those who flee persecution elsewhere can find safety and opportunity. In recent years, this self-image has been increasingly challenged by large flows of refugees and asylum seekers who have sought admission to the United States.

The Guarded Gate: The Reality of American Refugee Policy by Norman and Naomi Zucker focuses on whether or not this nation has been prepared to treat refugees fairly and generously and in accordance with its legal and humanitarian obligations. In a clear and articulate manner, the Zuckers have written a thought-provoking account of American refugee policy. *The Guarded Gate* is a book that should be read by all well-informed citizens, and the book's recommendations should be given serious consideration by our nation's decision makers.

As chairman of the former Select Commission on Immigration and Refugee Policy, I share the authors' concern for creating a U.S. refugee policy that is both pragmatic and fair. Seven years ago, Congress passed the Refugee Act of 1980. This law appeared to signal a fundamental shift in the nation's approach to refugees. The implementation of this law, however, has been badly flawed. *The Guarded Gate* details just how unjust and inequitable the application of the Refugee Act of 1980 has been. It considers the harmful ramifications of the government's narrow interpretation of U.S. laws that govern asylum; of long-term detention of asylum applicants; of interdicting Haitians on the high seas and returning them to their country; and of the arrest and forcible return to their countries of tens of thousands of desperate Central Americans seeking protection here.

The recommendations in this book to establish a just, impartial, and fair basis for determining refugee status and for choosing refugees for admission to the U.S. deserve careful attention. The recommendation to establish an independent refugee authority was first made by members of the research staff of the Select Commission, and it should be seriously reconsidered now. The Zuckers recommend the setting up of a Refugee Admission Priority Scale to help make our policy toward refugees more responsive to those refugees most in need of our assistance. The authors also suggest upgrading the importance of refugees in our national policy by enhancing the status and decision-making power of the U.S. Coordinator for Refugee Affairs.

How the United States responds to the world refugee problem is one of the crucial issues facing policy makers today. Public opinion polls demonstrate that the American people believe it important for the U.S. to abide by humanitarian standards that conform to the nation's image of itself. It is also essen-

tial that the U.S. exercise world leadership in the area of refugees because, through its actions, America has the ability
to bolster or to weaken the international system of refugee
protection.

Rev. Theodore Hesburgh, C.S.C.

Introduction:
Who Goes There?

Every refugee who journeys from the House of Bondage to the Promised Land must first cross a Red Sea, a border; he is never sure whether he will pass through on dry land or will drown.

Elie Wiesel has expressed the inexpressible essence of what it means to be a refugee, for whom a border divides not countries, but lifetimes. Remembering his own exodus, Wiesel writes, "If ever time was a metaphysical notion, that was it: when good and evil were separated by a man-made frontier. Any frontier is man-made, and yet, on one side people died, while on the other they went on living as though the others didn't die."[1]

The United States, protective of its own border, has yet recognized, both for humanitarian reasons and for reasons of self-interest, that we must take into our country numbers of refugees, must offer haven to some who do not live in freedom. We also permit entrance, and eventual citizenship, to larger numbers of people, people whose motives are no more complex than the wish to improve their lives. Still greater numbers, motivated by the same wish, are denied legal entrance and enter illegally.

Refugees, immigrants, illegal aliens. The people multiply. The words proliferate. Asylum seekers, special entrants, nonimmigrant visa abusers, parolees. The words separate as decisively as a political frontier, decide with as great finality, how, indeed whether, an individual will be permitted to re-create his life. When we distinguish between words, we distinguish between the forces that have shaped people's lives, and we make the decisions that will continue to shape their futures.

Refugees are neither immigrants nor illegal migrants, although, like immigrants, they have foresaken their homelands for new countries and, like illegal migrants, they may enter those new countries without permission. But a refugee is, in the end, unlike either. Both the immigrant and the illegal migrant are drawn to a country. The refugee is not drawn but driven; he seeks not to better his life but to rebuild it, to regain some part of what he has lost. The immigrant and the migrant are propelled by hope; for the refugee, whatever hope there may be must arise from the ruins of tragedy.

The refugee, unlike other migrants, has lost or been denied a basic human need—the legal and political protection of a government. Accompanying that loss has been the loss, as well, of culture, community, employment, shelter—all the elements that contribute to a sense of self-worth. Refugees, whatever their origins, are in need of protection.

The words matter. Whether one is called a refugee or a special entrant, an applicant for asylum or an illegal alien—in short, what status one is given by the receiving country—determines not only one's right to remain, but also a wide range of rights and entitlements, from the right to citizenship, through legal rights, to the rights to be employed and to receive federal assistance. The United States has many gates of entry. We can understand them best if we create a continuum of entry legitimacy. Schematically, the continuum would look like this:

Legal	Indeterminate Categories	Illegal
Immigrants and refugees	Asylum applicants, special entrants, extended voluntary departure groups	Visa abusers and illegal aliens

An immigrant enters the United States legally to take up permanent residence and, in time, to become a citizen. To be eligible for entry, an immigrant must fit within a preference system according to which he either has a close family relationship to an adult United States citizen or possesses employment skills needed in the United States. Although there are annual ceilings on the total number of immigrants admitted worldwide and the number from each country, parents, spouses, and children of adult American citizens are exempt from the ceilings.

Like an immigrant, a refugee enters the country legally, intending to remain permanently. Refugees are approved for entrance overseas and must fit within an annual numerical and regional ceiling. Unlike immigrants, refugees need no special job skills or even the capacity to be self-supporting. On the contrary, because of their traumatic circumstances, refugees are entitled to resettlement assistance and various time-limited benefits. Both immigrants and refugees, once in the country, have an assured status and the right to remain.

Those who fall into the indeterminate categories, on the other hand, have no such certainty. If it is determined that they are not eligible to remain in the United States, they are subject to deportation. Asylum seekers come directly to the United States and ask for protection from persecution. Unlike a refugee, who has already been approved for admission, an asylum seeker must plead for the right to remain.

The category of special entrant is an anomalous status that applies only to those Cubans and Haitians who arrived during a six-month period of 1980, during the Mariel boatlift. The special-entrant status is an ad hoc arrangement that confers the right to remain in the United States but does not lead to citizenship. The Justice Department, however, has found a loophole in Cuban refugee legislation that permits Cubans to acquire permanent residency, the first step to citizenship; only under the Immigration Reform and Control Act of 1986 will Haitians, along with other illegal aliens, be permitted to become permanent residents.

The last of the indeterminate categories is extended voluntary departure (EVD). This category includes members of particular national groups who are within the United States, but who have found that since their entry, conditions in their homelands have changed so as to make return unsafe. The Justice Department withholds deportation for given periods of time, until a group's return home is once again possible.

The demarcation between people holding EVD status and those who are nonimmigrant visa abusers is clearcut. Visa abusers enter the country on valid visas (for example, as tourists, students, or business people), but remain beyond the time they are permitted to stay. Once their visas expire, their sojourn on American soil becomes illegal, and they are subject to deportation.

The final category, illegal aliens—sometimes more charitably referred to as undocumented persons—enter the country illegally, either with fraudulent documents or by stealing across America's permeable borders.

The focus of this book will be on the refugees, the special entrants, those granted extended voluntary departure, and the applicants for asylum—those individuals who have been, or who assert that they will be, subject to persecution. We will not discuss, except peripherally, either those who enter as normal-flow immigrants or those undocumented persons who have not asked for the protection of asylum.

We shall ask many questions about America's policy toward these refugees, but they can all be expressed quite simply: Who gets in? Why? How are they resettled? Simple as these questions are, however, they are not serial questions, but circular. Knowing *why* refugees are admitted will inevitably reveal *who* will be admitted. For refugee policy does not in fact serve refugees; rather, it designates as refugees those who serve the policy.

It has generally been acknowledged that foreign policy is often a dominant factor in refugee decisions. While foreign policy may determine who is *eligible* for admission, however, a combination of two other factors determines who *is* admitted.

These two factors are the numbers of those pressuring for admission and the likelihood of low-cost and domestically unopposed resettlement. When a particular group of refugees serves our foreign policy goals, does not threaten to overwhelm us with its numbers, and can be resettled with little cost or domestic resistance, the members of that group are usually assured of admission. Conversely, members of a group that does not meet any of these criteria may be certain that admission will be denied.

Prior to the passage of the Refugee Act of 1980, the United States recognized as refugees only those who came from Communist countries or from the Middle East. The Refugee Act, by removing geographic and ideological limits from the law, intended to raise our refugee policy to the fairer and more universal standard expressed in the United Nations Protocol Relating to the Status of Refugees. In the end, however, our refugee policy has once more bowed to the demands of the least generous and bent to the shape of short-term policies.

Our responses to refugees have been characterized by conflicts in our basic attitudes. Polls show that most members of the public do not know the difference between immigrants and refugees, between refugees and illegal aliens. This confusion is compounded by the public's simultaneous feelings of hostility and humanitarianism. Many Americans feel hostile toward faceless newcomers—less so toward immigrants, more so toward refugees, insisting, when asked, that the United States admits too many foreigners, too many refugees. But when these same Americans are presented with a prototypical immigrant or refugee, most will say they favor his admission. Americans, thus, may be hostile to a foreign group, but accepting of the individual stranger. We fear the hordes, while we welcome the family.[2] Perhaps groups and classes of people unleash floodgate fears—worries about being inundated by large numbers of foreigners—while individuals do not evoke this same fear.

When Americans, in 1979, were asked whether they believed

Introduction: Who Goes There?

Indochinese boat people should be permitted to come to the United States, fewer than one third thought they should. Yet more than half, even among those who opposed the admission of the Indochinese, responded that if they did come, the refugees would be welcomed into American communities.[3] A poll taken just before the celebration of the centennial of the Statue of Liberty revealed that forty-nine percent of all adult Americans want immigration decreased. But, reaffirming earlier findings, even opponents of immigration, paradoxically, would welcome immigrants to their neighborhoods.[4]

The United States is a signatory to the Helsinki Accords, which guarantee free movement by citizens of all countries. Yet, even as we chastize the Soviets and other Communist countries for not permitting free emigration, the United States, under an agreement made with a repressive and now deposed dictator, interdicts Haitian nationals who attempt to escape their country and returns them to it. We urge Southeast Asian countries to grant temporary asylum to refugees from Indochina, yet refuse to grant temporary asylum in our country to Central Americans.

We insist that ours is a system of law based in fairness, but the United States Commission on Civil Rights has accused the Immigration and Naturalization Service and the Justice Department of discrimination that deprives aliens and citizens of their legal rights, while federal courts find the government guilty of denying the due process rights of asylum seekers.[5] We criticize the imprisonment policies of other nations, but here in the United States we strip search young girls, incarcerate children to bring their undocumented parents out of hiding, and detain asylum applicants in jails for indefinite periods until federal courts order their release. These problems and paradoxes are inherent in American immigration and refugee policy because we are, as a nation, genuinely ambivalent about receiving newcomers.

It is a further paradox that many of the refugees whom we have resettled and many more whom we have refused safe haven became refugees as a consequence of American foreign policies. American involvement in Indochina made us feel responsible for the Indochinese refugees, many of whom were received into our country. United States policy toward Castro led us first to welcome all Cuban émigrés who left the island, a welcome that suddenly chilled when Castro himself decided to encourage the migration. For nearly three decades, we generously assisted a repressive Duvalier dynasty in Haiti, generating tens of thousands of escapees who clamored for an asylum that was not forthcoming.

Along with our foreign policy, our domestic history has shaped our current policies and practices toward refugees. Chapter 1, "In Search of Entry," traces aspects of immigration history, with its competing wills to welcome and to exclude.

When the United States passed the Refugee Act of 1980, it appeared that the will to welcome had prevailed, that this country was at last affirming in law our obligation to the refugees of the world. But Chapter 2, "The Guarded Gate," shows that the law has, in the years since its passage, given way to the restrictive demands of foreign and domestic policies.

In two major areas, however, the Refugee Act broke new ground. The act established the principle that refugees are to be assisted in making the transition to citizenship in an alien community. Chapter 3, "The Stranger within the Gate," discusses the development of federal resettlement strategies, the resettlement system, and the burdens and benefits refugees create as they become new Americans.

In a second area, the Refugee Act established in law the principle of asylum, that an alien who fears persecution in his own country is entitled to ask for temporary protection from return. Chapter 4, "Breaching the Gate," shows that, although embodied in law, the principle of asylum is being debased in practice. The following chapter, "The Rejected," discusses how asylum seekers have sought redress in the courts for the abuses and illegalities of asylum practice.

Comprehensive as the Refugee Act was, however, it looked at refugees and refugee movements in the limited terms of the past: at refugees as individuals singled out for persecution, at refugee movements as episodic and aberrational. But the world is witnessing a new kind of refugee—a refugee not protected by the present law—one who is driven from his country by social injustice, or by civil war, as well as by political oppression. Chapters 6 and 7 discuss the the newest refugees, the unprotected, and two different responses to the problems they present: the temporary safe haven being proposed in Congress, and the extralegal sanctuary being offered by American churches.

To analyze what has been and what is our policy toward refugees, or even to project what that policy should be, however, is not enough. If refugee policy is to respect the larger principles on which the Refugee Act was based, we must find a way to translate those principles into workable practices, practices that are at once just, fair, and functional. The concluding chapter will make a number of proposals that would change the ways in which we select, protect, and resettle refugees.

The Guarded Gate

And before them, rising on her high pedestal from the scaling swarmy brilliance of sunlit water to the west, Liberty. The spinning disk of the late afternoon sun slanted behind her, and to those on board who gazed, her features were charred with shadow, her depths exhausted, her masses ironed to one single plane. Against the luminous sky the rays of her halo were spikes of darkness roweling the air; shadow flattened the torch she bore to a black cross against flawless light—the blackened hilt of a broken sword. Liberty. The child and his mother stared at the massive figure in wonder.

CALL IT SLEEP
Henry Roth

1 In Search of Entry: The Refugee in American History

American immigration and refugee history has been a variegated scene. Time and history arrange the pattern of arrivals. English, Irish, Germans, Scandinavians, Italians, Slavs, Greeks, Jews, and now Asians and Hispanics. Every schoolchild knows, almost mythically, of the Statue of Liberty on Liberty Island in New York Harbor. Liberty, with upraised arm holding high the torch of freedom, stands in enduring welcome at the gateway to America, a gateway that is always open, and open to all. But few schoolchildren know of the wooden structure on Angel Island in San Francisco Bay—a two-story, nondescript building where Chinese were detained—that represents rejection. For over a century, America has had a guarded gate, a gate always closed to some, a gate opened selectively to others. In American refugee history, myth and reality, welcome and rejection merge.

Why the gate was, and is, open to some and closed to others is a blend of many elements: presidential and congressional personalities and policies, judicial decisions, bureaucratic agendas, prejudices and conventional wisdom, pressure from groups and public opinion, the health of the economy and the happenstance of history. Together these elements are like the bits of colored glass in a kaleidoscope. Shaken at one time, they form a particular immigration and refugee policy. Shaken at another time, they take shape as another immigration and refugee policy.

The distinction between an immigrant and a refugee was unknown to immigration law until after World War II, and America did not have a comprehensive refugee law until the passage of the Refugee Act of 1980. From the end of World War II to 1980, well over one million refugees were admitted to America's shores. Yet their admission was always under special legislation or through the strained interpretation of the parole authority of the attorney general. Both mechanisms to admit refugees were extraordinary measures, and both required exceptions to the numerical limits of established immigration law and policy.

Refugee admissions in the immediate postwar period were brokered through a Congress as indifferent as the rest of the world to the special needs of refugees. Guilt or humanitarianism could make only small incursions into a solidly established immigration system. The Statue of Liberty mythologized America as a society welcoming immigrants and refugees, but historical reality reminds us that even before Liberty's dedication, Congress had enacted legislation excluding Chinese.

Immigration and refugee policies have been, and probably will remain, entangled in the political thicket. At stake are competing values and conflicting interests. Two sets of antithetical values and interests—admission and restriction—have tried to define immigration policy. On one side is the will to admit newcomers. On the other side is the will to restrict foreigners.

American immigration policy has been dominated not by the will to admit, but by the will to restrict immigration. Who the newcomer is and where he comes from are significant. Race and ethnicity influence demography, and demography shapes the body politic. Resistance to the admission of newcomers arises not only from those who fear change and from such easily discredited sources as the xenophobic and the racist, but from those who support such legitimate causes as labor unions, population control, and environmentalism.

Restrictionism has roots deep in American history. Representative Harrison G. Otis of Massachusetts implored his colleagues to shut the gate on immigration, saying, "When the country was new, it might have been good policy to admit foreigners. But it is so no longer."[1] Otis made his remarks in 1797, when the United States had a population of around four million. Otis's restrictionist logic, however, did not prevail for nearly a century.

Meanwhile, waves of newcomers flooded into American ports. They crossed the Atlantic, pulled by prospects of a better life and pushed by poverty, religious intolerance, demeaning class distinctions, and political upheavals. America, expanding across the continent, needed settlers and laborers. The first wave of mass immigration brought the Irish and the Germans, and in its wake, nativism. The number of immigrants was not disturbing; what was disturbing to those already established here was the increasing proportion of Roman Catholic immigrants. From 1830 to 1840, about one-third of all immigrants were Catholics; during the next decade almost one-half were Catholic. Virulent anti-Catholicism rose with the rising tide of Roman Catholics, finding political expression in the Native American Party and the Know Nothing movement.[2] Like the Irish, the Germans found hostility. The German Forty-Eighters, the refugees from revolution, with their unorthodox political ideas and hostility to slavery, triggered another form of xenophobia—one that feared the threat posed by immigrant radicals to American institutions.

Just as restrictionism has prevailed in the national ethos, so too has it prevailed in immigration legislation. In general, such legislation has pursued one of three strategies: curtailment of immigration, as with the exclusion of specific groups or proposals to suspend all immigration; barriers to immigration, such as the institution of a literacy test or a test of economic self-sufficiency; and finally, the strict regulation of the numbers and types of immigrants permitted entry, as through quotas or provisions for deportation.

The Immigration Act of 1875 marked the beginning of federal
regulation of immigration. Under the act, prostitutes and con-
victs were designated as excludable classes of aliens and banned
from entry. From the reasonable exclusion of undesirables,
however, the step was short to the exclusion of a particular
ethnic group. In 1882, Congress passed the Chinese Exclusion
Act. No more could Chinese seek their fortunes on the Golden
Mountain. The gates were sealed to Chinese until 1943, when,
in a gesture of good will toward our wartime ally, the exclusionary statute was repealed, only to be invidiously replaced
by a quota—105 Chinese each year would be permitted entry—
a quota that remained in effect until the major immigration law
reforms of 1965.[3]

During the 1880s, the ethnic composition of immigration
changed. The Irish, Germans, and Scandinavians no longer pre-
dominated. The "new" mass immigration now came primarily
from southern and eastern Europe—Italians, Slavs (Russians,
Ukranians, Slovaks, Poles, Croatians, Serbs), Magyars, Greeks,
and Jews flooded America's shores. (Fortunately for the entering Jews, who were fleeing poverty, systemic political repression, and bloody pogroms, admission regulations at that time
made no complicating distinctions between economic migrants
and refugees.)

This second wave of new foreigners once again aroused the
nativists. The Immigration Restriction League, organized in 1894
by Boston bluebloods, launched a campaign to alert the country
to the social and economic dangers posed by the arriving hordes.
The restrictionists believed that one way to reduce the influx
was to require a literacy test. Such a test would not seriously
interfere with the older immigration, but would halve the numbers from southern and eastern Europe. A literacy bill sponsored
by the League passed Congress, but was vetoed by President
Grover Cleveland.

But restrictionism, with its demand for a literacy test, lost
ground as the Spanish-American War dissipated the fin-

de-siècle depression, encouraged industry, and spurred a need for unskilled immigrant labor. The conservative Chamber of Commerce and the National Association of Manufacturers now lobbied against restriction. But when President McKinley was shot by Leon Czolgosz, an American-born anarchist with a strange foreign name, antiradical nativism once again rose up.

McKinley's assassination forced his successor, Theodore Roosevelt, to take action against the foreign invasion. Roosevelt demanded comprehensive legislation to bar "all persons who are anarchists . . . of low moral tendency or of unsavory reputation," as well as all "who are below a certain standard of economic fitness to enter our industrial field as competitors with American labor."[4] Roosevelt also called for a barrier to entry— an educational test. Congress responded with the passage of the Immigration Act of 1903. The act deemed anarchists, beggars, and white slavers inadmissable, but failed to impose a literacy test.

Four years later, in 1907, Congress appointed a joint Senate-House commission to investigate what it now viewed as a serious immigration problem: southern and eastern immigrants outnumbered northern Europeans by four to one. The new commission took the name of its chairman, Senator William Paul Dillingham of Vermont. In 1911, the Dillingham Commission issued a forty-two-volume report which was the first comprehensive study of American immigration. The report, which mirrored the beliefs and prejudices of its time, would serve as the rationale for the rigidly restrictive national-origins quota laws of the 1920s.

The Dillingham Commission had imbibed an amalgam of the "scientific" ideas then current, among them a theory of "eugenics," which endorsed the superiority of the Anglo-Saxon. The commission regarded immigrants from northern and western Europe as more desirable; it believed southern and eastern European immigrants to be prone to commit crimes, willing to accept a lower standard of living, less skilled, and more ignorant. The commission, concluding that immigration restriction was "demanded by economic, moral, and social considerations," advocated a literacy test and suggested that immigrant numbers be based on a percentage of each nationality group already in the country.[5]

The first fruit of the Dillingham Commission and the first twentieth-century victory for the restrictionists was the Immigration Law of 1917—a law which moved from regulation to restriction and proclaimed a white-America policy. Passed over President Wilson's veto, on the eve of America's entry into World War I, the 1917 act contained four key provisions: literacy, Asiatic exclusion, alien deportation, and an expanded list of excludables.

Presidents and congresses had battled over the literacy or educational test during the prewar decades. Since the closing of the frontier, successive congresses had voted for the literacy test. But vetoes by Presidents Cleveland, Taft, and Wilson in 1915, had defeated it. When the literacy test finally became law in 1917, it contained two important exemptions: the immediate family members of an admissable alien and persons who could prove they were fleeing from religious persecution. (Refugees from political persecution, significantly, did not receive an exception.) When immigration revived after the First World War, the literacy requirement (one had to be able to read thirty to forty words in some language) was as a barrier more symbolic than real.

A stronger barrier was the exclusion of Asians. Practically all Asian peoples, with the exception of the Chinese and Japanese, came from the geographical area designated as an "Asiatic barred zone." The Chinese had already been excluded, while the Japanese, under a gentlemen's agreement President Theodore Roosevelt made with Japan in 1907, also could not enter.

The act provided that aliens who preached revolution or sabotage could be deported at any time after entry; this signaled an important change. Deportation in the nineteenth and early twentieth centuries was a bureaucratic procedure designed to buttress existing immigration laws. It was used to return recently admitted aliens who, having specific excludable qualities, should have been denied admission at the port of entry. But during the war period, deportation, a purely administrative device, emerged as a potent weapon in support of public policy and in the arsenal of the "one-hundred-percent Americanists" who demanded social and cultural conformity. Through the threat and the actual use of deportation, the nation could purge itself of newcomers with divided loyalties. "We are going," said the chairman of the Iowa Council of Defense, "to love every foreigner who really becomes an American, and all others we are going to ship back home."[6] The law permitted the Labor Department to deport aliens, but only if they advocated subversion; membership in a subversive organization was not a sufficient basis for deportation. The bill was but the first step in what the distinguished historian John Higham has called "a trend, extending down to the 1950s, which progressively curtailed the civil liberties of aliens."[7] A trend, it should be noted, that has been revived in the 1980s.

The First World War had temporarily curtailed immigration, while it fueled patriotism and conformity. The 1920s were characterized by conservatism, racial and ethnic prejudice, isolationism, and xenophobia. Restrictionism again prevailed. A doctrine of racial superiority was given credence by Madison Grant, a patrician Manhattan socialite and founder of the New York Zoological Society, whose *The Passing of the Great Race*, published in 1916, warned of the debasement of the Nordic race. Grant's ideas were taken up after World War I by a bevy of prominent scientists. Carl Brigham, a Princeton psychologist, on the basis of a study of army wartime mental tests, concluded that Alpine and Mediterranean people were inferior to Nordics in native intelligence. Brigham warned that "American intelligence is declining, and will proceed with an accelerating rate as the racial mixture becomes more and more extensive." Harvard's William MacDougall asserted that Nordics possessed a self-assertiveness that enabled them to dominate in history. And Harry H. Laughlin, the biologist and eugenicist who was the expert for the House Immigration Committee, concluded that "the recent immigrants, on the whole, present a higher percentage of inborn socially inadequate qualities than do the older stocks."[8] "Scientific racism" was an important influence on the national-origins laws that would govern immigration to the United States for more than forty years.

The Russian Revolution added to the fear of things foreign and radical. Domestic bomb scares compounded the fear. Extremists sent through the mails several bombs which reached their destination and exploded with devastating effects. But the most sensational outrage was the 1920 explosion outside the offices of J. P. Morgan and Company on Wall Street, in which thirty-eight people were killed. Attorney General A. Mitchell Palmer began rounding up aliens and deporting them. In Indiana, a naturalized citizen was acquitted of having killed an alien who had shouted, "To hell with the United States."[9] The Ku Klux Klan—anti-black, anti-Semitic, anti-Catholic, and anti-immigrant—flourished. Labor leaders, whose unions were losing members, feared cheap labor. Immigration historians Leonard Dinnerstein and David M. Reimers have written, "Given the intense nativism of the 1920s, the issue was not *whether* there would be immigration restriction but *what form* it would take."[10]

To the dismay of the restrictionists, the literacy requirement was not as high a barrier as had been expected. It is estimated that between 1918 and 1921, 1,487,000 entered the United States, but only 6,142 persons were rejected for failure to pass the literacy test.[11] Southern- and eastern-European immigration continued. Literacy had improved in Europe; Italy, one of the leading senders of immigrants, had even established schools in areas of high emigration to prepare peasants for the literacy test.[12] Something stronger than qualitative restriction was needed.

The idea of suspending all immigration—an idea never seriously considered at any time previously in American history—began to gain currency.

The time was ripe for such an idea. While a postwar depression descended, immigration was rising. By September 1920, an average of five thousand immigrants daily were pouring into Ellis Island.[13] Support for the suspension of immigration came from organized labor and the one hundred percenters. Labor wanted to reduce the competition for jobs that would occur if there were an ever larger pool of immigrant workers. The one hundred percenters were terrified that American culture and institutions would be contaminated by "bestial hordes" and the Bolshevik menace. Between 1919 and 1921, a variety of bills were introduced that called for suspension of immigration. One bill would have suspended immigration for three years, one for four years, and one for five years. The most extreme bill proposed to prohibit immigration from Germany, Austria-Hungary, Bulgaria, Turkey, and their possessions for fifty years; immigration from other countries was to be prohibited for twenty years.[14] In such a climate, the House of Representatives easily passed a bill that would suspend immigration for two years.

After the Senate Committee on Immigration conducted extensive hearings on the House measure, Senator Dillingham offered a substitute bill which restricted immigration to three percent of the foreign-born population, as determined by the 1910 census. With a single day's discussion, the Senate passed its bill. The House, in conference, acceded to the Senate's wishes and passed the modified bill. The bill then went to President Wilson. But he, in his final days in office, killed it with a pocket veto.[15]

The restrictive immigration bill, however, was not dead. In the new Republican-controlled Congress, a House bill virtually identical to the one Wilson vetoed was speedily passed without a roll call. The Senate report on the bill approvingly quoted the House Committee:

There is a limit to our power of assimilation. A speaking and reading knowledge of English is the key to assimilation. The process of assimilation and amalgamation are [sic] slow and difficult. With the populations of the broken parts of Europe headed this way in ever-increasing numbers why not preemptorily check the stream with this temporary measure, and in the meantime try the unique and novel experiment of enforcing all of the immigration laws on our statutes?[16]

In the Senate, the vote was an extraordinary seventy-eight to one. Wilson's successor, Warren G. Harding, a mediocrity who well personified the Babbittry of the twenties and who had vowed to return America to "normalcy," signed the law. "Normalcy" was to include, by legislative fiat, the restriction of European immigration.

The Quota Act of 1921, also known as the Johnson Act, was the country's first general immigration restriction act; national origins quotas were now law. The act established an immigration ceiling of 355,000 European immigrants yearly: fifty-five percent from northwestern Europe and forty-five percent from southeastern. It established quotas for European countries, the Near East, Africa, Australia, and New Zealand, but significantly, no limits on immigration from Western Hemisphere countries. This was, in part, for diplomatic reasons, but also in response to pressure from southern and western agricultural lobbies that wanted the flow of cheap farm labor from Mexico to continue.[17] Pressure for some form of cheap migratory labor continues to plague the framers of present-day immigration legislation.

Adopted as a temporary measure until permanent policy could be worked out, the 1921 Quota law was a watershed in American immigration policy. The myth of welcome was being replaced by the reality of rejection. George Washington's exhortation that the United States should ever be "an asylum to the oppressed and needy of the earth" was forgotten. Not Emma Lazarus's "huddled masses yearning to breathe free," but Thomas

Bailey Aldrich's "wild motley throng" were pressing for entrance. The rhetoric of welcome had been replaced by the rhetoric of fear. Out of the nativism that led to the passage of the 1921 act, and in the debates preceding the final enactment of restrictionism in 1924, two major themes emerged: fear of opening the floodgates and fear of a threat to the existing social order. Foreshadowing the present-day conviction that the United States is being engulfed by illegal entrants was the conviction in the twenties that the floodgates would be opened and America would be awash in foreigners. In a widely read series of articles in the popular *Saturday Evening Post*, Kenneth Roberts ominously told of masses of Europeans wanting to emigrate. Only the limited space on transatlantic ships could control their numbers. Consular reports, particularly from southeastern Europe, lent support to this fear. The European hordes were threatening the social order, bringing into the country anarchists, bolsheviks, and criminals. The case of Sacco and Vanzetti darkened the formulation of immigration policy. The melting pot was a failure; foreigners were changing America. The European inundation had produced "alien indigestion."[18] (Immigration and refugee polemics seem to produce colorful images; compare the phrase *alien indigestion* with the phrase *compassion fatigue* used in contemporary debates on the admission of refugees.)

Congress extended the life of the Quota Act in May of 1922 for two years, while it fine-tuned a permanent law. In summing up the case for a tighter law, Representative Albert Johnson, who had led the fight to restrict immigration, proclaimed that the American people

have seen, patent and plain, the encroachments of the foreign-born flood upon their own lives. They have come to realize that such a flood, affecting as it does every individual of whatever race or origin, cannot fail likewise to affect the institutions which have made and preserved American liberties. It is no wonder, therefore, that the myth of the melting pot has been discredited. It is no wonder that Americans everywhere are insisting that their land no longer shall offer free and unrestricted asylum to the rest of the world. . . .

The United States is our land. If it was not the land of our fathers, at least it may be, and it should be, the land of our children. We intend to maintain it so. The day of unalloyed welcome to all peoples, the day of indiscriminate acceptance of all races, has definitely ended.[19]

A small minority of antirestrictionists, most of them from metropolitan districts that had large numbers of foreign-born, challenged Johnson's position in the House. They argued that the bill, by establishing a distinction between the peoples of Europe, would breed disunity; Congress was creating arbitrary divisions in the American population. But restrictionist arguments prevailed in Congress, and President Coolidge signed the Johnson-Reed bill which became the Immigration Act of 1924. In the crude words of Kansas Congressman J. M. Tincher, the gate had been shut against "Bolshevik Wops, Dagoes, Kikes, and Hunkies."[20]

The 1924 act was more draconian than all previous legislation. It retained the literacy test and the list of exclusions. It reduced the annual admissable total to 164,667, and it set the annual quota for each nation at two percent of that nationality as determined by the 1890 census. The 1890 census was chosen as the base year because at that time few southern and eastern Europeans had come to America. This scheme, however, was replaced in 1927 by a national-origins plan, under which quotas were to be computed by a special executive board composed of the secretaries of State, Commerce, and Labor. The board would use the 1920 census, with its broader calculation of the white population, as the basis for national origins. But when the national-origins clause went into effect in 1929, the annual admissions were further reduced to 153,714. As before, Canada and Latin America were exempt from the quota system. The law also established a tentative overseas screening procedure that required the intending migrant to secure a special immigration visa from an American consul abroad. The consuls were to issue immigration visas based on the established exclusion tests and the annual quotas.

A clause of the law that barred all aliens who would be ineligible for citizenship reaffirmed the exclusion of Orientals. Since the Supreme Court had ruled recently that Japanese could not be naturalized, the intent of the clause was obvious. Japan took umbrage and there were diplomatic difficulties. The Japanese, who had scrupulously adhered to the gentlemen's agreement of 1907, would have been willing to accept restriction under a treaty, but the language of the act was an affront to national pride. Both houses of the Japanese Diet passed resolutions protesting the discrimination, and the Japanese government proclaimed a day of national humiliation. President Coolidge and the State Department were concerned about the implications of Congress's actions, but an isolationist Congress remained heedless of the link between foreign and immigration policy. In a *Foreign Affairs* article, "Our New Immigration Policy," Robert Ward, commenting on the 1924 act, wrote, "This law settles it once and for all that immigration is a domestic matter which Congress proposes absolutely to control."[21] History has proven him wrong.

The nativists had won. Senator David A. Reed, one of the act's sponsors, called the 1924 enactment "the second Declaration of Independence."[22] America henceforth was to be for Americans. Isolationism prevailed; Wilsonian idealism was repudiated. Conservatism dominated. America wanted restricted immigration. Immigration would remain restricted even in the next decade for Europe's refugees.

While America was wrestling with the issue of immigration and how to restrict it, Europe was struggling with the problem of refugees and how to accommodate them.

The Soviet Revolution in 1917 and subsequent counterrevolutionary attempts created over a million and a half refugees. Scattered throughout Europe and the Far East, the émigrés found themselves penniless and stateless. Initially, the Red Cross and other private charitable organizations and individual host governments provided relief. But these efforts were short-term. The refugees, unable or unwilling to return home, had to resettle. There were, however, numerous legal obstacles to re-settlement. Most of the refugees had no identity papers; those who did had papers issued by the overthrown Tsarist govern-ment. The refugees found themselves trapped. Without valid passports, they could not be admitted to other countries. In addition, most of the refugees were without sufficient funds, and no country was eager to accept persons with a double disability.[23]

In Turkey and Asia Minor, the Russians were living in camps. Their treatment differed according to the locality. Most of the countries had given the refugees temporary residency papers. Some countries had given them the legal right to work. But in most cases, when the residency permit expired, the refugee was forced to depart and forbidden to return. If he returned and was caught, he could be imprisoned. Legally, refugees were on the same ground as immigrants.

By 1921 the refugee problem was onerous. In February of that year, the International Committee of the Red Cross re-quested that the Council of the League of Nations appoint a high commissioner who would define the status of refugees and coordinate the various assistance measures. Fridtjof Nansen of Norway became the first high commissioner.

Nansen was a fortunate choice. Universally respected as a polar explorer, he had enhanced his reputation in the postwar years in the complicated negotiations between the Central Pow-ers and Russia over the repatriation of prisoners. Nansen's ap-proach to solving the Russian refugee problem was simple: "Repatriation if possible, resettlement in countries of refuge or other areas, if necessary."[24] Nansen knew that without some form of legitimizing document, a stateless person would have difficulty obtaining work, receiving social benefits, and obtaining a residency permit. Identification was even more important to those trying to move between countries. Nansen devised a certificate of identity for refugees and asked the League to finance the provision of such documents. The League and the international community turned Nansen down, but finally Great Britain gave £420,000 to finance issuance of the certificates. The Nansen certificate, known as the "Nansen passport," won approval by the League Council. Issuance of the passport, however, was the responsibility of each country.

The Nansen passport was a poor substitute for a nation's own passport. The issuing country reserved the right to deny return to that country. The passport's validity was for one year only; and renewal was at the discretion of the issuing country. The passport, nonetheless, improved the position of the stateless Russians: the passport holder now had the protection of the high commissioner's office.

While Nansen was trying to solve the Russian problem, a new group of refugees arose, Armenians fleeing Turkish persecution. Beginning in 1924, the Armenians were made eligible for Nansen passports. But Nansen had difficulties in resettling the Armenians. League members were unwilling to fund resettlement in the new Armenian Soviet Republic. And a scheme to resettle Armenians in Latin America had to be abandoned because the Latin American countries, in a foreshadowing of their policies in the next decade, were unwilling to relax their stringent immigration restrictions. Nansen worked tirelessly to regularize refugee identity certificates, and in 1926 the League Council adopted a definition of refugee that was limited to Russians and Armenians.[25] In May 1930, Nansen died, and with him died his hope that refugee work would become a permanent function of the League's Secretariat.

In 1931 the League established a Nansen Office, which immediately faced a deteriorating refugee situation. In a worsening world depression, with increasing unemployment, countries were unwilling to extend Nansen passports and ordered refugees to leave their temporary host countries; for the same reasons, other countries were unwilling to receive refugees. It became common practice to return refugees to their country of origin. Thousands of refugees languished in prisons for having violated border laws. To try to ameliorate this situation, in 1933, the Nansen Office called an international convention on the status of refugees, but the practical results were negligible.[26]

The 1930s were a bleak decade, a decade of depression and flight. The refugee problem was worsening. The newly created nation of Iraq was slaughtering its Assyrian population. Jews and others began to flee from Nazi persecution. In Spain, the Civil War forced refugees over the borders. As the League's prestige diminished, the refugee crisis intensified.

As the 1930s began, Herbert Hoover was president of the United States. Although opposed to the national-origins quotas as a mechanical basis for restriction, Hoover was, in his own words, "strongly in favor of restricted and selected immigration."[27]

Even before Hoover proclaimed the 1929 national-origins quotas, restriction by administrative device was being used to close off immigration from Mexico. The State Department had sent special instructions to its consuls in Mexico to tighten the standards for admission. Traditionally, the two principal bases for refusing a visa had been failure to pass a literacy test and violation of the contract-labor provision. Now a third basis came into use. The 1917 law had denied admission to anyone who was "likely to become a public charge," a vague phrase that left much to the consuls' discretion. Each applicant was asked about his finances; if he replied that he had a job waiting for him in the United States, he was denied a visa on the basis of having violated the contract-labor provision. On the other hand, if the applicant answered that he had no job in prospect, he could be rejected as likely to become a public charge.

As the Depression deepened, restrictionist voices in Congress rose. Some called for a sharp reduction in the immigration quotas. Others urged that immigration be totally suspended until the economic crisis abated. Hoover, uncertain what steps Congress would take, ordered the State Department to curb immigration worldwide by rigidly enforcing the "likely to become a public charge" (LPC) provision.[28] The intending immigrant had to be sufficiently affluent to be able to support himself without a job, or failing that, had to produce affidavits declaring that friends or relatives would provide for him if he could not find work. (European immigrants had learned to avoid the job/no job trap by replying that they intended to look for work.) The use of the LPC clause caused worldwide immigration to drop so significantly that the State Department issued a press release announcing the success of its program. Restriction by administrative regulation had proven effective.[29]

The Hoover administration had intended to use the LPC device as a stopgap until Congress passed new legislation that would reduce the quotas. But in the 1930 congressional elections, Democrats captured the House of Representatives. With the change in party came an important change in the chairmanship of the House Immigration Committee. Samuel Dickstein of New York, an antirestrictionist, was now chairman. From his strategic position, Dickstein succeeded in keeping quota-reduction bills from reaching the floor of the House. The administration's strict interpretation of the LPC clause, however, remained in effect throughout the Hoover years.

In March of 1933, Franklin Delano Roosevelt was inaugurated as president of the United States and Adolph Hitler assumed dictatorial powers in Germany. Joined in time, but separated by an ocean and a continent, these events touched each other. With Hitler's formal ascension to total power came a flood of Jewish and antifascist refugees from Germany. As Germany forced out her own citizens, the *Anschluss* (the incorporation of Austria into Germany), the annexation of the Sudetenland, the occupation of Czechoslovakia, and the invasion of Poland and the start of World War II swelled the refugee stream.

Even after the war had begun, it was still possible for refugees to emigrate from Europe. Indeed, the Hitler regime, anxious to be *Judenrein*, encouraged the emigration of German Jews through the summer of 1941. (The Jews were transported in sealed railroad cars from Berlin to neutral Lisbon and asylum. Later Jews, who could not get passage on those trains to the west, went east in cattle cars to their final destination and death.)

The transnational mass movement of refugees forced the nations of the world to respond. America responded to the refugee crisis, as did most other countries, by creating barriers to entrance. Shanghai's International Settlement was the only place open to refugees "where there were no restrictions on immigration, where no visas, affidavits, or other guarantees were required." Some twenty thousand who fled there survived the war.[30]

America would not be invaded by European refugees. Humanitarian considerations were irrelevant. No distinction was to be made between immigrants seeking opportunity and refugees fleeing persecution. Only much later would that distinction be codified in the immigration laws. The face of restriction in the 1930s sat solidly on a body of time-honored economic argument and unyielding prejudices.

When there was an abundance of jobs and a need for labor, immigrants were welcome. When there was a scarcity of jobs and little need for additional labor, immigrants—and refugees were simply thought of as immigrants—were unwelcome. (The counterthesis that immigrants and refugees are consumers who create jobs and wealth and pay taxes was not, and still is not, part of the conventional wisdom.)[31] America, staggering and bewildered by massive unemployment and social and economic breakdown, was in no mood to accept newcomers.

Economic arguments were reinforced by one-hundred-percent Americanism. Nativism, which had recently triumphed in the quota legislation, remained a vigorous force throughout the Depression and the war years, and was buttressed by anti-Semitism. Many of the refugees were Jews, and anti-Semitism became a major factor in opposing refugees.[32]

Cherished restrictionist principles, enacted into national policy after hard years of politicking, now confronted new and different pressures. Unlike the previous newcomers, those fleeing Europe were not peasants tired of eking out a marginal existence, but skilled and educated urbanites. Prior to the Nazi seizure of power they had been economically secure and comfortably settled in their homes. They had not planned to leave, but had been forced to flee. They were, in short, not migrants, but refugees.

Nonetheless, the restrictionists rallied to their principles. Despite the stark differences between the old immigrants and the new refugees, those who clamored for admission remained hordes. Even refugee admissionists, attuned to the temper of the times, argued not for the abandonment of restrictionist rules, but for an emergency modification of their application. In the public and private corridors of power, the restrictionist stand-patters and the refugee admissionists battled. In public, Congress debated. In private, conflicts festered within the executive branch. Restrictionists and admissionists fought over visa policy, FDR's refugee executive orders, and plans and policy for internationalizing the refugee problem.

In Congress, from 1933 through 1938, refugee advocates introduced a variety of bills to help German refugees. One bill proposed to admit refugees outside the quota. Another bill wanted the unused quota allotments to be made available to refugees. Still another bill would have had President Roosevelt widen quotas for refugees and exempt unaccompanied minors and refugees sponsored by organizations from the likely-to-be-a-public-charge provision of the immigration law. Neither these nor other refugee relief measures received much attention. Only the Wagner-Rogers bill, the quintessential confrontation, was given serious consideration.[33]

The Wagner-Rogers bill, named after its sponsors, New York

Senator Robert Wagner and Massachusetts Representative Edith
Nourse Rogers, proposed the admission of twenty thousand
German refugee children, under age fourteen, on a nonquota
basis over a two-year period (ten thousand in 1939 and ten
thousand in 1940). To avoid provoking anti-Semitism, the bill
was deliberately termed a *German*, rather than a *Jewish*, refugee
children's bill, while the public committee created to support
the bill was carefully called the Non-Sectarian Committee for
German Refugee Children. For the same reason, at hearings on
the bill in April and May of 1939, only a few Jews testified,
while Clarence Pickett, the executive secretary of the American
Friends Service Committee and chairman of the Non-Sectarian
Committee, stressed that the proposal dealt with "children of
all faiths." Thousands of people and a diverse assortment of
interdenominational groups supported the bill. Pillars of the
Christian establishment—Mrs. Calvin Coolidge, Herbert Hoover, Alf Landon, and William Allen White, among many others—lent their names to the bill. The Federal Council of Churches
of Christ in America, the American Unitarian Association, the
National YMCA, the Methodist Federation for Social Service,
and the executive of the Boy Scouts of America supported the
bill. And in a noteworthy about-face, the traditionally anti-
immigrant AFL and the CIO went on record as approving its
passage. Senator Wagner read into the *Congressional Record* scores
of editorials from across the country supporting the bill.[34] There
was an amazing outpouring of humanitarian support.

But the humanitarian outpouring met a wall of nativist resistance. John B. Trevor of the American Coalition of Patriotic
Societies called for protests to Congress "to protect the youth
of America from this foreign invasion." The wife of the commissioner of immigration, Mrs. James H. Houghteling, opined
that "twenty thousand charming children would all too soon
grow up into twenty thousand ugly adults." The national legislative chairman of the Grand Army of the Republic claimed
that it was impossible to "Americanize" any immigrant over

the age of four. The Daughters of the American Revolution, the American Legion, and other patriotic groups that were strong in the 1930s, presented a quixotic variety of arguments against the bill. Helping refugee children would deprive American children. German children should not be helped because children of other nationalities were also suffering. Since all were not welcome, Americans should not discriminate in favor of any. America's children were America's responsibility; refugee children in Europe were Europe's responsibility. Two thirds of those sampled in a Gallup poll believed that refugee children should not be admitted. Other polls also demonstrated a strong antipathy to welcome. Underlying all the restrictionist arguments against the admission of refugee children was the overriding fear that any opening of the gates would countervail the restrictive legislation of the twenties.[35]

While Senator Wagner was swamped with hate mail, support surged for North Carolina's Senator Robert R. Reynolds's countermeasure which would have suspended indefinitely *all* immigration. Another bill, the epitome of yahooism, proposed that "every alien in the United States shall be forthwith deported."[36]

The refugee-children bill failed. Despite the nonsectarian cast of its title, most people perceived the modest bill as intended for the rescue of Jewish children. One year later, Congress, with alacrity, passed a measure to allow the entrance of British children.

Official Washington had followed, or perhaps shaped, public opinion. The Department of State opposed the children's bill. The Labor Department waffled, neither supporting nor opposing it. FDR, in the White House, was eloquently silent.

No less than the Congress, the executive formulated refugee policy. The Congress did so by erecting legislative barriers. The executive constructed, in historian David S. Wyman's felicitous term, "paper walls." Paper walls remain today a potent tool in the arsenal of regulatory devices, admitting or barring refugee groups at the will of the executive or the bureaucracy. President

Hoover had initiated the policy of invoking the LPC clause, a policy at first continued by Roosevelt. Roosevelt, however, softened under the pressure of refugees fleeing Germany, and, after the *Anschluss*, opened fully the German and Austrian quotas. After *Kristallnacht*, on November 10, 1938—"The Night of Broken Glass," during which the Nazis systematically looted and ransacked Jewish shops and homes, burned synagogues, and attacked and arrested thousands of Jews—in another administrative softening of the rules, FDR announced that persons on "visitors' " visas would not be forced to return to Germany. (This device of executive discretion is now called extended voluntary departure, and, in the 1980s, has been granted to Afghans, Ethiopians, Iranians, Poles, and Ugandans.) Between the *Anschluss* and the invasion of Poland (March 1938 to September 1939), American immigration policy—without any change in the basic quota system—"was more liberal than at any other time between 1931 and 1946." But *liberal* is a relative term. Aliens were not flooding the country. At a time when the nation's population was around 130 million, fewer than eighty-five thousand refugees were admitted in the eighteen-month period. Moreover, the "liberal" admission policy was short-lived. It did not extend to the period after 1939, when such a policy would surely have saved lives.[37]

After the war began, the State Department impeded the intake of refugees by imposing stricter administrative requirements. Affidavits of financial support were no longer accepted from relatives, and evidence of paid ship passage was required. On the pretense that the Nazis were infiltrating the refugee flow, the State Department instructed its overseas processing staff to withold visas from anyone about whom they had "any doubt whatsoever." A circular telegram amplified the new policy:

Although a drastic reduction in the number of quota and nonquota immigration visas issued will result therefrom and quotas against which there is a heavy demand will be underissued, it is essential to take every precaution at this time to safeguard the best interests of the United States.[38]

During the critical years from 1940 to 1944, Assistant Secretary Breckenridge Long was primarily responsible for the State Department refugee matters. Long, who as ambassador to Italy had written approvingly to FDR that Mussolini's trains "are punctual, well-equipped, and fast," was by temperament and philosophy a restrictionist.[39] Under his direction, the barrier of paper walls grew insurmountable. In a memorandum, he spelled out his modus operandi:

> We can delay and effectively stop for a temporary period of indefinite length the number of immigrants into the United States. We could do this by simply advising our consuls to put every obstacle in the way and to require additional evidence and to resort to various administrative advices which would postpone the granting of the visas.[40]

(Long's insistence on calling the harassed people fleeing for their lives *immigrants* rather than *refugees* cloaked a harsh policy in a facade of reasonableness. Similarly, today's bureaucrat refers to all people incarcerated in Immigration and Naturalization Service detention centers as *aliens*.)

The State Department piled regulation upon regulation. A "relatives rule" stipulated that any visa applicant with a close relative remaining in German, Italian, or Russian territory had to pass a security test. A subsequent broadening of this rule required that *all* immigration applications undergo a security review by a special interdepartmental committee. An applicant's papers moved with painstaking delay through the screening bureaucracy. "Even when an applicant faced immediate danger," notes Professor Wyman, "the State Department would not expedite the case."[41]

By July of 1943, the visa application form was more than

four feet long and had to be filled out on both sides and submitted in sextuplicate. Unsuccessful applications could be reconsidered six months after rejection. Since the Department of
State, however, never explained why the original applications
were rejected, the applicant had little chance of reapplying successfully. (At present, the Immigration and Naturalization Service denies applications for asylum without giving specific reasons for the denial.) Consulate officers overseas well understood
Washington's intentions; a consulate officer who desired advancement would only progress if he did not contravene these
intentions. Better to reject than to accept large numbers of applicants.

After 1941, consuls were given unlimited authority to deny
a visa to anyone who, in the consul's judgment, would "endanger the public safety of the United States."[42] Years later, in
1978, Fidel Castro agreed to the release of three thousand political prisoners if they could be admitted to the United States.
Attorney General Griffin Bell, fearing the infiltration of "Communists, terrorists, and criminals," insisted on personally
screening each prisoner. After two months, he had screened
and approved only forty-six prisoners, at which rate more than
ten years would have elapsed before the political refugees, many
of them no longer young or in good health, would have been
given their freedom.[43]

To a large extent, administrative reluctance to admit refugees
has only reflected an unwillingness to recognize that for refugees, future dangers are real. When, in 1939, the SS *St. Louis*
was not permitted to discharge its human cargo in Cuba, it
proceeded to American coastal waters. If the ship had been
sinking, American vessels almost certainly would have rescued
the passengers and brought them to shore, but the liner was
seaworthy. Instead, an American Coast Guard cutter patrolled
the waters off the Florida coast to prevent anyone from trying
to reach shore.[44] The desperate passengers sent a wire to President Roosevelt, but he did not respond. The State Department,

fearing that a precedent would be set, ruled that no one without a proper visa could land. Since none of the passengers had visas valid for the United States, haven was not granted. The *St. Louis* returned to Europe, where some of its passengers became part of "the final solution."[45] Today, other Coast Guard cutters patrol the waters off Haiti, interdicting Haitian émigrés and returning those without valid exit visas to their homeland.

If those in positions of power had wanted to liberalize policy, they could have done so without violating the law. FDR had made modest changes in policy when he softened the LPC clause and when he ordered the extension of visitors' visas. Certainly a more humane refugee policy could have been effected without breaking or changing the Immigration Act, simply through more liberal interpretation. The Treaty-Merchant provision, which permitted entrance to businessmen who showed promise of generating employment, was one option. Temporary immigrants might have been settled in the Virgin Islands. Greater use might have been made of visas for visitors, clergymen, and professors. Children could have been exempted from the quota. Unused portions of quotas could have been redistributed. And "temporary havens" or "free ports" could have been created.[46]

In a free port, merchandise lies duty-free while it awaits transshipment. This same principle could have been applied to human cargo, to refugees. The refugees would have been allowed to enter the United States and held in "free ports," or camps, until the end of the war, when they would have been "shipped on" to their native or other lands. When the idea of free ports was discussed, Secretary of War Henry L. Stimson cautioned against "inundations by foreign racial stock out of proportion to what exists here."[47] Stimson need not have feared such inundations. The United States created only one free port, Camp Ontario in Oswego, New York, and took in fewer than one thousand people. (The camp, an example of tokenism rather than rescue, is now memorialized by a permanent exhibition in the State Museum of New York.)

FDR, after initially approving the free-port idea, soon terminated the rescue scheme. What could have been a mechanism to save lives was itself short-lived. If free ports had been established on a broad scale, many could have been saved. Had the United States set an example of generosity, other nations would perhaps have felt a moral pressure to follow. Moreover, countries of asylum, particularly Spain and Turkey, would have been willing to shelter refugees temporarily had they been assured that the refugees were only in transit.[48] (Today the concepts of safe haven and temporary asylum have particular relevance to refugee situations in Indochina and Latin America.)

The eventual fate of the Oswego detainees was decided not by President Roosevelt, who died shortly before the European war was won, but by his successor, Harry S. Truman. Truman was aware that the refugees confined to Fort Ontario were a minuscule part of the much larger problem of Europe's displaced persons (DPs). The term *displaced persons*, new to the lexicon of human misery, denoted the survivors of the Holocaust and others uprooted by the war, who had been expelled or had fled from their homelands and could not return. With the surrender of Hitler's military, countless unfortunates were displaced.

Responding to the DPs' misery, Truman issued a presidential directive that declared, ''The immensity of the problem of displaced persons and refugees is almost beyond comprehension. . . . This period of unspeakable human distress is not the time for us to close or narrow our gates.''[49] Truman hoped to set an example for other nations. The directive's new administrative procedures eased the immigration of DPs under existing quotas. The Fort Ontario refugee-internees were the immediate beneficiaries of the directive. Rather than having to return to Europe to become eligible for immigration visas, the refugees simply crossed the nearby Canadian border, then returned to the United States later as permanent quota immigrants.[50]

But Truman's directive brought in only a trickle of DPs. Dissatisfied with the program, the president announced that he would ask Congress to admit DPs outside the quota system, thus setting the stage for another battle between the restrictionists and the admissionists.

Spearheading the admissionist forces was a newly created pressure group, the Citizens Committee on Displaced Persons (CCDP). The CCDP persuaded Congressman William G. Stratton to introduce a bill to allow one hundred thousand DPs to enter the United States annually for four years. The administration supported the bill and sent Secretary of State George C. Marshall, Secretary of War Robert H. Patterson, and Attorney General Tom C. Clark to testify. They urged passage of the bill for foreign policy reasons: America had a unique responsibility as a world leader. The bill drew expected endorsements from religious leaders. And, unexpectedly, the AFL reversed its traditional restrictionist position and favored the admission of DPs beyond the quotas. Restrictionist testimony was provided by patriotic societies and the veterans' organizations.

Two basic issues were in contention. There was the old arguing point: What effect would the newcomers have on American society? And a new arguing point: To what extent was America obliged to aid the DPs? To the tired arguments that refugees would take jobs was added the specter of deleterious effects on America. The DPs were a security menace. Russia had planted spies among them. Others, if not actual spies, carried intellectual germs which would infect America's ideology. America had no obligation to accept DPs. The admissionists countered with testimony from the Department of Labor that four hundred thousand additional immigrant-refugees would not deprive Americans of jobs. Further, the refugees would be screened to weed out subversives. The United States had a moral obligation to accept its fair share of DPs. The Senate, as a delaying tactic, authorized an overseas investigation.[51]

During the delay, support grew for the enactment of a refugee relief measure. The CCDP had worked extensively to educate the general public and enlist elite organizational support. The American Legion, after its own investigation of the DP camps, changed its position to support the admission of a limited number of DPs. A special subcommittee of the House Foreign Affairs Committee reported in favor of DP resettlement. Truman's State of the Union message in January 1948 urged Congress to admit DPs. With the pressure mounting and its overseas investigation completed, the Senate Judiciary Immigration Subcommittee under William Chapman Revercomb, a staunch restrictionist, realized that a tactical change was necessary.

The DP bill that was written and eventually enacted outwitted the admissionists. Truman signed it reluctantly. Under the Displaced Persons Act of 1948, to be eligible for admission to the United States a DP had to have been in Germany by December 22, 1945. This rendered ineligible the Jewish survivors of concentration camps who had fled to the west after the Polish pogroms of 1946. Priorities were also given to Balts and those involved in agriculture, thus limiting the numbers available to Jews. The act repealed the Truman directive while it provided that one hundred thousand DPs would be admitted under mortgaged quotas, a practice introduced to prevent the modification of the existing immigration laws. Under the quota system, if all visas for the current year were exhausted, half of the visas for subsequent years could be "mortgaged." The quota numbers thus used by the DPs would not be available for later immigrants from the same countries. The results were ludicrous. By 1951 the Latvian quota had been mortgaged to the year 2255, the Estonian to 2130, and the Lithuanian to 2079.[52]

With all its restrictionist flaws, the Displaced Persons Act was, nonetheless, the first significant refugee legislation in American history. Reflecting a humanitarian attempt to admit refugees, the act relaxed earlier restrictive and exclusionary legislation. In mortgaging future quotas, its framers recognized that refugee numbers might not be contained within normal immigration quotas, a concept that would later lead to the flexible admissions numbers of the Refugee Act. The act was amended in 1950 and extended in 1951, allowing over four hundred thousand refugees to find new homes in America. Although restrictionists had imprinted their bias on the act itself, the Displaced Persons Commission (DPC) administered it liberally. The DPC, Leonard Dinnerstein has written in the definitive study of the legislation, "was so creative in its operations that many legislators would later wonder how the bill they had voted for contained so many loopholes."[53]

The 1950 amendment of the Displaced Persons Act liberalized the original bill. It extended the cutoff date, eliminated the Baltic and agricultural worker priorities, and increased the number of refugees who could be admitted.[54] In the Senate, however, Patrick A. McCarran made amendment difficult. McCarran, then chairman of the Senate Judiciary Committee, believed that immigrants were a danger to American society and that immigration-refugee policy should be dictated solely by domestic considerations. McCarran warned the Senate of his "inescapable conclusion that the floodgates of the nation are being pried open for the entrance of millions of aliens, from the turbulent populations of the entire world, who are seeking admission into the United States under the guise of displaced persons."[55] Immigration and refugee policy had become an adjunct of foreign policy.

While the Displaced Persons Act was being debated, Senator McCarran was concluding the first comprehensive study of immigration since that of the Dillingham Commission. McCarran submitted his report to Congress in 1950, and two years later the McCarran-Walter Immigration and Nationality Act became law over President Truman's veto. The controversy over the McCarran-Walter Act recalled the arguments of the 1920s. On one side were the restrictionists who insisted, though less stridently than before, on retaining the national-origins quotas and who clung to an ethnic theory of immigration. Countering them, the admissionists used recently published anthropological data to refute the distinction between the "old" and the "new" immigration. They also argued that a generous immigration policy was necessary to support an effective foreign policy. Truman's veto message gave forceful point to the admissionist position:

> This quota system—always based upon assumptions at variance with our American ideals—is long since out of date and more than ever unrealistic in the face of world conditions. . . . The country by country limitations create a pattern that is insulting to large numbers of our finest citizens, irritating to our allies abroad, and foreign to our purposes and ideals. . . . It denies the humanitarian creed inscribed beneath the Statue of Liberty proclaiming to all nations: "Give me your tired, your poor, your huddled masses, yearning to breathe free. . . ."

The president emphasized that the bill offended America's NATO partners, Italy, Greece, and Turkey. "Through this bill we say to their people: You are less worthy to come to this country than Englishmen or Irishmen . . . you Turks, you are brave defenders of the Eastern flank, but you shall have a quota of only 225!"[56]

Truman's veto was overridden by two votes. The restrictionists had won again. But their ranks had diminished, and legislative inroads had been made into racial exclusion. The McCarran-Walter Immigration and Nationality Act of 1952 retained the national-origins quota system and the Western Hemisphere exemption, established stringent controls to bar radicals, Communists, and subversives, and provided quotas for independent, self-governing, and UN trustee areas found within an Asia-Pacific triangle. (The triangle consisted of all countries from Pakistan to Japan and the Pacific Islands north of Australia and New Zealand.) The act also repealed Japanese exclusion, assigned Asian nations tiny quotas, and gave their immigrants the right to naturalization.

The exclusionists' victory was being assaulted on still another front. Beginning with the Truman administration and continuing under Eisenhower, refugee admissions had become an important tool in anti-Communist foreign policy. The two administrations encouraged the first major postwar stream of refugees—European escapees from Communism—to flow into the United States. Every subsequent administration has maintained that commitment. Refugee-escapees who "vote with their feet" against Communism validate American foreign policy and offer vital proof of the inadequacies of the Communist system.

Both the executive and the Congress were committed to encouraging escape from Communism, even to the extent of abandoning numerical limits and quotas and allocating funds for escapee assistance. The President's Escapee Program (PEP), begun in 1952 and directed by the State Department, provided for financial assistance to escapees from Communist countries (except Yugoslavia), for reception services, vocational training, language instruction, and resettlement help.[57]

The Refugee Relief Act (RRA) of 1953, which followed, relaxed United States immigration law. Congress, responding to the heightened tensions of the Cold War, ignored the long-established national quotas and the practice of quota mortgaging, and instead authorized the issuance of over two hundred thousand nonquota visas for persons escaping from Iron Curtain countries. By executive order, the State Department (rather than the Immigration and Naturalization Service in the Justice Department) was to administer the act. In short, in order to fight Communism, in the economically comfortable fifties, the United States was ready to abandon the sacred shibboleths of numerical limits and national-origins quotas, to sanction additional immigration, and even to bestow federal dollars on the newcomers.[58]

It was anti-Communist fervor, as well, that led to the first mass parole of refugees into the United States. In 1956, just prior to the expiration of the RRA, an anti-Communist revolt had taken place in Hungary. When Soviet troops crushed the revolt, thousands of Hungarian "freedom fighters" fled to neighboring Austria. President Eisenhower authorized their admission to the United States. Some were given visas available under the RRA; others, however, at the President's direction, were admitted under the obscure attorney general's parole provision of the Immigration and Nationality Act. This was a new and elastic interpretation of parole. Congress had intended that parole be granted individually, on a case-by-case basis, and that the alien would be required to depart when the purpose of his parole had been satisfied. (One such purpose might have been coming to the United States for a specialized medical procedure.) Although Eisenhower was the first to use the parole on behalf of a group of refugees, he would not be the last.[59]

The Refugee-Escapee Act (REA) of 1957 admitted still more Hungarians. The REA was significant in two respects. First, in a shift in the immigration law, the act repealed the existing mortgages against the quotas. Second, the REA defined *refugee-escapees* as victims of racial, religious, or political persecution fleeing Communist or Communist-occupied or -dominated countries, or a country in the Middle East. This definition would stand until the Refugee Act of 1980 amended it.[60]

The Hungarians were followed by a second group, whose entrance signaled a major shift in American immigration and refugee policy—the admission of a large group who were, for the most part, Asian. In contrast to the highly publicized entrance of the Hungarians, the entrance of the Dutch-Indonesians was quiet and without fanfare. The Dutch-Indonesians—as their name suggests, a racial and cultural blend of Dutch and Indonesians—had been displaced when Indonesia gained its independence from the Netherlands. Facing an uncertain future, they migrated first to Holland, but were never fully integrated there. Special legislation allowed them to enter the United States outside of existing immigration quotas.[61]

Still another incursion into the pattern of immigration law occurred in 1960 with the passage of the Refugee Fair Share Law, the United States' response to the United Nations Declaration of a World Refugee Year. More comprehensive than previous refugee admission programs, the Fair Share Law was designed not to assist refugees of a particular nationality or to meet a particular emergency, but to provide an ongoing mechanism for the admission of refugees for a limited time. Congress authorized the attorney general to use his parole authority to admit twenty-five percent of the total number of refugees from Europe and the Middle East who were not yet permanently resettled. In 1962, the Fair Share Law was extended indefinitely. In 1965, the refugee parole program of the Refugee Fair Share Law was terminated and a permanent provision for the admission of refugees was incorporated into basic immigration law.[62] In piecemeal fashion, refugee admission policy was being developed.

An important influence in the development of refugee policy was America's anti-Communism. When Fulgencio Batista fell and Fidel Castro came to power in Cuba, in 1959, America began welcoming Cubans. For the first time, the United States became a country of refuge for a large group of refugees, receiving, over the years, some one million Cubans.[63]

A warm welcome was extended to the Cubans, in contrast to America's grudging attitude toward refugees in the 1930s and 1940s. From the early days of the Castro revolution until the diplomatic break in relations in January 1961, Cubans flowed directly to the mainland, the beneficiaries of an extraordinarily liberal nonimmigrant visa policy in Havana and a pro-forma grant of political asylum in the United States. From the October 1962 missile crisis until late in 1965, Cubans went first to other countries, where they were given parole visas for the United States. The exception to this procedure occurred in May and June of 1963, when some ten thousand Cubans came to the United States on the cargo ships that returned from Cuba after having delivered the ransom for the Bay of Pigs invaders.[64]

The Bay of Pigs fiasco was the most dramatic instance of the interplay of foreign policy and refugee movement in the Kennedy administration. But John F. Kennedy had long been aware of the connection between foreign policy and refugees. As a senator, even before the World Refugee Year had officially begun, Kennedy introduced a joint resolution urging the adoption of a permanent law for the admission of refugees into the United States. It was the Fair Share Law rather than Kennedy's proposal that was enacted, but the Migration and Refugee Assistance Act (MRAA), passed at the urging of President Kennedy, gave statutory recognition to refugees. When Kennedy sent his proposal for the Migration and Refugee Assistance Act to Capitol Hill, he set forth a rationale which combined humanitarianism with realpolitik:

> From the earliest days of our history, this land has been a refuge for the oppressed and it is proper that we now, as descendants of refugees and immigrants, continue our long humanitarian tradition of helping those who are forced to flee to maintain their lives as individual, self-sufficient human beings in freedom, self-respect, dignity and health. It is, moreover, decidedly to the political interests of the United States that we maintain and continue to enhance our prestige and leadership in this respect.[65]

The Migration and Refugee Assistance Act of 1962 was the first comprehensive refugee assistance statute and, until the passage of the Refugee Act of 1980, remained the basic law in that area. The MRAA supported programs of assistance to refugees, escapees, and migrants. It provided for annual contributions to the United Nations High Commissioner for Refugees (UNHCR) and to the Intergovernmental Committee for European Migration (now the Intergovernmental Committee for Migration) and authorized assistance to refugees overseas and to Cuban refugees in the United States. It also made available to the president annual monies to meet urgent refugee and migration needs. For the first time, the executive was given a broad, permanent, and flexible mandate to conduct refugee affairs.

In May of 1962, a month before the MRAA became law, on the other side of the globe, a new refugee emergency arose. Communist China relaxed its border controls, and Chinese began pouring into Hong Kong, already surfeited with Chinese refugees. The Kennedy administration saw a unique opportunity for both propaganda and a humanitarian act. JFK announced that, under the parole provision, he would admit several thousand Chinese into the United States. Eligible for admission, however, were not the new May refugees, but those Chinese who had been cleared for immigration to the United States since 1954, but had been unable, because of the minute Chinese quota, to enter. In actual effect, Kennedy's gesture served more to reunify families than to aid refugees, but it presaged a more liberal policy toward Asians.

In the third year of his presidency, Kennedy submitted legislation which, if enacted, would have altered basic immigration policy. The Kennedy proposals would have given the president power to admit refugees, would have abolished the Asian-Pacific Triangle, and, over a five-year transition period, would have eliminated the national-origins quota system.[66] It appeared that reform was in the offing. But Kennedy's assassination and Lyndon Johnson's campaign for the presidency intervened, keeping immigration reform in abeyance until 1965.

Johnson's landslide victory in the 1964 election and the large Democratic majorities in the Senate and House reflected the country's liberal mood, a mood that spilled over even into immigration issues. In 1965, President Johnson sent a special message to Congress urging immigration reform. The admissionists mounted a well-organized campaign to support Johnson's efforts. On Capitol Hill, the administration assembled a chorus of witnesses who urged the abandonment of the national-origins provision; they argued that the change in immigration policy would be in concert with our foreign policy and assured Congress that increased immigration levels would benefit the economy. Outnumbered, the restrictionists fought a rearguard battle, unable in the 1960s to defend the position of the 1920s.

The Immigration Act of 1965 began to liberalize immigration policy. The act abolished the national-origins quota system and the Asian-Pacific Triangle provision and, in so doing, radically altered the ethnic balance of future American immigration. Henceforth, 170,000 non-Western Hemisphere immigrants would enter each year while the traditionally favored Western immigration would be held to a numerical ceiling of 120,000 annually. Eastern Hemisphere entrants were admitted under a preference system in which priorities on a scale of one through six were assigned on the basis of family ties and occupational skills. In 1976, Congress gave the Western Hemisphere a preference system similar to that of the Eastern Hemisphere. And continuing the liberalization process, President Carter in 1978 signed a bill that combined both hemispheres under a worldwide ceiling of 290,000 with a single preference system. Two years later, the Refugee Act reduced the worldwide ceiling by twenty thousand.

With the passage of the 1965 Act, the major source of immigration shifted from Europe to Asia and Latin America. By 1985, only five percent of all immigrants came from Europe; Asians accounted for nearly half of the 570,000 newcomers, while Latin Americans, mainly Mexicans, made up roughly forty percent. This demographic shift, a reversal of a trend of almost two centuries of European immigration, nourished a resurgence of anti-Asianism and the fear of a Hispanic invasion.[67] (Current manifestations of antiforeignism are reflected in the widespread violence against Asians and in the movement to make English the official language.)

The 1965 act also specifically addressed the problem of refugees, for the first time providing for their annual admission. (Most of the special refugee admission laws had lapsed, and the act repealed the Fair Share Act of 1960, the only remaining law that permitted further nonquota entry of refugees.) Congress, however, attached little importance to the admission of refugees, placing them seventh—last—in the preference system and giving refugees the smallest proportion (only six percent or 10,200 admissions) of all entrants. Family reunification and needed occupational skills took precedence over refugee admissions. The refugee policy that Congress wrote into law made refugees ancillary to immigration and imposed geographic, ideological, and numerical restrictions. A refugee continued to be defined as an individual fleeing racial, religious, or political persecution from any Communist, Communist-dominated, or Middle Eastern country. Congress also specifically rejected the use of the parole provision for mass admissions. The Senate and House reports had stated:

> Inasmuch as a definite provision has now been made for refugees, it is the express intent of the Committee that the parole provisions of the Immigration and Nationality Act, which remain unchanged by this bill, be administered in accordance with the original intention of the drafters of that legislation. The parole provisions were designed to authorize the Attorney-General to act only in emergent, individual, and isolated situations, such as the case of an alien who requires medical attention, and not for the immigration of classes or groups outside of the limit of the law.[68]

Congress' attempt to incorporate refugee policy into the 1965 act was a Maginot Line—obsolete as it was being constructed. Within the decade, refugees, first Cubans, then Soviet émigrés, and finally Indochinese, would enter the United States in circumvention of statutory policy. In September 1965, the Cuban government announced a new departure policy. Those Cubans who had families in the United States would be permitted to emigrate. President Johnson responded immediately. Showman that he was, Johnson signed the Immigration and Nationality Act of 1965 at the Statue of Liberty and proclaimed an open gate for Cubans. LBJ's policy to admit, under parole, all those whom Castro permitted to depart, however, was in clear contravention of the act he had just signed.

Johnson's declaration triggered a second major wave of Cubans. From Florida, hundreds of boats ferried to the small Cuban port of Camarioca and brought some five thousand Cubans speedily to the mainland, before the United States and Cuba established an orderly departure program. This program, the Freedom Flight Program (FFP), established an airlift between Miami and Varadero. During the FFP period (1965 to 1972), an "aerial bridge" brought in some 270,000 Cubans, while another 70,000 came in from Spain under a parole program. In 1973, Cuba terminated the FFP, and direct movement from Cuba ceased. Nonetheless, from 1973 to 1979, thirty-eight thousand Cubans came to the United States through third countries.[69]

The Carter administration brought about a thaw in relations with the Castro government. In the fall of 1978, the Cuban government announced its willingness to release three thousand political prisoners and six hundred others who had been caught trying to escape the island. The United States soon initiated a parole program, under which more than ten thousand former political prisoners and their families came to this country. With the passage of the Refugee Act of 1980, this Cuban parole program was converted into a refugee program. After the act, the next wave of Cubans would be the Marielitos.[70]

During the period in which the second wave of Cubans entered the United States, Soviet emigration policy—enigmatic to Westerners and dictated by Soviet objectives—softened. Like other totalitarian societies (and despite its international obligations), the Soviet Union does not allow its citizens to emigrate freely. The only recognized bases for emigration are repatriation and family reunification. Accordingly, only three groups of Soviet citizens have been allowed to emigrate in significant numbers. Those groups are ethnic Germans who have gone to the Federal Republic of Germany, Armenians who emigrated to Lebanon and the United States, and Soviet Jews who emigrated to Israel and other Western countries.[71]

While one can only speculate on the motivations of the Soviet government, the degree of détente between East and West, and particularly the United States and the U.S.S.R., seems to be related to the rate of emigration to the West. American foreign policy, anxious to embarrass the Russians ever since the President's Escapee Program in the early cold-war days, has encouraged anti-Communist refugee flows. Like the Cubans, Armenians and Soviet Jews are beneficiaries of this policy.

Most of the Armenians who emigrated were not born in the Soviet Union. After World War II, they had migrated to the U.S.S.R. from Lebanon, Syria, Iran, and Greece. Needing labor in the newly industrialized Armenian Soviet Socialist Republic, Stalin mounted a propaganda campaign to entice Armenians to return to their "homeland." But the Armenians were disappointed with life in the Soviet Union, with its restrictions on religious and economic freedom, and asked to leave. The Soviets, since 1970, have permitted some twenty-three thousand Armenians to depart. In the early 1970s, the majority of Armenians who were permitted to leave resettled in Lebanon. But when the 1976 civil war in Lebanon closed that country's borders, Soviet Armenians changed their destination and came to the United States.[72]

The exact number of Armenians entering the United States is difficult to calculate because ethnic groups exiting the Soviet Union are differentiated only as "non-Jewish" and "Jewish," and because Armenians came in as both immigrants and refugees. Armenian emigration reached its highest point in 1980, when six thousand were allowed to leave the U.S.S.R. for the United States. Since then, Russian policy has changed, and the number of Armenians allowed to leave has been reduced drastically.[73]

Like the Armenians, Soviet Jews also have been subject to

the caprice of Soviet emigration policy.* The state-sponsored persecution of Jews, however, is endemic. Jews are no longer subjected to pogroms; nonetheless, an official policy of oppression exists. Jews are systematically shut out of higher education. The dissemination of Jewish culture and the teaching of Hebrew are forbidden. Anti-Semitism and anti-Zionism are harsh realities. Those who apply for permission to emigrate, especially Jews, lose their jobs and are treated as outcasts. "Refusenik" and "prisoner of Zion," are phrases applied uniquely to Soviet citizens. One becomes a refusenik by having his request for an exit permit repeatedly denied. Similarly, one becomes a prisoner of Zion and is internally exiled or jailed for the crime of having pushed too hard for an exit permit, or for being too active in teaching Hebrew or Jewish culture.

Between 1966 and 1985, more than a quarter of a million Jews were granted exit visas and permitted to emigrate. (Significantly, Jews who are allowed to leave Russia must renounce their nationality; thus, on departure, they become stateless.) From 1966 through 1975, the great majority of exiting Soviet Jews went to Israel. But beginning around the middle of the 1970s, a shift occurred. In the years 1975 to 1980, before the Soviets again began to curtail emigration, some ninety thousand Soviet Jews arrived as refugees in the United States.[74]

The number of Soviet refugees was significantly smaller than the number of Cubans, whose influx was ongoing, or of Indochinese, who began to arrive at the same time as the Soviets. But unlike either the Cuban or the Indochinese emigrations, Soviet emigration had become hostage to U.S.-Soviet relation-

---

* There is an old story told about the emigration of Soviet Jewish refugees. Two officials, one a Soviet, the other an American, are talking. The American says to the Russian, "It is very difficult to tell how many refugees are going to be leaving Russia under your emigration program." "Ummmm," says the Russian. "You really can't tell?" "Yes," replies the American. "From year to year, from month to month, it is impossible for us to know." "Ah ha," says the Russian with a smile, "our program is working."

and was a stalking horse in domestic American politics. In the United States, Jewish pressure groups kept Russian anti-Semitism and discriminatory practices against Jews and other dissidents in the forefront of public opinion. In this, a wide spectrum of anti-Communist labor, ethnic, and religious groups have aided them substantially. It is good domestic politics for both Republicans and Democrats to be anti-Communist, pro-religion, and pro-human rights. Ordinarily, congressional actions of an anti-Soviet nature (for example, the Ribicoff Amendment condemning Soviet religious persecution, a sense-of-Congress resolution supporting free emigration, or votes for appropriations for Soviet refugee assistance) are straightforward issues. But the major congressional attempt to influence Soviet emigration policy, the Jackson-Vanik Amendment to the Trade Reform Act of 1974, initiated during the Nixon administration, was and remains complex and problematic.[75]

The Nixon administration, in its policy of détente with the Soviets, had, in 1972, worked out a comprehensive commercial agreement with the Soviet government. As part of the agreement, the U.S. would extend most-favored-nation (MFN) import-tariff treatment to the Soviets. But Senator Henry Jackson introduced an amendment to the East-West trade bill which would have blocked the extension of MFN status and credits to those countries that restricted or taxed the emigration of their citizens. Congressman Charles Vanik introduced a similar bill in the House of Representatives.

The Jackson-Vanik Amendment had widespread support for a number of reasons. It suited America's selective application of human-rights policies. It was good politics. Nineteen seventy-two was an election year. Nixon, the entire House of Representatives, and one-third the Senate were up for reelection. There was no political advantage in not supporting Jackson-Vanik, but there was a decided political disadvantage in failure to support it. Jews, human rights groups, academic-scientific groups, and a wide variety of anti-Soviet groups were for the amendment. Labor, especially the AFL-CIO under George Meany, opposed the Trade Reform Bill and supported the Jackson-Vanik Amendment. Meany, the consummate anti-Communist, feared the export of American technology and the loss of American jobs. Those who disliked the tilt of Nixon's foreign policy toward rapprochement with the Russians endorsed the Amendment because it was antidétente. Other congressmen felt the U.S. had been "taken" on an earlier wheat deal with the Russians. And finally, there were those in the Congress who supported the amendment as a display against what they considered to be Nixon's executive usurpation of power (since the bill gave the executive the authority to set tariff rates, Congress wanted to attach conditions).

In response to the Jackson-Vanik Amendment, Henry Kissinger, speaking for the administration, warned of the dangers of trying to transform the internal structure of other nations. He pointed out that the restriction would endanger détente and that the administration was trying by diplomatic means to induce the Soviets to relax emigration restrictions. Kissinger's main support came from big business which, seeing the opportunity for additional markets, supported the trade bill and opposed Jackson-Vanik.

The dispute waged for many months against the background of the 1973 Arab-Israeli War, Watergate revelations, Nixon's impeachment imbroglio and resignation, and Gerald Ford's assumption of the presidency. Kissinger, meanwhile, tried to work out an agreement with the Russians and an accommodation with Senator Jackson. They finally achieved a compromise. The new Ford administration would waive the provisions of the original Jackson-Vanik Amendment and grant MFN status and credits to the Soviet Union for an initial period of eighteen months. After eighteen months, further waiver extensions would be subject to congressional approval. The Trade Reform Act of 1974 was finally enacted, but the Russians announced shortly afterwards that they would not put it into force. Moscow objected that linking MFN to emigration violated the principle of noninterference in the domestic affairs of other states.

The Jackson-Vanik Amendment seemed to produce the opposite of the desired result. In the years immediately following the nonimplementation of the trade agreement, the Soviets restricted emigration drastically. During the Carter administration, however, the Soviets permitted more emigration. (The usual explanation for this is that the Kremlin wanted a favorable resolution of the Strategic Arms Limitation Treaty [SALT] talks.) Some prominent prisoners of Zion and refuseniks were permitted to emigrate, and Jews wishing to emigrate were less harassed. By 1979, extending MFN status to the Soviet Union seemed economically and diplomatically wise, especially since the United States and China had initiated a trade agreement. But the Soviet Union's invasion of Afghanistan at the year's end rudely terminated the possibility of softening trade relations between the superpowers. From the invasion of Afghanistan through the first Reagan administration, emigration continued to plummet. Indeed, in 1984, 1985, and 1986, the Soviet Union allowed on average only some one thousand Jews to depart each year, an all-time low. Jewish emigration continues to be tied to the general state of American-Soviet relations. The Jackson-Vanik "Freedom of Emigration" Amendment remains more a testament to the mingling of international and domestic politics than a vehicle for liberalizing Soviet emigration policies.[76]

Like the Soviet Jews who were, and remain, pawns of superpower politics, the Indochinese—the largest inflow of refugees after the Cubans—were also victims of global rivalries. President Ford, along with the contretemps over the Jackson-Vanik Amendment, inherited from Richard Nixon the denouement of the Vietnam War. In the spring of 1975, the Saigon government disintegrated. America was unprepared for the events which quickly followed. In April 1975, after the United States had begun evacuating Americans and Vietnamese from Saigon, President Ford appointed Ambassador L. Dean Brown to head a special interagency task force for the evacuation and resettlement of Indochinese refugees. The evacuees were to be admitted into the United States under the parole provisions of the Indochina Refugee Act, and their number was set at a maximum of two hundred thousand. Guidelines limited evacuation to United States employees and other Vietnamese whose lives would be endangered by the Communist takeover. In Saigon there was chaos, and the guidelines were not adhered to.

In May 1975, while the evacuees were being brought into the United States, a Harris poll revealed that only thirty-six percent of all Americans thought Indochinese should be admitted, and fifty-four percent thought they should be excluded. In a wash of nativism, governors, senators, and congressmen urged the federal government to proceed with caution in admitting the Indochinese. California Congressman Burt Talcott succinctly summed up racist prejudice when he urged the government not to bring in the refugees because, in his words, "Damn it, we have too many Orientals."[77]

Despite nativism and racism, Congress responded to the new refugee emergency with the passage of the Migration and Refugee Assistance Act of 1975. The act provided statutory authorization for a temporary program of relief and resettlement. As originally envisioned, the program was to last no later than 1977. In all, some 135,000 Indochinese refugees were evacuated, screened on Guam and Wake Island, and processed through reception centers in the United States. By the end of 1975, the temporary refugee relocation camps had been closed, and it appeared as if the Indochinese refugee problem would fade from the national consciousness. But the agony of Indochina was not over.[78]

Refugees continued to leave Vietnam, Cambodia, and Laos. In Vietnam, the "new order" fed waves of "gold bar" refugees and "boat people." In Cambodia, first the Khmer Rouge's takeover, then Vietnam's invasion produced turmoil and bloodshed, and with them, refugees. In Laos, shortly after the fall of Saigon, the Communist Pathet Lao took control of the government. Those associated with the Royal Lao government and the mountain-dwelling Hmong, America's wartime ally, were targets of Pathet Lao reprisals and were forced to flee.

As the numbers of Indochinese refugees grew, the neighboring states of Thailand, Malaysia, and Singapore found that the continued admission of the exiles created unprecedented political and economic problems. Unwilling to exacerbate their own difficulties, the neighboring states closed their frontiers. Other countries in the region were equally reluctant to offer asylum.

The boat people, often in unseaworthy boats and lacking adequate provisions, found that passing ships, in violation of maritime custom, refused to pick them up. Ships which had boarded boat people were often forbidden to discharge their cargoes or send their crews ashore at ports of call. And so, rather than disrupt commerce, passing freighters left boat people afloat. Norway and Israel acquired small numbers of refugees when captains of their merchant ships boarded boat people and no Asian port would give them haven. Now the UNHCR guarantees ship captains who board boat people that the United Nations agency will assume responsibility for those rescued.

In July 1978, President Jimmy Carter ordered American carriers and ships with United States registry ("many of which have been refusing to pick up refugees to avoid difficulties at their next ports of call") to pick up boat people and promised that, if they wished, the boat people could settle in the United States.[79] It was hoped that other countries would emulate the American policy of sea rescue and the resettlement offer. Moreover, by using established world refugee aid organizations, Carter tried to internationalize rescue efforts.

In December 1978, the United Nations High Commissioner for Refugees called a special consultative meeting of thirty-eight nations in Geneva, Switzerland, but the meeting produced meager results. Some months later, in response to an appeal from the High Commissioner and the United States, the Philippines and Indonesia offered to provide temporary haven on isolated islands to twenty thousand Indochinese refugees, if the United States and other nations would guarantee to cover all costs and assume the responsibility of resettlement.

While the administration was trying to internationalize the Indochinese refugee dilemma, Congress also grappled with the problem. Representative Joshua Eilberg, chairman of the House Subcommittee on Immigration, Citizenship, and International Law of the Committee on the Judiciary, began a series of hearings on the admission of refugees into the United States. Eilberg's opening statement was significant, for it encapsulated congressional-executive differences that had been building for years. Eilberg pointed out that the vast majority of refugees who entered the United States yearly did so at the discretion of the attorney general, rather than under the regular refugee provisions of the Immigration and Nationality Act of 1965. It was clear that "Congress had abdicated its responsibility." While there was some consultation with Congress when the attorney general exercised his parole power, there was "little if any meaningful input by the Congress or by the members of the Judiciary Committee." Some administrative flexibility was required, but it was not "reasonable or proper for the Congress to delegate to the executive branch its constitutional obligation to enact laws establishing the Nation's refugee policy." The attorney general should not be the sole decision-maker, particularly when there were no legislative guidelines or administrative criteria. Eilberg designed a bill to "establish a uniform refugee policy."[80]

The Eilberg bill, both in its initial and subsequent versions, was restrictive. Parole admission was limited to twenty thousand; no more than five thousand of such admissions would be available for adjustment to permanent resident status. Fair Share provisions and consultations with the House and Senate were required. In addition, if either house disapproved of the admissions, they could be terminated by resolution. The Eilberg bill never passed. In the November 1978 election, Eilberg, under the cloud of a kickback indictment, lost his seat.

Although it never reached the floor, the Eilberg bill indicated that Congress was growing distressed with the response by the executive branch to the refugee situation. After much delay, in March 1979, the Carter administration submitted a bill which was introduced in the Senate by Edward M. Kennedy and in the House of Representatives by Peter Rodino and Elizabeth Holtzman. A year later, President Carter signed the Refugee Act of 1980.

The Refugee Act was enacted at a time when America was psychologically awash in post–Vietnam War ambivalence—shame at America's ignominious departure from the Indochina Peninsula, coupled with feelings of guilt and responsibility for those who escaped from the area's Communist regimes. The media brought the Southeast Asian refugee problem into everyone's home. The parallels to the pre–World War II refugee movements of Europe were obvious, and also a painful reminder that refusal to help was a decree of death. The *Southern Cross, Tung An, Huey Fong, Hai Hong* and countless other nondescript vessels crammed with desperate people were reminiscent of other boats, other ports, other times. During the Hitler era, cattle and cargo boats went from port to port over the Atlantic, the Mediterranean, and the Black Sea. Four decades later, ancient tugs and worn fishing vessels sailed the Gulf of Thailand and the South China Sea. Jews and antifascists then, now ethnic Chinese (who, like the Jews in Germany, were forced to purchase their way out), Vietnamese, Laotians, and Cambodians fled their homelands. Then, as now, people jammed together on boats, or in unhealthy detention camps, became sick, starved, and died. Physical and mental deterioration were the norm. The people, vessels, ports, countries, and even hemispheres have changed. But the moral issue has not. America, recognizing the permanence of refugee exoduses, now has a legislative means, a Refugee Act, to respond to refugee tragedies.

2 The Guarded Gate: Refugee Law and Policy

When Congress passed the Refugee Act of 1980, declaring "that it is the historic policy of the United States to respond to the urgent needs of persons subject to persecution in their homelands," the United States recognized its moral responsibility and its international obligation to the world's refugees. Shortly after the Refugee Act became law, Ronald Reagan, accepting the Republican nomination for the presidency, reaffirmed the credo of welcome and of hope for the world's persecuted:

> Can we doubt that only a divine Providence placed this land, this land of freedom, here as a refuge for all those people in the world who yearn to breathe free? Jews and Christians enduring persecution behind the Iron Curtain, the boat people of Southeast Asia, Cuba, and Haiti.[1]

But as students of America's refugee history know, the words of welcome have always been shadowed by the reality of restriction, the shining rhetoric dulled by the tarnish of rejection. Not all are welcome. It has been "the historic policy of the United States" to guard the gate of entrance; the gate remains guarded today. The Refugee Act notwithstanding, refugees who would begin their lives anew in the United States still must scale a wall of rejection, a wall built from the bricks of foreign policy and the mortar of budgets.

Since candidate Reagan became President Reagan, his rhetoric has been transmogrified. The numbers of Southeast Asian boat people have been "managed down"; Cuban admissions have fallen hostage to the realpolitik of Washington-Havana negotiations; Haitians are interdicted by American ships in international waters. Not a humanitarian law, but the exigencies of a restrictive policy govern the admission of refugees. The outlines of current American refugee policy have been clearly drawn by the Department of State:

> The Administration seeks to resolve refugee problems without resort to large programs for resettlement to the United States, but will continue to provide resettlement opportunities to maintain first asylum for refugees and to aid refugees with links to the United States. The Administration also seeks to encourage other nations to assume a greater level of responsibility for resettlement of refugees.[2]

United States refugee policy is based on a precedence of solutions. The preferred solution is to repatriate the refugee. If repatriation is not possible, then the United States seeks to resettle the refugee outside the United States. Only a select few will be accepted for admission to this country.

Repatriation, while it may be the most desirable solution, may be the hardest to attain. The forces that create refugees—wars, political turmoil, tyrannical and totalitarian regimes—are not easily undone. Until the cause of a refugee's flight has been removed, he cannot be repatriated. Nor is the second goal, resettlement outside the United States, always attainable. When a refugee flees his homeland, he attempts to gain entry to a country of first asylum; but, except for countries in Africa, first-asylum countries are loath to open their gates to large numbers of refugees. Non-African asylum countries fear that the refugees will resettle permanently in the asylum country, creating economic burdens and political and social tensions. In order that the countries of Southeast Asia and Central America will continue to provide safe havens for refugees, the United States encourages other countries to assume some of the burden, usually by donating money or commodities, either directly or through the United Nations High Commissioner for Refugees (UNHCR). However, when the countries of first asylum begin to stagger under the weight of many refugees, they threaten to seal off their borders, to turn away any refugees who seek asylum there. At that point, the United States will selectively admit refugees.

When Thailand and Malaysia began denying asylum to Indochinese refugees, before the United States could ask other countries to resettle them, this country had to demonstrate its own willingness to do so. The United States has admitted more Indochinese than all the other resettlement countries combined. The United States also eases entry to further other anti-Communist foreign-policy goals. For decades, America has encouraged and welcomed migration from the Soviet Union and other Communist countries. And, not insignificantly, America has become a country of first asylum for Cubans. But we admit only those refugees who serve our foreign policy ends. The United States has admitted very few Central Americans; in that region, we give precedence to repatriation and resettlement of refugees within the region.

When a refugee flees political persecution, which response—repatriation, resettlement abroad, or resettlement in the United States—will he meet? Who will be admitted? The answer to these questions is found in part in United States law, but more fully in United States policy.

The law, the Refugee Act of 1980, was intended to replace the patchwork of varying programs that had developed in response to individual refugee crises. "From the end of World War II until 1970," Deborah E. Anker and Michael H. Posner have observed, "the history of refugee admissions into the United

States is the story of a series of temporary responses to emerging crises."[3] The 1965 legislation was inadequate for the admission of refugees and had to be circumvented by means of the attorney general's parole. The executive reacted to refugee crises, and Congress acquiesced and grumbled about losing control of refugee admissions.

The Refugee Act was designed to be comprehensive and "to provide a permanent and systematic procedure for the admission . . . of refugees of special humanitarian concern to the United States, and to provide . . . effective resettlement and absorption." Laudable as these objectives might have been, however, the law has not resolved the persistent questions of who is a refugee and whom the United States should admit.

While the term *refugee* is an ancient concept, only under the League of Nations did it become an internationally recognized legal category.[4] A refugee is one who has a

well-founded fear of being persecuted for reasons of race, religion, nationality, membership of a particular social group or political opinion, is outside the country of his nationality and is unable or, owing to such fear, is unwilling to avail himself of the protection of that country; or who, not having a nationality and being outside the country or his former habitual residence as a result of such events, is unable or, owing to such fear, is unwilling to return to it.

This definition, part of the United Nations Convention Relating to the Status of Refugees, was adopted in 1951. The United States, however, was not a signatory to the convention and thus not bound by the United Nations definition. The first act to have the word *refugee* in its title, the Refugee Relief Act of 1953, even though it was enacted at the height of the Cold War, defined a refugee rather broadly as a person who had been driven from his country by "persecution, natural calamity, or military operations." This all-inclusive classification was soon narrowed in the Refugee-Escapee Act of 1957, under which the term applied only to those who were victims of racial, religious, or political persecution, fleeing from Communist or Communist-occupied or -dominated countries, or from a country in the Middle East. This definition remained in effect until the 1965 Immigration and Nationality Act, which created a permanent statutory authority to admit refugees. The 1965 act retained the ideological and geographic restrictions in the definitions, but also included persons uprooted by catastrophic natural calamities.

Three years later, the United States assented to the UN Protocol Relating to the Status of Refugees, with its nongeographic and nonideological definition. Now the United States statutory definition of a refugee was at odds with its international obligations.

It remained for the 1980 act to jettison the political restrictions that did not conform with the United Nations definition. The Refugee Act no longer recognizes as refugees those fleeing from natural catastrophes. (Victims of natural catastrophes theoretically are eligible for admission through private bills, parole, and emergency legislation.) The nonideological definition in the Refugee Act represented a victory for refugee advocates, the domestic human-rights lobby, and the United Nations High Commissioner for Refugees.[5] There was to be a single, universal standard: a "well-founded fear of persecution." Refugees from both right-wing and left-wing governments, and from anywhere in the world, could lay equal claim to the possibility of resettlement in the United States. Furthermore, the United States recognized a new category of refugees, those who remained within the country in which they were being persecuted. The latter provision offered haven to those persecuted persons who could not flee their countries, either because they were not permitted to emigrate or because they were being forcibly restrained, in political imprisonment or in internal exile.

As the United States definition expanded, so too did the number of refugees who could be considered for admission. Arnold H. Leibowitz, who as special counsel to the Senate Subcommittee on Immigration and Refugee Policy helped draft the Refugee Act, observed, "More and more, our policy was going to be transformed into a poststatutory debate as to who among the various claimants could enter the United States."[6]

Even though the refugee definition had been expanded, there were, and there remain, those who believe the definition did not go far enough, that it should also include people who have not been persecuted, but are simply in distress.[7] Whole groups of people fleeing from dangerous circumstances are now covered by the Organization of African Unity's (OAU) Convention on Refugees. The OAU definition adds to the protocol definition of a refugee:

> every person who, owing to external aggression, occupation, foreign domination or events seriously disturbing public order in either part or the whole of his country of origin or nationality, is compelled to leave his place of habitual residence in order to seek refuge in another place outside his country of origin or nationality.

This definition would cover the hundreds of thousands of noncombatants who are displaced by civil violence. But the United States and other nations, already besieged by myriad claimants who are individual targets of persecution, are unlikely to join the small number of countries which are signatories to the OAU's Convention on Refugees.

There is no dispute that those who run from civil disorder and generalized violence are, in every sense of the word, refugees. The United States acknowledges that they require humanitarian assistance, but denies that they also require resettlement in the U.S. Similarly, the law does not afford refugee status to those who have been driven from their homes by intolerable economic circumstances. Yet repressive governments may persecute their citizens precisely by restricting their ability to earn a livelihood. Such governments may retain power through enforcing the poverty, and powerlessness, of whole groups of citizens. In such cases, the distinction is tenuous between the political refugee and the economic migrant. It is sobering to recall that the expression *economic migrant* was first applied to Hitler's victims.[8]

Finally, what is to be the fate of the migrant who, though he had not been persecuted in his own country, departs without permission, a crime for which he may be punished? Has his act of unauthorized departure, by rendering him subject to possible reprisal, created refugee status for him? Has he become a refugee *sur place*? America's obligation to accept refugees is determined solely by law and policy. However, the UN Protocol Relating to the Status of Refugees obligates the United States not to return a refugee to a country where his life or freedom may be threatened. What, then, is to become of the refugee whom the United States does not accept and who can find no other country willing to resettle him? Though few in number, these refugees are sent from country to country, refugees in orbit.

The criteria for refugee status arise from the troublesome issue of admissions numbers. The more restricted the definition (and the application of that definition in actual practice), the smaller the number of eligible refugees. Like the debate over the refugee definition, the debate over admissions numbers antedates the Refugee Act and remains ongoing. How many should be admitted? Should there be separate ceilings for refugees and immigrants? Or should there be a single ceiling for both? These questions over refugee numbers are superimposed on the traditional background of contending restrictionist-admissionist philosophies.

Refugee admissions numbers have been a vexatious point with Congress. At issue are not only actual admissions numbers, but just as importantly, legislative prerogative. Prior to the passage of the Refugee Act, Congress was decidedly unhappy about the executive's use of the parole power for mass admissions. Mass parole, which had begun with the Hungarians, became an accepted means of admitting Cubans; between 1962 and May 1979, over 690,000 Cubans entered. The Cubans, in effect, entered neither under normal immigration procedures nor under the refugee provision of the Immigration and Nationality Act of 1965. Congress was further frustrated by the series of parole authorizations between 1975 and 1980 that permitted the entrance into the United States of large numbers of Indochinese.[9]

In the Refugee Act, Congress attempted to reassert its control over admissions by reworking the parole provision, instituting a flexible numerical ceiling, and requiring that the executive consult with the legislature. Although the act restricted the attorney general's parole authority for refugees, individuals and groups of aliens who were not refugees under the act's definition (for example, persons displaced in their own countries by military upheaval or natural disaster) conceivably could still be admitted under parole.

The issues of numbers and the linkage between immigration and refugee admissions still smolders. The drafters of the Refugee Act incorporated both a linkage and a limitation. The Refugee Act reduced the worldwide immigration quota from 290,000 to 270,000 and raised the annual limitation on regular refugee admissions from 17,400 to 50,000. The increase in refugee numbers, a Senate report noted, would be "accomplished without really increasing overall immigration to the United States" because the parole authority had been used repeatedly to exceed the 17,400 limit.[10] The act, in consonance with the restrictionist demand for limits, established a guideline of 50,000 "normal flow" refugees for the first three years. Thereafter in succeeding years, the president, after consultation with the Congress, would set the number of refugees to be admitted. During the first three years of the act, the executive prevailed upon the Congress to exceed the normal flow numbers. Foreign policy required that the Indochinese who were escaping into first asylum countries be resettled.

Some in the Congress argued that the Refugee Act had failed to keep the refugee numbers from expanding and that, furthermore, Congress had little role in the consultations. Leading the restrictionists, Kentucky's Senator Walter D. Huddleston in 1982 introduced an amendment to the Simpson-Mazzoli bill that would have included refugees within the overall total for immigrants. If more refugees were accepted, correspondingly fewer immigrants could enter. Huddleston, arguing for his amendment, stated that the Refugee Act "has created a vague, open-ended admission process that has never come close to keeping refugee flows anywhere near the fifty thousand-per-year normal flow." In the three years the Refugee Act had been in effect, admissions were running at over three hundred percent of normal flow. This had come about, Huddleston maintained, because "the consultation process is not adequate for assuring congressional control over refugee admission policies."[11]

Senator Alan K. Simpson, chairman of the Immigration Subcommittee, rebutted Huddleston's arguments. Simpson, himself no radical admissionist, defended the effectiveness of the consultation process and warned of the dangers of emasculating the refugee program. Simpson stated:

Refugees and immigrants are two distinct groups. . . . They should not be competing with each other for admission to the United States. . . . Immigration policy is principally concerned with family reunification; . . . refugee policy is concerned with the United States accepting its fair share of persons who are fleeing persecution in their homeland. Both policies obviously have a humanitarian purpose, but the two groups should never be allowed to compete for admission.

This administration strongly opposes the amendment also because of the severe limitations it would place on the flexibility that it requires in addressing domestic and foreign policy interests.[12]

The Huddleston Amendment failed (as did an amendment for a single-house congressional veto of refugee admission numbers), but the concerns it addressed have not disappeared. Until refugee admissions fall to "normal flow" levels or below, the issue of linkage is certain to reappear.

Despite the restrictionists' desire for tight statutory control over admission numbers, it was evident that the United States must respond flexibly to the fluctuations in refugee numbers. The act instituted a Solomonic compromise that reconciled the principle of executive flexibility with the principle of congressional control. After 1983, annual refugee ceilings were to be established by consultation between the president and the Congress, but, in the event of an unforeseen emergency, the ceiling could be raised after further congressional consultations.

Along with creating a procedural mechanism for arriving at refugee numbers, the Refugee Act also recognized statutorily the principle of asylum. Both the refugee and the asylee come under one definition and must demonstrate well-founded fear of persecution in their home country. The refugee, however, requests admission to the United States from *outside* its borders; he is brought to this country only after he has been accepted for resettlement. By contrast, the asylum seeker arrives on America's shores and asks for safe haven, a grant of asylum. Such status can be withdrawn if circumstances in the asylee's country change and he no longer has reason to fear persecution. Unlike refugees, all of whom are entitled to apply after one year for permanent resident status, each year no more than five thousand asylees may apply for such status. At the time of the passage of the Refugee Act, it was assumed, incorrectly, that few people would request asylum.

The Refugee Act also gave statutory recognition to the existing Office of the U.S. Coordinator for Refugee Affairs, and it

created an Office of Refugee Resettlement within the Department of Health and Human Services. The coordinator, to be
appointed by the president and confirmed by the Senate, was
given the rank of ambassador-at-large and had both foreign
and domestic responsibilities. He was authorized to represent
the United States and to negotiate with foreign governments
on refugee matters. The coordinator was responsible for developing policies and programs for refugee admission and resettlement.

The act called for consultation with the coordinator, the director of the Office of Refugee Resettlement, states, localities,
and voluntary agencies on refugee sponsorship and placement
distribution. And finally, it authorized programs for domestic
resettlement and assistance to refugees.

The Refugee Act of 1980 had scarcely been launched when
it was all but submerged in the backwash of the Mariel boatlift,
a crisis that would test every major provision of the untried act.
More threatening, however, to our refugee policy than the boatlift itself would be the responses it aroused, both in government
and in the American public. Thereafter, American refugee policy
would be less enlightened by the humanitarian policies of the
Refugee Act of 1980 than shadowed by fears of another Mariel,
another mass migration. Not the Refugee Act, but the Mariel
boatlift would become the benchmark against which all refugee
policies were measured; xenophobia and fear would, once again,
influence United States refugee policy and direct our practices.

Ironically, the Mariel disaster did not come about because of
any omissions or failures of the Refugee Act, but because of
earlier cold-war policies that the Refugee Act had been intended
to supplant, policies toward which the Reagan administration
has been inexorably returning. The Cubans who were brought
to the United States by the Mariel boatlift were only following
earlier migrations from Cuba, migrations that the United States
had actively encouraged and assisted.

Although the first Cubans to flee from Castro's takeover had been admitted as immigrants, the federal government assumed a substantial share of their resettlement costs, underwriting a full range of needs, from the communities' education and medical-attention costs, through food assistance, to the costs of job retraining and professional recertification. In 1961, the United States severed relations with Cuba; thereafter, Cubans were admitted as refugees under the parole power of the attorney general. Cuban immigration was effectively halted when, in 1962, the United States imposed a full trade embargo on Cuba, cutting off the commercial flights that had been bringing Cubans to this country. By that time, nearly two hundred thousand Cubans had been resettled in the United States. For the next three years, Cubans who wished to come to the United States had to leave without exit visas and travel via a third country.

As the embargo increasingly straitened Cuba's economy, the Cuban people became increasingly dissatisfied. Then, in 1965, Cuban president Fidel Castro, attempting to provide a safety valve for the mounting popular unrest, threw open the port of Camarioca, announcing that all who wished were free to leave. The American president responded to the challenge: Lyndon Johnson proclaimed that all Cubans "who seek refuge here will find it."[13] Cuban exiles in the United States hastily assembled a flotilla of boats which began ferrying Cubans from the port of Camarioca to the shores of south Florida. The voyage was far too dangerous for the small and overcrowded boats, and President Johnson instead instituted a regular airlift—two flights a day, five days a week—to carry the Cuban émigrés. By the time Cuba ended the flights in 1973, 270,000 Cubans had come to the United States. But an additional 135,000 Cubans, who had been approved for departure from Cuba and for resettlement in the United States, remained behind.

The time bomb that would be Mariel was slowly being assembled. A large and powerful community of Cuban exiles had been established in the United States. This community had, furthermore, been led to expect a generous welcome and preferential treatment for their compatriots. The cessation of Cuban emigration in 1973, rather than having cooled the potentially explosive situation, only inflamed it: families in Miami waited to be reunited with their relatives; Cubans who had been promised resettlement saw no hope of it. The final pieces of the bomb were put into place in 1978 and 1979, when Castro permitted the Cuban-Americans to return for visits to Cuba, to an island that Castro acknowledged was "sailing in a sea of difficulties, primarily economic in nature."[14] The Cuban-Americans flew in on a dream of wealth, spending huge sums of money that only aroused the frustrated longings of their countrymen. One hundred thousand exiles returned home, with all the apparent trappings of American luxury. When, in 1980, the port of Mariel was opened, the Cubans were ready to sail, and the Cuban-Americans were ready to receive them.

Edward A. McCarthy, the Catholic archbishop of Miami, who worked in resettlement for many years, saw the crisis building. Early in the Mariel crisis, Archbishop McCarthy spoke before the Senate:

The present exodus was an accident waiting to happen. . . . When the freedom flights slowed down and financing expired in 1973, no reasonable process for uniting Cuban families was substituted even though the need was evident. . . . The enormous frustration thus created on both sides of the Straits of Florida among separated families was bound to seek an outlet once the opportunity occurred. . . . In December 1978, we had the opportunity to talk to Secretary of State Vance and Assistant Attorney General Eagan about these matters and we predicted, unfortunately too accurately, what occurred at the American interest section last Friday. Our only surprise was that it took so long to occur.[15]

Archbishop McCarthy's had not been the only warning. Six weeks before Fidel Castro opened the port of Mariel, the Cuba

Analytic Center of the CIA had sent to the State Department a report predicting "that the Castro regime may again resort to large-scale emigration to reduce discontent caused by Cuba's deteriorating economic condition."[16] Over the succeeding weeks, the warning was repeated and was reinforced by other reports that the Cuban government was considering the reopening of Camarioca and wanted the United States to permit more Cuban immigration. Castro himself, in early March, threatened that if the United States continued to offer asylum to those who escaped on hijacked ships, in contravention of the antihijacking agreement between the two countries, Cuba might have "to take measures," as it had once by opening the port of Camarioca.[17] The State Department remained unruffled by either the CIA's warnings or Castro's threats. Instead, the department assured the Cuban government that under the soon-to-be-passed Refugee Act, the United States could admit Cubans at the rate of one thousand per month.[18]

The Department of State's response was both narrow and short of vision. From 1959 to 1980, the United States had admitted, under the attorney general's parole power, more than 750,000 Cubans. Although, in the terminology of the earlier legislation, these Cubans were considered refugees, their parole was essentially an immigration program. The refugee bill, however, if enacted, would terminate the attorney general's power to parole in national groups and, more importantly, would qualify for admission as refugees only those who had a well-founded fear of persecution. Some twenty thousand political prisoners and their families could be admitted under the Refugee Act, but a number of Cubans many times greater also waited to join their families, Cubans who could not qualify for refugee admission. American policy had, in the past, created a *presumption* that all Cubans were refugees and were to be given specific entitlements. Although that presumption no longer existed in law, it persisted in the plans of the Cuban exile community and in the expectations of their friends and relatives still in Cuba. That same presumption would continue to exist in the minds of United States immigration officials even after the Refugee Act had become law.

The persistence of that presumption, and with it the conviction of the Cuban exile community in the United States that the door remained open to Cuban entrants, made possible the success of Fidel Castro's dangerous stratagems. On April 1, 1980, six Cubans crashed through the gate of the Peruvian embassy and asked for political asylum. Infuriated, Castro withdrew the guard that protected the embassy and, within three days, the embassy grounds were teeming with 10,800 Cubans who wished to be given asylum. Conditions at the embassy rapidly grew unsafe, and Castro was persuaded to allow the asylum seekers to leave. Regular flights were begun, on April 12, to evacuate the refugees, and a number of countries volunteered to resettle them; the United States agreed to take thirty-five hundred. Three days later, Castro again reversed himself and, in a fit of pique, terminated the airlift.

The Cuban-American community needed no planes. On April 17, the day the airlift halted, they had assembled a small fleet of boats to bring a mercy shipment of food and medicine to the Peruvian embassy. The first boats returned with Cuban émigrés, and other boats were already leaving for Cuba when Fidel Castro, grasping the opportunity, proclaimed that any Cuban who wanted to leave for the United States was free to do so. The Cuban exile community immediately launched its sealift. Within a week, over two thousand Cubans had been brought to the United States, and there were reports that more than one thousand vessels were waiting at the port of Mariel to take on émigrés.[19]

The Department of State could do no more than warn that boat owners could be fined or imprisoned and that their boats could be seized. Although the State Department continued to maintain that the boat owners were subject to punishment, the highest immigration official in Miami ventured that if the Cuban entrants applied for political asylum, the boat captains would have broken no law in bringing them to this country.[20] The State Department conceded, however, that those Cubans who were brought into the country would suffer no penalties if they were given asylum, a status that the Cuban community had every reason to expect would be granted. As Refugee Coordinator Victor H. Palmieri told a House subcommittee, "We have had twenty years of accepting any Cuban who can get out, and you don't turn that situation around overnight. I don't know whether we should want to turn it around."[21]

In the event, however, what the administration wanted to do was irrelevant. The Cuban exile community, not the administration, was at the rudder. The State Department, on April 26, met with leaders of the Cuban community, asking that they cooperate in ending the sealift. The Cuban leaders unequivocally refused to do so, half of them turning their backs on the talks and, instead, countering with the demand that the United States return to its earlier immigration policy of bringing to this country all Cubans who wished to come and awarding them legal resident status.[22]

Nor were the Cuban exiles the only group exerting pressure on the administration. Nineteen eighty was an election year; Jimmy Carter's campaign was foundering in Florida, and Ronald Reagan, who was known to be a relentless foe of Fidel Castro, had been demanding, even before the Cubans had begun their boatlift, that the U.S. launch a "rescue . . . akin to the Berlin airlift—massive and swift," of the Cubans in the Peruvian embassy. Candidate Reagan at first proposed that the rescued Cubans be given asylum in Latin American countries.[23] When questioned, however, he became expansive and recommended that if no other country were willing to take in the refugees, the United States should take them all.[24]

But foreign policy was only one issue of the 1980 campaign. Of far more concern to the majority of the American public were questions of the domestic economy. The nation was in a

recession; Jimmy Carter had been pressing for budgetary aus-
terity; officials in Florida were demanding assistance in meeting
the needs of the newcomers. Interviewed in Florida, Refugee
Coordinator Palmieri explained that this consideration—the
economic burden to the United States that large numbers of
Cuban immigrants would impose—was constraining the
administration to reverse its policy of welcome and, instead, to
try to halt the sealift.[25]

Jimmy Carter was caught between the economy and the
campaign; for a brief, but ill-fated moment, Carter the cam-
paigner prevailed. Speaking before the League of Women Voters
in Washington, the president, in a burst of rhetoric, declared
that the United States would receive the Cubans "with an open
heart and open arms," and that he would request from the
Congress the monies necessary to meet their needs.[26] Within
days, to the distress of the Cuban community, Carter was qual-
ifying that welcome. The president proposed to substitute a
government air- and sealift to bring to the United States only
those Cubans who had been screened in Cuba and who qualified under one of several categories: Castro's political prisoners,
those who had sought asylum in the Peruvian embassy, and
immediate relatives of Cubans in the United States who had
permanent resident status.[27] It was, perhaps, too late, but Carter
was trying to reimpose on the Mariel crisis some legal standards
for admission.

On Capitol Hill, members of Congress were arguing whether
legal standards could be imposed, whether the Refugee Act
could be applied to what was being called a mass-asylum emergency. Senator Edward M. Kennedy, in a letter to President
Carter, maintained that the president could invoke the emergency provisions of the new legislation. Under these provisions,
if the president determines that there is "an unforeseen refugee
emergency," and that the admission of those refugees is "justified by grave humanitarian concerns or is otherwise in the
national interest," and if the refugees cannot be admitted through

the regular provisions of the Refugee Act, the president may then ask that a given number of those refugees be admitted to the United States. Senator Kennedy felt that the president should have invoked and used his emergency powers.[28]

Victor Palmieri, the new refugee coordinator, took the opposing position. Palmieri argued that the Refugee Act contained no provision for the admission of large numbers of people arriving directly on our shores, without any prescreening for admissibility. Others in the administration agreed, arguing that the Refugee Act had been intended to impose order on the process of admissions, whereas the Mariel influx could most charitably be described as disorderly. Many in the White House felt that new legislation was required.[29] Senator Kennedy, however, feared that "if we fail to use the Refugee Act now, with the flexibility and scope for which it was intended, we will likely compromise its future use just as it has been signed into law."[30]

The two sides remained unalterably apart, primarily because each defined differently what the responsibilities of the United States ought to be. Senator Kennedy, with the more forward-looking view, recognized that the United States was becoming a country of first asylum. As such, we had to respond as any other place of first asylum would—he used the examples of Malaysia and Hong Kong—by providing safe haven only until the refugees were either admitted to the United States or resettled elsewhere.[31] The White House, on the other hand, clung to the historic policy of the United States that all Cubans who arrived on our shores would be resettled in this country.

Representative Elizabeth Holtzman, chairman of the House Subcommittee on Immigration, Refugees and International Law, took a third position. Representative Holtzman maintained that refugee status should not be granted to an entire class of people, but should be determined, as required by the Refugee Act, on an individual basis. "Political prisoners," she argued, "and others who can demonstrate that they meet the refugee definition in individual adjudications should be granted asylum, given benefits in accordance with the Refugee Act of 1980, and allowed to adjust their status after one year. No one who does not meet the refugee definition should be granted refugee status; individual adjudications, not class determinations, should be the rule." Cubans who qualified under the immigration laws to be reunited with their families could be admitted as immigrants. For the remaining Cubans, Holtzman recommended a possible parole, under which the entrants would remain in the United States but could not become legal permanent residents unless under specific legislation.[32]

Much more was at stake here than the admission of a group, no matter how large, of Cuban asylum seekers. Also at issue was the role of the Refugee Act, whether it would enlighten our refugee and asylum admissions in the future or merely impede them. In this regard, Representative Holtzman was correct in insisting that refugee admissions be made individually and not revert to the kind of group parole that had been the earlier practice. A second critical consideration was to avoid establishing a sense of entitlements for the future, like those that had been established through past policies toward Cuban immigrants. Finally, however, it needed to be borne in mind that Mariel Cubans were not, for the most part, refugees. This was not, as many called it, a mass-asylum emergency, but a mass migration.

It was rapidly becoming evident that, among the thousands landing each week on the Florida shores, a number of people were neither refugees nor even immigrants, were not legally admissible to the United States. Fidel Castro wanted to cleanse his country of those who opposed his revolution—political opponents he had released from prison and asylum seekers who had immured themselves within the Peruvian embassy. He was also pleased to release those Cubans who wanted to work not for the Cuban revolution but for the American dream. Together they were seen as antisocial elements; but it was not long before

Castro was forcing onto the American boats other antisocial elements—inmates of Cuba's prisons and mental institutions, drug dealers, the retarded, the unwanted.

Nor did everyone who arrived during the Mariel boatlift set sail from Mariel, from Cuba. For some years, Haitians had been coming in a small, but steady stream. The Haitians, who fled a cruelly repressive and brutally impoverished country, came for many reasons: some were forced out by persecution, others by poverty. None were acknowledged by the United States as genuine refugees. Successive administrations had taken the position, now become dictum, that Haitians were all economic migrants, best dealt with through measures designed to discourage their arrival and hasten their departure. These practices persisted throughout the Mariel emergency; a State Department official would later explain that Cubans and Haitians had to be treated differently because the "foreign-policy aspects" of their migrations were different. The Cubans, it was said, had been forced out by a totalitarian and unfriendly government. The Haitians, on the other hand, came by choice from a country whose "friendly government is interested in enforcing its laws and . . . wishes to cooperate with the United States in bringing illegal migration under control, . . ."[33] In other words, it mattered not whether an individual was or was not a refugee, but only whether the United States could prevail upon that individual's government not to permit undocumented departures. The Immigration and Naturalization Service was equally committed to the status quo, in the first weeks of the emergency giving each Cuban entrant an application for political asylum, while classifying the Haitians as undocumented entrants.

It was not long, however, before Haitian supporters in this country had made public the disparity of treatment, and forced the administration to aver that it would now classify Haitians as applicants for political asylum and would process and assist them in the same manner as Cubans. The latter promise would not be fulfilled.

As word spread that all were being welcomed to the United States, the numbers of Haitian arrivals increased; fifteen thousand would join the Cuban exodus. When the last American boats had left the port of Mariel, Haitians continued to come.

Because so many Cubans and Haitians could qualify as neither immigrants nor refugees, and because the United States was unwilling to grant refugee status to the Haitians, the administration, rather than follow Representative Holtzman's suggestion, created a new status for *all* the Mariel arrivals: special entrant. The status applied to all Cubans and Haitians who were within the United States before the cut-off date (originally June 20, 1980; later extended to October 10, 1980). But the inequities had not been put to rest. The special entrant status did not allow one to apply for permanent resident status, the first step toward citizenship. In 1984, however, the Reagan Justice Department did conclude that under a 1966 law, Cubans could become permanent residents and then citizens. Haitians could not.

When the government decided that the Mariel Cubans and Haitians were to become special entrants, it was also deciding that they would not be considered for either refugee status or asylum. The provisions of the Refugee Act had, in a single stroke, become moot. For the Mariel entrants, the refugee definition was irrelevant and the provisions for reimbursement of resettlement costs were inapplicable. The refugee coordinator was reduced to no more than a figurehead. As the Mariel crisis progressed, the role of the coordinator became increasingly peripheral until, in the end, Ambassador Palmieri chose to withdraw from administering the crisis and to concentrate his attentions on those areas in which he had clear authority.[34]

When the Mariel boatlift began, the refugee coordinator had not yet been given either the authority or the appropriations that he would need to perform effectively. The White House, therefore, seeing the boatlift as a crisis in need of immediate resolution, gave responsibility not to the coordinator's office but to the Federal Emergency Management Agency (FEMA), the expertise of which lay in dealing with natural disasters. Although FEMA was experienced in providing for the physical needs of displaced people, the refugee crisis presented problems for which FEMA was totally unprepared. Such a basic process as screening for refugee admission was beyond the ken of the agency. Yet it is significant that the administration, in appointing the Federal Emergency Management Agency, had decided that Mariel, though an emergency, was not a refugee emergency. Later, a new agency was created—the Cuban Task Force, which, with the inclusion of the Haitians under the special entrant status, became the Cuban-Haitian Task Force. The Cuban-Haitian Task Force was to work under the refugee coordinator, out of the Department of State. Yet the White House continued to regard Mariel as though it were, in the words of Mario Rivera, a participant and researcher, a "domestic-policy—and political—problem."³⁵

The office of the refugee coordinator would never attain the stature or the presence that the Refugee Act envisioned. Indeed, the coordinator's role would become less that of policymaker and more that of chief bureaucrat, so that eventually the office was able to operate for months with no coordinator at all.

Of equal significance, however, with the effect of the Mariel emergency on the Refugee Act, was its effect on the attitudes of the American people. An unready Miami reeled as the numbers of Cuban arrivals outran available sponsors and shelters, and newcomers were "housed" under the bleachers of a football stadium, in armories and churches. In Dade County, Florida, the newcomers crowded into firetrap apartments, filled the jails, and overburdened the hospitals; food stamps ran out; the crime rate rose; and many among the aged in Miami's population grew fearful.

Attempting to impose some measure of control on the influx, the federal government moved newly arriving Cubans from Florida to camps in Maryland, Arkansas, Pennsylvania. In camp after camp, Mariel Cubans rioted and rampaged, and the National Guard moved in with tear gas and billy clubs; the uneasy townspeople protested.

In time, the majority of the Cubans were resettled in receiving communities, the criminals were jailed, and the mentally ill placed in hospitals. But another kind of order had also asserted itself; in the words of Monsignor Bryan Walsh, head of Catholic Charities for the Archdiocese of Miami, "Mariel has made it respectable to be anti-Cuban."[36] The spirit of welcome that had been cautiously emerging during the years of the Indochinese Refugee Program was frightened into withdrawal. After Mariel, restrictionism once again became respectable, and xenophobia could step from the shadows.

A woman in Florida wrote that "we are living in an alien society. It is geared to Latins everywhere we go—shopping centers, recreation areas, neighborhoods, churches, and schools. We would like to see an ethnic balance in our county and state. That way everyone is equal and shares the same problems."[37] Another wrote, "Legal and illegal aliens are settling here in unprecedented numbers. Can we afford more? The influx into Florida has caused more crime, higher taxes, greater unemployment, a squeeze on housing, inflated welfare and food-stamp costs, and educational expenses that are staggering. It is time we firmly said 'no' and declared a moratorium on all immigration, at least until we balance the budget."[38]

Through all the anger and hatred, a single refrain seemed to best reassure the American public of its rightness—the rationalization that although the United States had been a nation of immigrants, a nation of people who came here for a better life, that way of life could be diminished if we did not now shut the door. In Miami, the grandson of Italian immigrants, a Mr. Del Russo, led a rally of suburban homeowners in protest against a proposed refugee-processing center. Their placards read: "In America, We Speak English," and "Deport Illegal Aliens. Save Your Jobs." Mr. Del Russo explained, "Our ancestors settled this country as political refugees. But we're in a different time now. Let's not overdo it. I don't think it's America's job to take care of the world. We can't afford to take care of ourselves."[39]

For many Americans, Mariel had come to symbolize the sense of helplessness they felt against the machinations of foreign powers, a failing economy, and a surpassing crime rate. It eased the frustration to give a face to America's problems—the face of the "illegal alien." Before long the face provoked a rallying cry: America must regain control of her borders.

Ronald Reagan took office with a mandate to reestablish the United States as a world power, to revive the economy, and to restore law and order. The Reagan administration quickly grasped the potential inherent in that rallying cry. A nation that controlled its borders would also be saying to the world that it brooked no violations of its sovereignty, that Americans would fill American jobs, and that we would not only enforce our immigration laws, but protect our citizens from lawbreaking aliens. The administration moved in two directions. For refugees, those who entered the United States after having been approved abroad for resettlement here, the goal was to "manage down" the numbers—to find other options than resettlement in the United States—so that fewer refugees would be admitted. For asylum seekers, the goal was "deterrence" and denial, to discourage or prevent the actual arrival of asylum seekers on our shores, or, for those who would not be deterred, to deny asylum to refugees from groups that threatened to arrive in large numbers.

The fledgling Refugee Act was again being put to the test. And once again, refugee policy diverged from the intentions of the law. Foreign policy, budgetary restraints, and concerns about resettlement continued to dominate refugee policy. For the Reagan administration, which refugees would be "of special humanitarian concern to the United States"?

Refugees, as in the past, could only enter the United States by passing through a series of gates guarded by both law and policy. The law guarded refugee admission through the definition of a refugee in the Refugee Act, and through eligibility for immigration as specified in the Immigration and Nationality Act. Policy regulated ceilings, allocations, and priorities, and determined which refugees were of "special humanitarian concern." Congress wrote the law; policy was the province of the State Department. Congress, aside from its annual approval of admissions ceilings and its linked concern over resettlement costs, has given but cursory attention, thought, and direction to other policy areas.

From the beginning, the annual refugee consultations have disclosed a decided imbalance in the partnership between the executive and the Congress. During the first consultation after the passage of the Refugee Act, Illinois Representative Henry J. Hyde voiced his concerns on four points:

> One, the dilution of congressional control over immigration by granting almost absolute power to the President to determine refugee admissions for the coming fiscal year. Two, the inadequate control the consultation process gives to Congress in adjusting numbers of refugees to be admitted. Three, the fear that political decisions would be the primary consideration in any refugee admissions program, rather than valid humanitarian concerns. And four, the only control which could modify a Presidential proposal would be exercised by a funding committee rather than the substantive committee, the Committee on the Judiciary.[40]

Five annual consultations later, Representatives Peter W. Rodino, Jr., and Hamilton Fish, Jr., chairman and ranking minority member, respectively, of the Committee on the Judiciary, wrote to President Reagan that "We are pleased to advise you that we interpose no objections to the number and allocations as recommended. We believe, however, that no reallocation of refugee numbers between regions should take place during the fiscal year without notifying the Committee on the Judiciary sufficiently in advance to permit an expression of an opinion should it be deemed advisable." Representative Romano L. Mazzoli, in his capacity as chairman of the Subcommittee on Immigration, Refugees, and International Law, also wrote to the president, and was more forceful. He "saw no valid reason why admissions cannot be reduced. . . . The United States should not admit any more refugees for resettlement than it is willing to properly finance." He voiced dissatisfaction with the consultation process because it was a "cut and dried notice," and he expressed his concern that the admissions program was tilted too heavily toward Indochinese refugees; a better regional and nationality balance was in order. Mazzoli concluded by reminding the president that "The Refugee Act of 1980 was intended to eliminate ideology and geography as the controlling factors in our refugee admissions program. We seem not to have accomplished this most important objective and a more balanced program would certainly be a step in the right direction."[41]

Ideology and geography, not solely humanitarian impulses, shape the policy. Before a person may be granted refugee status, two determinations must be made. First, whether refugee numbers have been allocated for the region of a person's nationality; and second, whether the person is within a group designated to be of "special humanitarian concern." Even an individual who could qualify for admission under the Refugee Act will not be admitted if no allocations exist for his country and his group.[42]

The president, in practice the State Department, presents to the refugee committees in the Senate and the House a report, "Proposed Refugee Admissions and Allocations," for the forthcoming fiscal year. The proposal allocates refugee numbers for each region of the world (Africa, East Asia, Eastern Europe and the Soviet Union, Latin America and the Caribbean, and the Near East and South Asia) and puts forth, as well, the administration's case for admitting certain groups within each region. In fact, the numbers apply to particular groups rather than entire regions. Thus, for example, the numbers for Latin America are intended primarily for Cuban political prisoners. These admissions are said to be justified "by humanitarian needs and domestic and foreign policy concerns." The report affirms quite clearly that the State Department evaluates refugees' cases on the basis of "the national interest of the United States, the refugees' situation in temporary asylum, the conditions from which they have fled."[43]

The report gives an overview of the world refugee situation, reviews refugee and resettlement policy, and highlights the past year's activities. It presents the actual numbers admitted in the past year and proposes refugee admission levels for the forthcoming fiscal year. (Since the passage of the Refugee Act, actual admissions have always been fewer than the congressionally approved "normal flow" ceiling.) Finally, it justifies the regional numbers and offers explanations as to why refugee programs have included some national groups and excluded others.

The critical designation of "special humanitarian concern" is frequently subject to differing interpretations. When the Refugee Act was being drafted, the House Judiciary Committee report emphasized "that the plight of the refugees themselves as opposed to national-origin or political considerations should be paramount in determining which refugees are to be admitted to the United States."[44] But the lofty rhetoric is at odds with the reality of policy. Foreign and domestic politics in fact determine who is of "special humanitarian concern."

The same policy considerations determine admission numbers and allocations. The consultation process, in theory, could work to change admission numbers and allocations in regions and countries. In practice, it does not. There is little cooperative decision-making between the executive and the Congress. Congress rarely challenges the State Department's allocations. Refugee programs fall within the purview of the Senate and House

Judiciary committees because the Immigration and Naturalization Service is within the Department of Justice. The Foreign Affairs Committee, although it possesses the expertise to check and complement the State Department's reports, does not participate in the consultation process.

The State Department's "Proposed Refugee Admissions and Allocations" report and the supporting State Department's "Country Reports on the World Refugee Situation" are generally taken at face value, this despite their having been questioned by nongovernmental groups. Americas Watch, the Helsinki Watch, the Lawyers Committee for International Human Rights, Amnesty International, and other respected groups have challenged findings of fact and interpretation.

The consultation process has other deficiencies. It takes place late in the fiscal year, generally just a few weeks before the new fiscal year is to begin. (The federal government's fiscal year begins on October 1 and ends on September 30.) By the time of the consultation, the budget which drives the policy process has already been developed, so admissions numbers and resettlement costs command the largest part of the hearings. In recent years, there has been less public testimony in the refugee hearings. The Refugee Policy Group, the respected independent center of policy analysis and research in refugee issues, has noted that "lacking now is regular, public input into the refugee determination process through formal, open testimony and presentation of perspectives."[45] The voices of the voluntary agencies, human rights organizations, the UN High Commissioner for Refugees, the Intergovernmental Committee for Migration, and other public interest groups are quieter.

The regional allocations submitted to Congress are not firm and can become a numbers game. When the number of refugees in a given region is high, policymakers have three alternatives: to increase or reallocate admissions numbers, to restrict eligibility (either by interpreting the refugee definition restrictively or changing priorities administratively), or to create a backlog of approved cases. As an example of reallocating admissions numbers, in fiscal year 1984, two thousand admissions that had been allocated to other regions were given to Southeast Asia, so that more refugees could be admitted from that region. Admissions numbers also can be manipulated. In recent years, the ceiling for the Soviet Union and Eastern Europe has been much higher than actual entries. The numbers have been inflated to embarrass the Soviet Union by encouraging emigration. In other regions as well, there is no real possibility that the available slots will be used. In 1985, Latin America was allocated three thousand entries, but these were intended almost exclusively for Cuban political prisoners. A mere 156 refugees were actually admitted.[46]

It is only after Congress has approved the State Department's formulae for refugees of special humanitarian concern and its geographical allocations that the actual decisions are made as to who will be admitted. Groups and individuals are processed for admission according to a Worldwide Priorities System (WPS), which in the noncommittal words of the State Department, "sets administrative guidelines to manage refugee admissions into the United States and ensures an organized processing of refugees within the established annual regional ceilings."[47] The key word here is *administrative*. Congress treats the WPS as an administrative matter, and by and large, shows little interest in the priorities process. But the priorities, fully as much as the allocations, decree which refugees will be eligible for resettlement in the United States.

There are six priorities for admission to the United States. The highest priority is given to refugees deemed to be of "compelling concern/interest," those whose lives are in immediate danger or those who are present or former political prisoners. The second and fourth priorities are given to those who have links to the United States, through having worked for the U.S. government or for American organizations or businesses. Priorities three and five are given to family reunification cases, relatives of persons permanently in the United States. The final priority is reserved for those in "specified regional groups whose admission is in the national interest."[48] Critically, while certain regions of the world are awarded all six priorities, others may have far fewer.

Priorities are not preferences. Processing for an entire national group takes place within all the approved priorities. Thus, someone in priority two does not usually get preference over someone in priority three, and priority three does not take preference over priority four, and so on. If an applicant satisfies any priority being processed, he gains a place in the pool of eligible applicants. On the other hand, no matter how well-founded a refugee's fear of persecution may be, if he does not fit into a priority for his country, he is ineligible for consideration.

In actual practice, people who have already departed their country of origin are no longer in priority one—"in immediate danger of loss of life." For the most part, priority one applies only to political prisoners. Priorities two through five, under which the refugee either has ties to the United States or has family here, form the basis for most refugee admissions. The emphasis on family ties, especially in the case of long-term refugee flows, blurs the line between persons who genuinely need refugee resettlement slots and persons who are eligible for admission through regular immigration. This distortion of the critical distinction between a bona fide refugee and someone who enters as a refugee, rather than wait for entrance as an immigrant, does a disservice to the spirit and intent of the Refugee Act.

Moreover, priorities are awarded to various regions according to the State Department's foreign-policy positions. Refugees from the Soviet Union and Eastern Europe (with the exception of East Germans and Yugoslavs) are eligible for admission under all six priorities. Since 1982, there has been a special refugee program for Poles who had been detained under martial law. This program has brought some three thousand Poles to the

United States. Rumania, which has been granted most favored nation status, deals out exit permits as bargaining chips to enhance its trade position. Rumanians are processed for admission directly from Bucharest in a Third Country Resettlement Program.

In Africa, refugee applicants from Ethiopia, Angola, Malawi, Mozambique, Namibia, South Africa, Uganda, and Zaire are eligible in all priorities. In the Sudan, priorities one through five are considered. The overwhelming majority of African refugees who are accepted for resettlement in the United States, however, are urbanized Ethiopians fleeing from the country's repressive Marxist government.

In Latin America, a spawning ground for refugees, and the Caribbean, only those who fall within priorities one and two—political prisoners or former employees of the United States government—are eligible for consideration. The United States has accepted only a handful of Argentinians, Chileans, Nicaraguans, and Salvadorans. The only Latin Americans the United States has admitted in large numbers are the Cubans.[49]

In the Near East and South Asia, the nationality groups eligible for refugee status are Afghans and Iranians who are within priorities one through four. However, the State Department expanded priority four to include persons who could show they suffered persecution because of their religion, making Baha'is, Jews and Christians from Iran, Iraqi Christians, Kurds, and Syrian Jews eligible.

In Southeast Asia (the region is officially East Asia), Vietnamese, Laotians, and Kampucheans (Cambodians) are processed from first asylum countries. Members of these three groups who arrived in countries of first asylum prior to April 1982 are eligible for processing in all six categories. Those who arrived after the 1982 cut-off date are eligible in priority categories one through five. In addition, there is an Orderly Departure Program (ODP), through which Vietnamese are processed directly from Vietnam.

ODP, established in 1979 under the auspices of the UNHCR, provides an alternative to the dangerous exodus by boat. Under the ODP, representatives of resettlement countries, in Vietnam, select Vietnamese who are permitted to leave. Since its inception, over 119,000 persons have left Vietnam, more than 47,500 of them to the United States. The operation of the program, however, is subject to the vicissitudes of Vietnamese–United States relations. On January 1, 1986, the Vietnamese government refused to allow further interviewing of ODP applicants until the fifteen thousand Vietnamese who had already been granted exit permits, and had been interviewed, were accepted for admission. But American processing, even after an interview had been conducted, took time; the authorities had to check for fraud, and the applicants had to obtain documentation to prove family ties. Those Vietnamese who had been interviewed and accepted for admission prior to the suspension of processing continue to leave. But the numbers of emigrants have dropped off sharply since the interviewing was halted.[50] Of those coming out of Vietnam, few are former U.S. government employees or current and former re-education camp prisoners; most of the migrants are accepted because of family ties.

ODP also brings in Amerasians, the children of American fathers and Vietnamese mothers, and their close relatives. The number of Amerasians who enter the United States under the Amerasian Act of 1982 is small. The Amerasian Act applies to children fathered by American servicemen since 1950 and abandoned in Korea, Vietnam, Laos, Thailand, and Cambodia. Under ODP, about thirty-six hundred children, along with some five thousand of their mothers and other close family members, have entered as refugees.[51] It is an anomaly that Amerasians enter under the Refugee Act, rather than the Amerasian law; this has come about because the Amerasian Act requires that the mother or legal guardian of the child release him irrevocably for immigration, and that a U.S. citizen or resident alien assume legal custody and support the child for five years. As the Amer-

asian children in Vietnam generally live with their mothers or
close family members, enforcing separation would not be in
the best interest of the child or the mother. The State Department believes "that entering the United States with their mothers as refugees under the Refugee Act of 1980 provides the most
humane and workable means for bringing Amerasian children
to the United States."[52] Bringing the children and their families
to the United States as refugees also qualifies them for overseas
English-language training, cultural orientation, and domestic
resettlement assistance.

In trying to ameliorate the plight of the pitiful *bui doi*, the
dust children of Vietnam, the State Department is acting hu-
manely. Children of mixed parentage lead harsh lives characterized by harassment and discrimination. These children are
an American obligation. But bringing them and their relatives
in under the refugee quota is inappropriate. Secretary of State
George P. Shultz commissioned the Ray Panel—named after
chairman Robert D. Ray, former governor of Iowa—to review
the Indochinese refugee situation and U.S. policies and options
in responding to it, and the panel recommended in April 1986
that Congress amend the Amerasian legislation. The legislation
should be changed to provide for the admission of mothers and
other close family members with Amerasian children and waive
or simplify the law's support and sponsorship requirements.
The panel specifically recommended "that there should be no
upper limit to the number of Vietnamese-American children
and their close relatives that the United States is prepared to
receive, regardless of allocations or ceilings that may be set for
other purposes."[53] Because by definition the numbers of
Vietnamese-American children are limited, and because they
are the direct consequences of the American presence, the Ray
Panel's recommendation makes good sense.

The present Worldwide Priorities System has been criticized.
The Refugee Policy Group (RPG), for one, has suggested that
there should be a broader category for refugees of compelling

concern, even those whose lives may not be in immediate danger. Another criticism is that the priority categories are treated as administrative matters and are offered or withdrawn at the discretion of the State Department. When the State Department removes certain categories from consideration, it also reduces the number of eligible applicants. The apparent logic behind the priorities appears to be that some refugees are more equal than others.

It is desirable that the United States respond flexibly to the needs of refugees. But the priorities, as opposed to preferences, work to discriminate against certain refugees. "The establishing and imposing of priority categories," a Refugee Policy Group report has noted, "is so major a determinant of refugee eligibility that it should be taken up as a formal part of the consultation process."[54] RPG believes there should be a formal public review not only of the rationale behind the priority system, but also on the adequacy of the categories. Such a review, obviously, implies a rethinking of the entire refugee program.

When the administration sets priorities, it creates policy; but the process by which the Immigration and Naturalization Service admits refugees can either further or thwart that policy. Before the Refugee Act was passed, persons who were eligible for admission were presented to an immigration official who would screen the applicant's background for anything that might make him excludable under United States immigration law. But with the passage of the Refugee Act, the INS had, in addition, to be satisfied that the applicant was a bona fide refugee. No longer could all Indochinese in refugee camps be given "categorical eligibility." Henceforth, each case had to be reviewed for its own merits. What seemed, at first, to be a minor bureaucratic modification became a major policy contretemps.

In early 1981, INS officers in Southeast Asia began to review each refugee's application to ascertain whether he or she met the definition of a refugee. By the spring of 1981, the INS had rejected nearly all of the thirty-one thousand Khmer applicants, as well as a large number of Vietnamese, as being "economic refugees." Morton Abramowitz, then the United States ambassador to Thailand, incensed about the high rate of rejection, cabled Washington: "Presumably after World War II, INS would have rejected as refugees the remaining Jews from Germany on the grounds they could go back to Germany."[55]

In Washington, a tug of war was taking place between those who wanted a large Indochinese admissions program to bolster foreign policy objectives and fight Communism, and those who wanted to restrict admissions to keep down resettlement costs and reduce domestic strains. Secretary of State Alexander Haig persuaded Attorney General William French Smith to overrule the INS. The Reagan administration agreed to return temporarily to presumptive eligibility for those refugees, and to suspend the case-by-case determination through September 30, 1981.

Haig, in consultation with Smith, established a special refugee advisory panel to resolve the issue. The panel, which reported its findings in the fall of 1981, upheld the State Department's presumption that all Indochinese were categorically eligible. However, in the 1982 congressional consultations, the executive and Congress reached a tacit agreement to reinstate case-by-case review, an agreement that, in the "Revised INS Processing Guidelines for Indochinese Refugees," gave the INS final say as to who was admissable.

Once again, the INS was deciding on a case-by-case basis. Robert P. DeVecchi of the International Rescue Committee subsequently observed:

The results again were devastating, both as regards articulation by the U.S. of a coherent rational refugee policy to countries of first asylum and resettlement, and determination in a decent, humane way the fate of thousands of innocent persons. The rates of rejection of otherwise qualified applicants . . . varied from post to post, week to week, and INS office to INS office. . . . The number of applicants who were rejected as not meeting the definition of a refugee grew to startling proportions—over 50 percent of the applicants for many weeks. Terms like "economic migrant" were used to describe anyone who said he had left Cambodia in 1979 because he was starving to death. "Intending immigrant" was the phrase invented to describe a survivor of Pol Pot who found his or her only living relatives in the U.S. and wanted to join them to rebuild their shattered lives. Of the applicant who had seen his family killed before his eyes by the soldiers of Pol Pot, INS interviewers found "persecution suffered under the previous regime was not germane."[56]

The case-by-case determination continued to vex. In late fall of 1982, in an attempt to remedy the processing problems, INS officials from the Washington office visited Southeast Asia and afterward issued a series of clarifying instructions, known as the Kamput cables, to officers in the field. The Kamput cables notwithstanding, differences persisted between, on the one hand, personnel of the Joint Voluntary Agencies and the State Department and, on the other, the INS inspectors. Finally, the National Security Council asked the attorney general to review Indochinese processing. As a result, INS commissioner Alan C. Nelson, in August 1983, issued the "Worldwide Guidelines for Overseas Processing."

The guidelines, an attempt at compromise, allowed that although the burden of proof continued to rest with the applicant, there were clearly defined groups of persecuted persons, within which individuals might be presumed to be eligible for refugee status. In short, a refugee who could prove that he fell within one of those categories was entitled to admission. Categories were established for Southeast Asia processing only and were "to be treated as subject to on-going review and modification as circumstances change."[57] In addition, it was noted that it would be well to develop categories for other refugee-producing areas of the world. Even with the new processing guidelines, however, problems remained.

United States law denies refugee status to those who have persecuted others, and in many cases, a refugee who had been affiliated with the Khmer Rouge was, for that reason alone, denied refugee status. The rejection rates for Khmer were high, and in 1984 the Senate Committee on Foreign Relations sent a staff member to investigate their processing. The study found "serious shortcomings," a lack of reliable information that could demonstrate whether an applicant for resettlement had been a Khmer Rouge or had participated in the persecution of other Cambodians. The INS in the field needed detailed guidance from Washington. Until such guidance could be provided, screening of the Khmer should be suspended. The study found, "Large numbers of refugees are probably unfairly branded as KR without appreciably increasing the chances of identifying the truly guilty."[58] The staff report further noted that "Washington writes off criticism from humanitarian groups and private refugee agencies as the special pleadings of do-gooders and advocates. Unfortunately real problems exist."[59]

One of those humanitarian groups, the United States Committee for Refugees, in April of 1986 issued a comprehensive and thoughtful analysis of the INS rejection of roughly 14,500 Cambodians in Thailand's Khao I Dang holding center. Stephen Golub, the author of the report, criticized the INS for "looking for phantoms that are not there."[60] Golub suggested that new guidelines be constructed. To date, new guidelines have not been instituted, but rejected cases are being reviewed. Dissatisfied with INS's high rejection rates and its review process, Senator Mark O. Hatfield of Oregon and Representative Chester Atkins of Massachusetts introduced in Congress the Indochinese Refugee Resettlement and Protection Act of 1987. The bill, among its other provisions, would give the State Department, rather than the Immigration and Naturalization Service, the authority to admit refugees in East Asia.[61]

Not only have INS processing procedures in Southeast Asia been criticized; so has processing in Europe. Refugee decisions in Europe, which should have been made on merit, were, in fact, being made on a group basis. In Southeast Asia, the INS had presumed against the Khmer, while in Europe, the INS was presuming that persons departing from Communist countries were refugees.

The processing of refugees can limit those who are eligible for consideration. Most Africans are not eligible for processing in Europe because it is felt that local settlement is available to them in Africa. Ethiopians were processed in Europe until February 1982; since then, only those Ethiopians who come directly from Eastern European countries (where many have been students) may apply. Prior to 1982, Cubans were processed from Madrid; since then, only former political prisoners may be processed there. If a person cannot apply for processing abroad, he is effectively blocked from requesting refugee status; his only choice is to journey to the United States and request asylum.

In Europe, there are no processing guidelines equivalent to those in effect in Southeast Asia. Patricia Weiss Fagan, of the Refugee Policy Group, investigated the processing by INS offices in Rome, Vienna, and Frankfurt. INS interviewers told her that because the INS received inadequate country information, the agency could not judge the substance of the refugee applications.[62] Then too, the INS European offices differ in approach and standards of evidence. It is possible for similar cases to be decided differently by different offices. Similar cases in the same office may also be decided differently according to what time of year they are presented. Early in the year, there is a tendency to apply the criteria for refugee status stringently; later in the year, if the numbers allotted to the office have not been used, the standards of proof may be relaxed, allowing migrants to qualify as refugees. The allotted numbers become less like a ceiling and more like a quota.

Determinations of special humanitarian concern, ceilings, regional allocations, priorities, and processing procedures all either reflect or affect refugee policy. The Refugee Act was intended to be geographically and ideologically neutral. The law has been neutral, the policy has not. Gil Loescher and John A. Scanlan, in their definitive study, *Calculated Kindness: Refugees and America's Half-Open Door, 1945 to the Present*, quote an anonymous State Department official: "The Refugee Act established a set of new procedures, but instituted no new policy."[63] The State Department officer was correct. Although admissions are no longer by parole, and numbers and allocations are now authorized by Congress, the refugees who are most likely to be resettled in the United States still come primarily from Communist countries. In the first six years since the passage of the Refugee Act, the United States took in approximately 800,000 Indochinese, 178,000 East Europeans and Soviets, and, from all the rest of the world, only slightly more than 78,800. And most of those 78,800 were Afghanis, Ethiopians, and Cubans—in short, refugees from Communist governments.[64] And the bias persists. For fiscal year 1987, the proposed regional ceilings are Africa, 3,500; East Asia, 40,500; Eastern Europe and the Soviet Union, 10,000; Latin America and the Caribbean, 4,000; Near East and South Asia, 8,000; and reserve for unanticipated admissions, 4,000.[65] Clearly refugees fleeing non-Communist governments have not been, and will not be, welcomed.

Refugee admissions have been "humanitarian" only insofar as they serve "the special interests of the United States," interests that, abroad, will embarrass the Communists and, domestically, will satisfy special interest groups. But in the last few years even these interests have fallen to the pernicious effects of what Senator Alan K. Simpson calls "compassion fatigue" and the growing disinclination of Americans to respond to those in need. Compassion fatigue has been reinforced by funding fatigue: refugee funds are being reduced. In fiscal year 1980, the U.S. budget for refugees was over $445 million. In

FY 1985, State Department expenditures for refugee programs totaled more than $390 million. In FY 1986, refugee expenditures were reduced to approximately $385 million, and in fiscal year 1987 the Reagan administration proposed a refugee budget of $347 million.[66] The pattern of future American funding seems clear: in the absence of a new refugee emergency and given budget deficits, it is unlikely that Congress will significantly increase refugee funding. More likely refugee programs will be restricted. Of the funds expended on refugees in fiscal year 1985, more than two-thirds were committed to international refugee assistance and less than one-third for all other aspects of refugee admissions. Robert Funseth, senior deputy assistant secretary for refugee programs, described budget decisions as a stark dichotomy. "We face," he told a refugee conference, "extremely difficult policy choices between applying very scarce dollars to fund the cost of a level of refugee admissions to the United States or applying those same dollars to meet severe international refugee relief requirements. The dilemma is this: do we spend $100,000 to bring 60 more refugees to America or do we spend this same $100,000 to help feed and shelter many more than 60 refugees in camps in Asia, Africa, Central America, or the Middle East?"[67] The way the question is phrased there can be only one answer, the Reagan administration's answer.

Resettlement abroad, always the preferred alternative, will, in the future, be pursued more vigorously. Where resettlement to the United States is an absolute necessity, costs will be reduced. The Ray panel, while genuflecting to the tradition of welcome, recommended vigilance:

> . . . We are part of a nation of refugees. . . . The Statue of Liberty . . . represents our commitment to freedom and our tradition of offering safe haven to those fleeing persecution. We recognize our obligation to keep faith with these principles and this tradition.

U.S. Refugee Admissions Ceilings and Actual Arrivals, Fiscal Years 1975–87

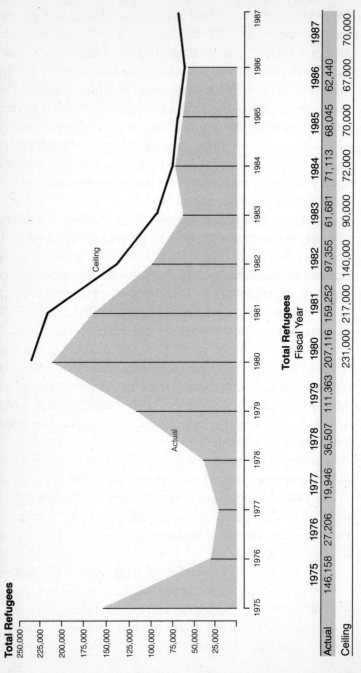

Total Refugees

Total Refugees
Fiscal Year

	1975	1976	1977	1978	1979	1980	1981	1982	1983	1984	1985	1986	1987
Actual	146,158	27,206	19,946	36,507	111,363	207,116	159,252	97,355	61,681	71,113	68,045	62,440	
Ceiling						231,000	217,000	140,000	90,000	72,000	70,000	67,000	70,000

U.S. Refugees, by Region of Origin, Fiscal Years 1975–87

Figures in shaded areas represent actual arrivals; figures in unshaded areas represent annual ceilings.

Region	Fiscal Year 1975	1976	1977	1978	1979	1980	1981	1982	1983[a]	1984[b]	1985[b]	1986	1987	Total
Africa (actual)						955	2,119	3,326	2,648	2,747	1,953	1,315		14,669
Africa (ceiling)						1,500	3,000	3,500	3,000	2,750	3,000	3,500	3,500	
Asia (actual)	135,000	15,000	7,000	20,574	76,521	163,799	131,139	73,522	39,408	51,960	49,970	45,454		803,584
Asia (ceiling)						169,200	168,000	96,000	64,000	52,000	50,000	45,500	40,500	
Eastern Europe (actual)	1,947	1,756	1,755	2,245	3,393	5,025	6,704	10,780	12,083	10,285	9,350	8,713		72,841
Eastern Europe (ceiling)						5,000	4,500	11,000						
Soviet Union (actual)	6,211	7,450	8,191	10,688	24,449	28,444	13,444	2,756	1,409	715	640	787		105,101
Soviet Union (ceiling)						33,000	33,000	20,000	15,000	11,000	10,000	9,500	10,000	
Latin America (actual)	3,000	3,000	3,000	3,000	7,000	6,662	2,017	602	668	160	138	173		29,298
Latin America (ceiling)						20,500	4,000	3,000	2,000	1,000	1,000	3,000	4,000	
Near East and South Asia (actual)						2,231	3,829	6,369	5,465	5,246	5,994	5,998		34,833
Near East and South Asia (ceiling)						2,500	4,500	6,500	6,000	5,250	6,000	6,000	8,000	
Unallocated Reserve (ceiling)													4,000[c]	4,000[c]
Total (actual)	146,158	27,206	19,946	36,507	111,363	207,116	159,252	97,355	61,681	71,113	68,045	62,440		1,060,290
Total (ceiling)						231,700	217,000	140,000	90,000	72,000	70,000	67,000	70,000	

[a] From fiscal year 1983 on, the Eastern Europe ceiling was combined with the ceiling for the Soviet Union.

[b] This chart shows the adjusted regional ceilings that were established at midyear consultations in fiscal years 1984 and 1985. The overall annual ceilings did not change.

[c] For the first time, the fiscal year 1987 admissions ceiling includes an unallocated reserve for "contingent refugee admission needs," to be used only after consultation with Congress and only to the extent that private sector funding is available to support admissions using the reserve.

SOURCE: BUREAU FOR REFUGEE PROGRAMS/U.S. DEPARTMENT OF STATE

> At the same time the Panel acknowledges its responsibility
> to keep our refugee programs in perspective. . . . Our refugee
> programs must take precautions to ensure that those coming
> as refugees truly deserve this special status.[68]

The panel's findings and recommendations were pragmatic. They
blamed Vietnam's repressive and expansionist policies for
nourishing the roots of the refugee exodus in Southeast Asia.
First asylum, they believed, must be preserved; the problems
of declining resettlement offers and the increasing residual populations in camps had to be addressed. Accordingly, an international effort must be mounted to find durable solutions for
long-stayers in first asylum countries. Here, the panel recommended that the United States should take the lead in "sharing-
out" long-stayers and should begin processing from the current
population refugees who have no ties to the United States (priority
six). Many of those arriving in first asylum countries now "appear to have less compelling claims to refugee status . . . than
was true in earlier years"; those seeking admission to the United
States solely on the basis of family ties should do so by means
of immigration procedures. As approximately forty-five percent
of refugee admissions in 1985 from Southeast Asia were based
on family reunification, shifting family admissions to an immigrant basis would reduce resettlement costs. The panel was
conscious that critics of refugee benefit programs "point to their
high costs and to the continued reliance on public assistance
by many refugees, including new arrivals with relatives in the
United States."[69]

Henceforth, the Ray Panel recommended, the Indochinese
Refugee Program should be restructured to have two components: a refugee program and an immigration program. For a
two-year transition period, new arrivals with close family ties,
if they cannot qualify as immigrants, should be processed as
refugees.[70] After that time, they should be processed as immigrants. Spouses and minor children of refugees would con-

tinue to enter as refugees. Family ties notwithstanding, one is either an immigrant or a refugee. To designate a genuine refugee as an immigrant is to ignore the special needs of the refugee, among them the need for resettlement assistance. It is, of course, precisely such assistance, with its additional expense, that the panel's recommendation is intended to avoid. This policy paradox is but one of many. Policy goals are most easily achieved if logical inconsistencies are ignored and subtle distinctions encouraged.

The paradoxes of United States policy are global. In Southeast Asia, some first-asylum Indochinese might be either refugees or immigrants; and in Vietnam, Amerasians and their close family might be refugees or immigrants. An individual is what policy wants him to be. And that policy may not be consistent, even within the administration. The Department of State and the Immigration and Naturalization Service sometimes differ on which Indochinese are "economic migrants" and which "political refugees." In Europe, both the Department of State and the INS are in closer accord. Communist countries produce fewer "economic migrants" than "political refugees."

If processing creates paradoxes for individuals, the regional ceilings produce policy paradoxes for whole nationalities. The United States pressures the Rumanian government to allow its citizens to emigrate, but the regional ceiling causes a backlog which prevents Rumanians from leaving. Representative Barney Frank of Massachusetts told James N. Purcell of the State Department that Frank believed the regional ceiling to be "a disgrace. . . . What you just told me is that our pressures on the Romanian Government to let out more people have somewhat succeeded, but because of our own self-imposed ceiling, we can't take advantage of that. I am embarrassed as an American by the fact . . ."[71]

In Africa, there is an ongoing presumption in favor of Ethiopians. The "Proposed Refugee Admissions and Allocations for Fiscal Year 1987" finds that "the continued economic crisis and political oppression in Ethiopia will account for the largest group of refugees from any single African country. Because the situation in some African countries continues to be unpredictable, other refugees accepted for admission during FY 1987 will be on a case-by-case basis.''[72] It is in Latin America, however, that our pursuit of an anti-Communist foreign policy brings policy paradoxes to flower.

Under every administration, this country's response to Fidel Castro has been implacable opposition. But in recent years, our responses to the Cuban émigrés have been inconsistent. The Cubans who came in the Camarioca boatlift were paroled in as refugees. The Cubans who came in the Mariel boatlift came in first as applicants for political asylum and then were suddenly designated special entrants, a category that applies only to those who came from Cuba or Haiti before October 10, 1980.

Those Cubans most in need of refugee resettlement, Castro's political prisoners, have been made pawns in a political power game. The Reagan administration, though it presses for the prisoners' release and professes its willingness to resettle them, predicates their acceptance on Castro's willingness to take back the 2,700 Cuban criminals and mental patients who remain incarcerated in this country. An agreement had been reached under which Castro would take back the unwanted residue of the Mariel boatlift in exchange for three thousand Cuban political prisoners and an annual quota of twenty thousand Cuban immigrants. When Castro took umbrage at the Voice of America's Radio Martí broadcasts from the United States, he refused to take back the Mariel undesirables. In return, the United States canceled the agreement. The few political prisoners who now come to the United States do so under the aegis of private persons and a voluntary agency.[73] That refugees—particularly political prisoners—should be accepted only in exchange for undesirables is in itself a paradox.

Paradoxes abound in our Latin American and Caribbean policy. In 1985, ninety-one percent of the 4,771 Nicaraguan asylum claims were rejected. Yet in 1986, Perry A. Rivkind, the chief official of the INS in Florida, announced that he would send no Nicaraguans back to their homeland because they might be persecuted by the Marxist Sandinista government. Although Rivkind is the only one of the thirty-three INS district directors to adopt such a policy, his unilateral stance is of significance because three-fourths of all asylum applications by Nicaraguans are in Florida. (In fiscal year 1986, the approval rate for Nicaraguan asylum applications jumped to nearly 38 percent.) Rivkind's *ex cathedra* pronouncement was particularly disturbing to those who felt the government had not administered the Refugee Act in an evenhanded manner, favoring asylum applicants from Communist countries over those from right-wing nations. Peter W. Rodino, Jr., a judicious voice in the House of Representatives, expressed his concern: "For some time," he said, "I have been urging the Justice Department to halt the deportation of Haitians and Salvadorans because of the intolerable situations in those countries. In my judgment, nationals of El Salvador and Haiti are deserving of relief, and it seems inconsistent to provide relief to Nicaraguans without providing identical treatment to Salvadorans and Haitians."[74]

Rivkind's policy statement was not rebuked or repudiated by anyone in the Reagan administration. It came at a time when the Justice Department was preparing to make it easier for Poles and citizens of other Communist countries to gain asylum in the United States. The new rules would establish a presumption that a person fleeing "totalitarian" governments had a well-founded fear of persecution, thereby meeting the statutory standard for refugee and asylee status. The new procedures, the *New York Times* correctly observed, appear to be designed to make asylum policy "conform to the Administration's antagonism toward Communist regimes and partly to respond to pressures from Polish-Americans for changes in American policy on asylum."[75] Mr. Rivkind's actions and a "presumption of persecution" to assist persons from "totalitarian nations" violate not only the nonideological definition of a refugee, but also the need for a uniform procedure for the adjudication of refugee status.

The Reagan administration's antagonism to "totalitarian" governments and its tolerance of "authoritarian" governments create an arbitrary distinction between refugees. A well-founded fear of persecution from the left is no more pernicious than it is from the right. Persecution makes no distinctions as to ideology; it is policy that makes the distinction.

Policy also generates refugees. In Central America, the Reagan administration's support of the Contras against the Sandinistas in Nicaragua, and its failure to pursue a vigorous human rights policy in Guatemala and El Salvador, are responsible for generating refugees.

The United States, as well as professing welcome, professes to support human rights. We are signatory to the Protocol Relating to the Status of Refugees and the Helsinki Accords. We affirm, by treaty and by word, the basic right of citizens of all countries to freedom of movement. We urge the countries of Southeast Asia to give asylum, at least temporarily, to fleeing Indochinese. We constantly chastize the Soviet Union and Eastern European states for their failure to permit emigration. We use the most-favored-nation tariff status as a tool of anti-Communist diplomacy and link it to the right to emigrate. But while the United States presses for free emigration from certain countries, we actively discourage it elsewhere.

The Reagan administration entered into an agreement with the dictatorial regime of Baby Doc Duvalier to prevent Haitian nationals from leaving the country. Duvalier is gone, and his successors are having difficulty running the country; the legal system suffers from desuetude; chaos and random killings have occurred. The agreement remains in force. The United States interdicts Haitian émigrés and, in international waters, rules on their claims of asylum. Lawyers may temporize over the legal issue of interdiction; decency says it violates the spirit of the right to free movement, a right we affirm against the Communist nations.

If the ethics of our policy are tailored to fit the situation, favoring refugees in one region over those in others, ignoring the critical distinctions between immigrants and refugees, and condemning other nations for human rights violations while we call similar actions immigration law enforcement, they are because our priorities are skewed.

In absolute numbers, the United States admits more refugees than any other country in the world, but in relation to our native population and per capita gross national product, we are seventh in the world. Our 1985 contribution to international refugee aid agencies was eighty cents per capita. In contrast, Norway, with a lower gross national product, contributed $4.43 per capita.[76]

The number of refugees we admit is declining. In 1975 the United States admitted 207,116 refugees. The ceiling of seventy thousand proposed for fiscal year 1987 should be seen in perspective. A recent Population Reference Bureau study found that the annual emigration from the United States was estimated at over 280,000 in the early 1970s. An estimated 100,000 to 150,000 residents leave annually.[77] More residents depart than refugees enter.

The public is ambivalent toward refugees, balancing antagonism with compassion—the antagonism a result of an inchoate fear of inundation by illegals. But this unfortunate linking in the public mind of refugees and illegal entrants arises from confusion over the two groups and their motives for, and methods of, entrance. Refugees enter legally; illegals infiltrate our permeable borders. Refugee entrant numbers are precise; the number of illegals present in the United States is speculative, ranging upward from a low of two million. Even the number of illegals actually apprehended and returned runs many, many more times than the refugee ceiling. Moreover, there are others who, though they enter through the immigration process, do so fraudulently. The INS estimates that nearly forty-five thousand aliens who entered the United States as spouses in fiscal year 1984 were involved in marriage fraud. The numbers of fraudulent entrants—those aliens who fail to surrender after the final order of deportation, added to the numbers of illegal entrants—make the refugee admissions numbers look paltry.[78]

Costs, too, must be seen in perspective. In fiscal year 1986, the estimated total costs for *all* refugee-related services—transportation, reception and initial placement, health, medical, welfare, and social services, and without any calculation of what refugees return to the government in taxes—was under eight hundred million dollars. In contrast, compare the sums which frequently make the headlines because of the government's faulty procurement practices or poor project planning. The Sergeant York antiaircraft gun, a major weapons project, was cancelled after an outlay of $1.8 billion.[79]

Our refugee admissions are linked to our foreign policy objectives. The Indochinese are the residue of a failed foreign policy; Eastern Europeans, Soviets, and Cubans, the fuel of an ongoing foreign policy. Foreign policy, however, can also keep refugees out. The determination that refugees are of "special humanitarian concern," the regional allocations and priorities, and the system of processing are not neutral.

Refugee admissions also reflect concern with another crucial area of policy—resettlement. If foreign policy determines which refugees are admitted, resettlement policy influences which and how many refugees we will accept. And like admission policies, resettlement policies are not neutral.

3 The Stranger within the Gate: Resettlement

When a refugee enters the United States, a new set of policy questions surrounds him, questions of resettlement. Outside the border, policy questions asked who; within the border, policy questions ask how and where. Resettlement, like admission, can evoke emotional responses. The refugee, the stranger, is no longer an abstract tug on America's collective conscience, out of sight in Europe, Asia, Africa, or Latin America. Now he is here, and he brings with him not only his strange language and strange ways, but also unique problems. The refugee must learn a new language and a new culture, and the American people must learn how to respond to the refugee with his burdens. The transition is difficult for both the new American and his receiving community.

Transition is at the core of resettlement, a transition that is both physical and psychological. For the refugee, the physical passage is easier: from Havana, Cuba, to Miami, Florida; from Saigon, Vietnam, to Westminster, California; from Odessa, U.S.S.R., to Brighton Beach, New York. The prototypical refugee follows a difficult path with clearcut way stations. Having a "well-founded fear of persecution" in his home country, he undertakes a journey with varying degrees of danger to a country of first asylum. A Russian émigré who boards a plane in the U.S.S.R. does not face the hazards of a Vietnamese who sur-

reptitiously leaves by boat and sails through pirate-filled seas
in the Gulf of Thailand, or a Laotian or Cambodian who walks
through unsafe countryside. Once in the asylum country, the
refugee's reception is predicated on the nation's current policy
toward refugees. In Austria, a major European entrepôt for
Soviets and East Europeans, the refugee is welcomed. In Southeast Asia, the refugee's reception is different. There he may be
pushed back to sea or, by Thailand, back across the border to
Cambodia or Laos, but more often he is placed in a refugee
camp.

In a refugee camp he is registered, processed, and allotted
food and shelter. The refugee's experience in the camp will
depend on the asylum country's policy toward his ethnic group.
In Austria, the Traiskirchen camp is open, and the refugee may
move freely in and out. In Southeast Asia, camp life is harsh
and unpleasant. Thailand, which has provided first asylum for
more Indochinese refugees than any other country, follows a
three-pronged policy designed to deter refugees: it detains them
in austere refugee camps; it provides only essential care and
maintenance services; and Thailand may even defer or deny a
refugee access to resettlement in third countries. Malaysia houses
its refugees in a camp on austere Pulau Bidong Island. Indonesia
maintains a first-asylum camp on Galang Island. Hong Kong
interns arrivals in "closed camps." Macau no longer accepts
refugees and operates a closed camp for those already there.
Singapore refuses to grant asylum or accept refugees for resettlement, but permits transit of refugees from the neighboring
countries of asylum.[1] Policies of "humane deterrence" and transit-
only, while hard, are still less hard than the closed-borders
policies that states instituted between the two world wars.

After he is processed and registered, the refugee must wait
in a camp until he finds a country willing to grant him admission. For many refugees, there is little, or no, hope for third-
country admission and resettlement. The psychological passage
from one nationality and culture to another is as difficult. The

refugee brings with him the vivid memories and habits of a past life, which continually color his present life. The refugee's hope for himself and his family is diminished by the guilt he feels for those he left behind.

One can think of the refugee's progress toward acculturation and assimilation as a climb up a ladder of transition. One upright of the ladder represents the economic and material side of resettlement, the achievement of successive levels of economic self-sufficiency; the other upright of the ladder represents the psychological side of resettlement, feeling and thinking like an American, with new attitudes and social behavior. Rungs connect the two uprights. But because the refugee makes economic and psychological progress up the ladder at different speeds, the rungs, which represent stages or levels, are not necessarily horizontal.

The climb up the ladder of transition is difficult; some, particularly the elderly, never attempt it. Others ascend the economic side of the ladder but do not progress as well culturally and psychologically. A refugee can succeed materially, even though he does not acculturate. A Cuban who speaks very little English can be quite comfortable (and successful) in Miami's Little Havana. Some refugees arrive with skills and education that place them high on the ladder of transition; others, lacking these advantages, must begin by first acquiring the cultural skills at the bottom rungs. A Vietnamese who has a Sorbonne education and speaks fluent English begins at a higher level than a Polish worker who speaks no English and has only a limited education. A Russian or East European with professional skills and English-language ability will find well-paid employment with high socioeconomic status, unlike a Hmong peasant who is preliterate and comes from a nontechnological society, with a slash-and-burn agriculture, in which time concepts are measured imprecisely. The closeness of the refugee's native culture to American culture, or his earlier exposure to American culture, positions the refugee on the ladder of transition. A Soviet doctor, with difficulty, can retrain and be licensed to practice medicine. A Hmong shaman, knowledgeable in the ways of herbs and the body's spirits, can never be licensed as a doctor in America.

The difference between the Soviet doctor and the Hmong medicine man highlights one of the challenges of resettlement—the difference between the "traditional" refugee and the "new" refugee. Refugee expert Professor Barry N. Stein has noted that the traditional refugee comes from a country that is culturally and ethnically similar to his new host country, where the level of development is likewise similar. He understands, in Stein's words, "most of the material aspects of our culture—appliances, subways, telephones, automobiles, clocks." He is likely to be assisted by ethnic kin who know the refugee's language and can help him adjust. In contrast, the new refugee is culturally and ethnically different from his hosts, comes from a less-developed country, and is likely to lack kin who can help ease his transition.[2]

Despite the tendency to homogenize all refugees from a country or a region, there are also important distinctions within groups. We speak of Cubans, Indochinese, or Russians, but refugees are subdivided into waves and vintages. Waves refer to the time of the refugees' arrival in their new homeland. They may depart from their old homeland long before arriving in a new country, spending time in asylum countries or in processing facilities. Refugees are of different vintages because they leave a country or a region at different times, under different circumstances, because of different pressures. A Cuban who fled in the early days of Castro's rule is of a different vintage than a Marielito who was expelled. A Vietnamese who worked for the United States and left Saigon with the departing Americans is of a different vintage than a Vietnamese who enters the United States a decade later, dissatisfied with life under Communist rule.

One should also be careful about what Stein calls "the public title" given to a refugee group.[3] Americans may think of Indochinese as a single entity, but Indochinese think of themselves as Vietnamese, ethnic Chinese, Laotian, Hmong, Khmer. The public title masks discrete ethnic groups that have little in the way of common culture, religion, or language. Historically, the relationships between these peoples have been marked by suspicion and hostility, and it is not easy to transcend ancient animosities, even in a new homeland. What the Indochinese do share are the experiences of war, self-exile, and of being foreign minorities in a strange land.

Soviets and *Russians* are loose, catchall terms for those emigrating from the Union of Soviet Socialist Republics. Here, too, the public title embraces distinct groups of people, each with its own cultural background. Most Soviets come from the heartland of the Soviet Union—territory that has been Soviet since the 1917 revolution. Some come from areas that were not incorporated into the U.S.S.R. until 1939 to 1940, or until after World War II. Others come from Georgia and speak principally Georgian, while still others come from central Asia, Bukharins whose primary language is not Russian, but Farsi.[4]

Yet all of those being resettled bring problems, no matter what their wave, vintage, or public title, no matter where they begin on the ladder of transition. Resettlement is the art of helping the refugee to transcend his problems and enabling him to ascend the ladder of transition. A complex nationwide system of federal, state, local, and private agencies has grown up to assist refugees in their resettlement. This system of interlocking entities, which developed incrementally, was institutionalized by the Refugee Act of 1980.

Before the federal government became a participant in resettlement, and before the law distinguished between immigrants and refugees, private, nonprofit voluntary agencies (volags) and their local constituents, relying solely on their own funds, helped all newcomers. Both the number of volags and the federal commitment grew in response to refugee outflows.

The oldest volag, the Hebrew Immigrant Aid Society (HIAS),

has roots which go back to the *landsmanshaften* established by Jewish immigrants in the late nineteenth century.[5] Somewhat later, in the 1920s, the forerunner organization of the United States Catholic Conference (USCC), now the largest of the volags, was organized. Both the American Council for Nationalities Service (ACNS) and the International Rescue Committee (IRC) were founded in the early 1930s. The ACNS began as urban international institutes that assisted the foreign-born in adjusting to American life. The IRC was founded to aid the victims of Nazi persecution. The Lutherans, in 1939, established a department of welfare, which was the forerunner of the Lutheran Immigration and Refugee Service (LIRS). That same year, Alexandra Tolstoy and other prominent Russian émigrés organized the Tolstoy Foundation to assist Soviet refugees (mainly White Russians) and to establish a center of Russian culture in the United States.

Shortly after World War II, Church World Service (CWS) and the Polish American Immigration and Relief Committee (PAIRC) were founded. CWS operates under the aegis of the National Council of Churches of Christ in the U.S.A. and is the service and umbrella organization for its constituent Protestant, Orthodox, and Anglican denominations. PAIRC grew out of the need to care for the masses of displaced persons in Poland and Germany after the war. The American Fund for Czechoslovak Refugees (AFCR) was organized in 1948, following the Communist takeover in Czechoslovakia. World Relief, the humanitarian arm of the National Association of Evangelicals, and the presiding Bishop's Fund for World Relief of the Protestant Episcopal Church ("The Fund") became active in resettlement in response to the Indochina exodus. And, recalling the earlier *landsmanshaften*, one of the newest volags is the Buddhist Council for Refugee Rescue and Resettlement (BCRRR), an organization of Buddhist congregations and mutual-assistance associations that caters specifically to the resettlement needs of Indochinese.[6]

As the voluntary agencies grew in numbers and organizational capacity, the federal government, responding to specific refugee crises, unwittingly assumed more and more of a national responsibility for resettlement. As it did so, the government gradually fell into partnership with the volags.

Today's resettlement system developed in several stages. It began with the Corporate Affidavit Program of 1946, which was carried over into the Displaced Persons Act of 1948, expanded during the Hungarian Refugee Program, and became firmly established in the Cuban and Indochinese Refugee Programs. These two specific programs were subsequently augmented by the catchall Soviet and Other Refugees Matching Grant Program. In 1980, the three ongoing discrete programs— Cuban, Indochinese, and Soviet and Other—were brought within the purview of the Refugee Act.[7]

The Corporate Affidavit Program grew out of President Truman's concern for Europe's displaced persons. Truman issued a presidential directive that permitted the DPs to enter more easily under existing quotas, through the device of the corporate affidavit. The corporate affidavit was a guarantee of financial support, given by the voluntary agencies, so that the refugee-immigrant would not become a public charge. Since most DPs had no means of support, the volags' affidavits qualified thousands for admission, for whom entrance to the United States would otherwise have been impossible. That private agencies could be responsible for new entrants was now officially recognized; the voluntary agency had become the cornerstone of resettlement. By 1948, when the Displaced Persons Act superseded the presidential directive, the volag affidavit program had become so successful that the act awarded responsibility for resettling DPs to the voluntary agencies and state commissions. The Displaced Persons Act, a harbinger of future refugee programs, was the first planned resettlement program under federal auspices in American history. It established state DP commissions that worked with private and public agencies

to use educational, health, employment, and community services for the benefit of the refugees.

The DPs were followed by the Hungarians. Impelled by the
1956 uprising, Hungarians surged across the borders to Austria
and Yugoslavia. By November, seven thousand persons were
crossing the frontier every day; in slightly more than a year,
over two hundred thousand fled from Hungary. Austria, the
primary first-asylum neighbor, was soon host to more escapees
than she could handle. Austria appealed for help to the United
Nations High Commissioner for Refugees, who called upon other
nations to admit the Hungarians.

The United States, along with other nations, responded. President Eisenhower established a reception and processing center
at Camp Kilmer, New Jersey, and created the President's Committee for Hungarian Refugee Relief to coordinate the various
public and private agencies involved in resettlement. At Camp
Kilmer, the Public Health Service provided health screening and
medical examinations. The Department of Labor's Employment
Service helped find housing and jobs. IBM designed and paid
for an employment and housing form, which the sponsoring
voluntary agencies used. Although Hungarians resettled
throughout the country, three states—New York, New Jersey,
and Ohio—became home to over fifty percent of the new arrivals.

The refugees were resettled by the private sector with only
modest financial assistance from the federal government for
health care and transportation costs—less than $40 per refugee.
In a classic example of miscalculation, the government insisted
that "the payments do not constitute a precedent for giving
payment to the voluntary agencies for similar costs for other
refugee movements."[8] The total costs for resettling the Hungarians ran to somewhat over $71 million, of which approxi-
mately $20 million was funded through the private sector.[9]
Federal and private outlays were small in relation to the foreign
and domestic benefits. The Hungarian migration visibly un-

derscored the shortcomings of Communism, while at home, Hungarian-Americans and other anti-Communist groups were gratified.

The Hungarians were resettled easily and successfully for a number of reasons: their numbers were small, only 38,121; they had a well-established community to receive them; they were white Europeans with educational skills, high labor-force participation rates, and relatively few dependents; their arrival coincided with a period of low unemployment; they arrived over a relatively short time period; and, finally, they were popularly perceived as brave anti-Communists. In contrast to the Hungarians, both the Cuban and Indochinese refugees have come in large numbers, over a long period, and have required high levels of federal and private aid.

When refugees began to arrive from Fidel Castro's Cuba, resettlement strategies and practices had to change. The United States was both the country of first asylum and the country of resettlement for the Cubans. The federal government, for the first time, assumed a significant financial responsibility for the refugees' resettlement, a responsibility that would continue and grow. The federal government would fund both public assistance through the states, and various resettlement activities through the voluntary agencies.

By November 1960, seventeen hundred Cuban refugees a week were pouring into Florida. These refugees, like others before them, had to leave their assets behind. Their needs were met, at first, by the voluntary agencies, using private resources, and by the state of Florida. It soon became apparent that federal help was needed. In December 1960, President Eisenhower established a Cuban Emergency Center in Miami and four voluntary agencies (National Catholic Welfare Conference, Church World Service, International Rescue Committee, and HIAS) received federal funds to aid in resettlement. A year later, Abraham Ribicoff, Secretary of Health, Education, and Welfare under President Kennedy, fashioned a comprehensive plan which later was given permanent form as the Cuban Refugee Program (CRP) by the Migration and Refugee Act of 1962. Under the CRP, various federal, state, and local agencies administered cash assistance, medical assistance, child-welfare funds, surplus foods, and food stamps. Federal monies helped finance education for children and adults, vocational training, student loans, and preparation for professional certification and licensing for doctors and dentists. In a giant step toward a federal commitment to resettlement, the federal government fully reimbursed the states for these services and also covered the administrative expenses involved.

In time, the CRP became well established; in fact, many critics felt it was too well established. By 1980, some 750,000 Cubans had entered the country, and the federal expenditures for the CRP had reached $1.4 billion. Congress, feeling that the program had become too costly and too long-lived, arranged to phase it out by 1983, but the Reagan administration, urging restraint in human-services expenditures, terminated the CRP in October 1981. Henceforth, Cuban refugees were to be treated like other refugees: the federal government would give them financial and medical assistance for only the first three years, though some might subsequently qualify for other state and federal programs, such as Aid to Families with Dependent Children.[10]

For more than a decade, the Cuban Refugee Program was the only program of domestic assistance to refugees. But with the abrupt end of the Vietnam War came a massive refugee exodus from Indochina. To impose some order and to coordinate the chaotic refugee outpouring—from mid-April to December 1975, more than 130,000 Indochinese were paroled into the United States—President Ford created an Interagency Task Force for Indochina Refugees (IATF). From the evacuation of the refugees to their eventual resettlement, the IATF took charge. Refugees were first brought to staging areas in the Pacific, then transported to stateside reception and processing centers, and finally, under volag sponsorship, were placed in communities throughout the nation.

Within weeks of the closing of the American embassy in Saigon, Congress, acting with rare alacrity, passed the Indochina Migration and Refugee Assistance Act of 1975, which authorized a temporary program of relief and resettlement. (It was thought incorrectly that the refugee eruption would be a solitary episode.) The Indochinese Refugee Assistance Program (IRAP) paralleled the Cuban program in services and in the full federal reimbursement to the states, a response to the concerns of state and local governments that the refugees would become economic burdens.

Congress, like the state and local officials, was wary. The House Committee on Appropriations, concerned that IRAP "could develop into a permanent federal undertaking similar to the present Cuban Program," stated categorically that this was not its intent.[11] As originally envisioned, IRAP was to expire in 1977, but refugee flows continued, and Congress extended IRAP until terminating it in the Refugee Act of 1980.

Nearly half a million Indochinese were resettled under the Indochinese Refugee Assistance Program. During its five-year existence, the program cost more than one billion dollars. In addition, IRAP was supplemented by the Indochina Refugee Children Assistance Act of 1976 which covered educational expenses to the states and localities. More than eight hundred thousand Southeast Asians have already fled to the United States, and the outpouring from Vietnam, Cambodia, and Laos continues.

The Cuban program was well established, and the Indochinese program was underway, when the Soviet and Other Refugees Matching Grant Program (MGP) began in 1979. During 1978, more than ten thousand Soviet Jews arrived in the United States. The receiving Jewish community paid for their resettlement, with no federal assistance, as other communities and agencies had done for other refugee groups before the special Cuban and Indochinese legislation. Other non-Cuban and non-Indochinese refugees were ineligible for special cash and medical assistance programs. The MGP was intended to introduce some equity into the provision of services not only for Soviet Jews, but also for other refugees whom the voluntary agencies were helping to settle.

Unlike the earlier Cuban and Indochinese programs, the Matching Grant Program was based on matching funds. Under the terms of the legislation, the Department of Health, Education, and Welfare (now the Department of Health and Human Services) was to provide federal funds to the volags, matching dollar for dollar, up to one thousand dollars per capita. The volags were to use the matching funds to provide such domestic services as English-language training and employment counseling. Unlike the Cuban and Indochinese programs, which were phased out under the Refugee Act, the MGP continues. The MGP was never a large program—at its height, in 1979, the volags received only twenty-eight million dollars—and by 1985, with the decrease in refugee admissions, volag awards were down to four million dollars. Because Moscow has drastically curtailed the numbers of Armenians and Jews permitted to leave the Soviet Union, the MGP now aids refugees from Eastern Europe (mainly Poles and Rumanians, to a lesser extent Czechs, Hungarians, and Bulgarians, and a scant number of Albanians and Yugoslavs), Afghanis, Iraqis, and Africans.[12]

Beginning in 1978, refugees were arriving in the United States in ever-larger numbers. By midyear 1979, some fourteen thousand Indochinese refugees were entering monthly. Congress was forced to expand its thinking from the narrow issue of admissions to a more comprehensive approach that included the problems of resettlement. Senator Edward M. Kennedy—who, as chairman of the Subcommittee on Refugees of the Senate Judiciary Committee, was instrumental in securing the passage of the Refugee Act—had early on seen the need for comprehensive refugee legislation. When S. 2752, a precursor to the 1980 Refugee Act, was under consideration, Kennedy wrote to the Carter administration that:

> . . . this basic reform of the immigration law deals with only half the problem—the admission of refugees into the United States. We must also consider the problems involved in their resettlement in communities across our land, and what the Federal responsibility is to help in the resettlement process.[13]

The Kennedy approach was finally adopted, and resettlement issues of policy coordination, the administration of federal refugee programs, and the availability and duration of federal refugee resettlement assistance were incorporated into the act. The act established an Office of Refugee Resettlement (ORR), within the Department of Health and Human Services (HHS), and delineated the conditions under which the office would provide domestic assistance. The act mandated state and local consultations, the designation by each state of a coordinator of refugee affairs, and, as a precondition for receiving federal assistance, the drawing up of state plans for refugee resettlement services.

The HHS Refugee Resettlement Office was empowered to give grants and to enter into contracts with public and private nonprofit agencies for a wide range of resettlement services, such as job training, employment counseling, day care, professional retraining and recertification, English-language instruction, physical- and mental-health care, and appropriate social services. The office could also authorize special educational projects for refugee children in elementary and secondary schools.

States were eligible for one hundred percent reimbursement for cash and medical assistance for the first three years of the refugee's residence in the United States, and for the administrative costs in providing this assistance. The three-year limitation was not to go into effect until April 1, 1981, thereby creating a transition period for affected refugees and states. The three-year cash and medical assistance limitation, combined with the one-year transition period, represented a political compromise between those who felt a two-year period of special federal assistance was adequate and those who wanted longer periods of aid. The limitation was written in to avoid an unlimited period of assistance similar to that of the Cuban program. The Cuban program was to be phased down, after which eligible Cuban refugees would come under the Refugee Act.

Finally, the ORR was authorized to use funds for cash and medical assistance and social services, as well as to reimburse states and local public agencies for applicants for asylum prior to November 1, 1979. Florida's Democratic representative Dante Fascell, speaking on the House floor, made it quite clear that the asylum assistance and services provisions were for some eight thousand Haitians who were then waiting for the adjudication of their asylum claims. The cost to Dade County, where most of the Haitians live, was at that time approximately two million dollars a year for various social services.[14]

In sum, the Refugee Act of 1980 included both foreign and domestic resettlement concerns. The road to resettlement had now been institutionalized. The refugee in a refugee camp is interviewed and assisted in preparing his application for admission by a joint-voluntary-agency employee, who works with the embassy staff and/or an officer of the Immigration and Naturalization Service. If the refugee has successfully met the criteria for admission to the United States, he waits for his resettlement, which begins with his being taken to an overseas processing center. There are three such processing sites in Southeast Asia. Ethiopians are processed in the Sudan. At their processing centers, Southeast Asians and Ethiopians receive English instruction and cultural orientation. In Europe, the State Department's Bureau for Refugee Programs provides a short cultural orientation program for East Europeans. The need for language and orientation courses, especially for many of the Indochinese, is apparent, and the effectiveness of these programs has been confirmed. One study concluded, "There is simply no doubt that pre-entry training should be regarded as an essential element of refugee resettlement." Aside from the benefits to the refugee, the cost of these programs in Southeast Asia is less than half of what it would be in the United States.[15]

While the refugee is overseas, his biodata forms are sent to New York City, where the American Council for Voluntary International Action, an umbrella organization of the voluntary agencies, uses State Department funding to run a Refugee Data Center. At the Data Center, the refugee is assigned to a sponsoring volag, which decides where to locate him. Initial placement is determined by any number of factors: location of family, cosponsorships, housing, or job availability. The language and orientation sessions completed, the refugee awaits transportation to the United States.

The Department of State finances the transportation from overseas to the United States through a revolving loan fund administered by the Intergovernmental Committee for Migration (ICM). ICM makes all the travel arrangements. Before leaving his asylum country, a refugee signs an interest-free promissory note with ICM, stipulating that he will repay most of the expenses of his move to the U.S. The refugee generally agrees to make monthly payments to his sponsoring volag and to liquidate the loan within three years. The volag retains twenty-five percent of the repaid amount to cover collection costs and remits the seventy-five percent remaining to the ICM-loan-fund account. In 1985, the General Accounting Office (GAO) investigated how well refugees repay their loans and concluded that "most refugees do not pay back their loans." ICM has lent about $200 million since refugee admissions increased dramatically in 1979. By 1985, $144 million should have been repaid in full and most of the repaid monies redeposited with ICM. However, $44 million of all loans has been repaid. Because of the low repayment rate, over $30 million is needed annually for the transportation program to continue. The GAO found that "low refugee loan collection/repayment rates have resulted from two types of problems—inefficient collection methods used by the voluntary agencies and the lack of enforcement." Aware of the need to demonstrate their responsibility, most of the volags have switched from manual to automated accounting and loan-collection systems, and are improving their loan collections.[16]

When a refugee arrives at his port of entry, a representative of his sponsoring volag meets him and arranges for his journey to his new home. There, a volag representative or affiliate or a cosponsor—family, friends, a civic or religious group—helps the refugee to settle in. The refugee's reception by others in the community ranges from enthusiasm through indifference to, frequently, hostility. The newly resettled refugee must confront problems that are both personal and communal—a personal maelstrom of culture shock, generational conflicts, and a range of physical and mental disorders, and, for some, a communal wall of hostility or even racism. Moving from the familiar to the unfamiliar is always difficult, but it is even more difficult for refugees, who must adapt to a new language, new patterns of thinking and behavior, while physically weakened by years of hardship, possible malnutrition, anemia, intestinal parasites, malaria, or tuberculosis, and mentally beset by anxiety and the psychiatric conditions known as survivor syndrome and post-traumatic stress disorder. The Indochinese, moreover, have added a new term, *sudden nightmare death syndrome* (SNDS), to the American medical lexicon. (SNDS is the trauma of repeated nightmares that strike healthy young men, causing death.)

The refugee's mental and physical problems require treatments which then, because of their cost, become a community problem. And there are other, more direct, community problems. As refugees compete for community aid services, low-income housing, jobs, and dwindling or already scarce resources, they are pitted against long-resident Americans, particularly those who are economically marginal and/or socially disadvantaged. Wherever refugees have congregated, from Maine to California, clashes have occurred.

Just such a clash took place on the Texas Gulf Coast. Many Vietnamese, drawn by the mild weather there and the possibility of familiar work, settled in fishing towns. Frugal and hardworking, they pooled their resources and bought fishing boats. The refugees were unfamiliar with the local fishing laws and customs and created additional competition for the dwindling supply of shrimp and fish. The Texans made it clear that the Vietnamese were not wanted. A young Vietnamese, fed up with the harassment and intimidation, shot and killed a local fisherman in August 1979, and the smoldering controversy exploded. Vietnamese boats were torched and refugees attacked. The Ku Klux Klan proclaimed a new cause; at Klan rallies, Vietnamese boats were burned in effigy. (The boats were sometimes named the U.S.S. *Viet Cong*, a special irony, since the refugees had fled the Communists.) Robed Klansmen burned crosses (even, in attempted respectability, inquiring of the Texas Air Control Board whether a permit was required for cross-burning!) and chanted "Death to the Gooks."[17] In time, state and federal officials established an uneasy truce and subdued the fishing war.

Similar, if lower-keyed, fishing wars were fought along the coasts of central California, Florida, and Louisiana.[18] On a smaller scale, other clashes have occurred across the country. Refugees have been accused of stealing and eating pets, poaching in the public parks, living together in such numbers as to create health hazards, receiving favorable treatment at the expense of the local residents, and undercutting the labor market.

When the number of refugees in an area is low, the expenses for these refugees are low. But refugees, like immigrants before them, congregate, for various reasons: to be with those who share their culture, to join with family, or because a particular location offers a better climate, housing, jobs, needed services such as English instruction or bilingual social services, or better welfare benefits. When refugees congregate, particularly in the refugee groups' early years when they require more community services, they cause impactment. Impactment has a negative connotation. It usually means the concentration in an area of a large number of refugees who need extensive support, draining the available resoures. All three major refugee groups— Cubans, Indochinese, Soviets—have caused impactment problems.

The Cubans, now the third largest group of Latin Americans living in the United States, settled principally in two areas. Nearly three of every four Cubans live in the metropolitan areas of Miami, Florida, and Union City–West New York, New Jersey. The rest are found in large cities in New York, California, and Illinois. One of the primary goals of the Cuban Refugee Program, along with job placement and assistance, was to lessen the burden of impactment on southern Florida by redistributing "relocatable" Cubans outside the state. Cubans with education, skills, and the ability to speak English were considered to be most easily relocated. If a Cuban refused an opportunity to settle outside of southern Florida, he would be denied assistance. Some sixty-one percent of the Cubans who registered with CRP agreed to be resettled under the terms established by the CRP. But the pull to Florida was strong. Once the relocated Cubans had adjusted to living in the United States, saved some money, learned English, and become independent of government assistance, they moved back to Miami. When the returnees were surveyed as to why they had returned, the majority cited as reasons climate and a desire to be close to relatives and friends. The returnees, who started out as a trickle, by the middle of the 1970s were a major migration stream. The number of Dade County's returnees is increasing and is likely to continue so in the future.[19] In the long run, the CRP's policy of geographic dispersal has not worked.

A policy of dispersal for the Indochinese also has not worked, but ORR is still trying various strategies to reduce impactment. When the United States first began bringing Indochinese into the country, the Interagency Task Force on Indochina Refugees described its placement policy in two general guidelines: "(1) to avoid resettlement in areas of high unemployment; and

(2) to avoid high concentrations of refugees in any specific community."[20] The prevailing sentiment in Congress in 1975 was that refugees should be dispersed widely, should be discouraged from settling in large groups, and would tend to remain in the community of their first placement and sponsorship. This has not happened. Of the Southeast Asian refugees, over fifty percent are settled in three states. California, with the highest concentrations of Indochinese, has nearly forty percent of the refugees. (Some counties in California are home to more refugees than forty states combined!) Texas, a distant second place, has 7.5 percent of the refugees. Washington follows with 4.5 percent. Another 23.4 percent are settled in eight states, and the remainder are scattered throughout the states and territories.[21]

Other refugees also tend to congregate. Soviet refugees are found primarily in four states—New York, California, Illinois, and Pennsylvania. Of the New York Soviet Jewish refugee population, more than fifty percent are located in fourteen neighborhoods. One neighborhood, the Brighton Beach area of Brooklyn, is known as Little Odessa because it has an estimated Soviet Jewish population of thirty thousand. Other recent refugees—Poles, Rumanians, Czechs, Afghanis, Ethiopians, Iranians, and Iraqis—also have gravitated toward sites where they have an existing ethnic community.[22]

One of the early tasks undertaken by ORR, under the Reagan administration, was to prepare a refugee placement policy. After considerable discussion among federal, state, and voluntary agency officials, ORR promulgated a formal placement policy in 1982, designed "to reduce the placement of refugees in areas of high concentration so as to achieve a more equitable distribution of refugees throughout the country." The policymakers however, could not agree on a statistically based definition of impactment, so they wrote a vague definition. Impactment was:

The existence of circumstances under which, based upon available data and the judgments of those most actively par-

ticipating in the resettlement effort, continued arrivals of refugees into an area would result in a drain on community
resources of sufficient magnitude to materially affect the quality of services to the general community, and would be det-
rimental to the refugees' prospects for the timely achievement
of self-sufficiency.[23]

A number of counties were identified as being impacted. The
volags agreed not to settle new arrivals who had no relatives
in the United States in the impacted areas.

Simultaneously with the development and implementation
of the placement policy, ORR funded two demonstration projects. One project, the Khmer Guided Placement Project, was
designed to create new clusters of refugees and reduce the number of Khmer who would have been initially settled in Long
Beach, California. The Khmer were to be resettled in groups of
three hundred to one thousand, in cities that already had Khmer
populations. The other project, the Favorable Alternative Sites
Project (FASP), was designed to settle refugees in cities with
favorable employment prospects. Those cities would receive
more in social service funds. The FASP, it was hoped, would
reduce welfare dependency, increase self-sufficiency, and reduce secondary migration among refugees.[24]

In January 1983, FASP projects began in North Carolina and
Arizona. A consultant's subsequent evaluation of the two sites
found that the increase in employment "was an unqualified
success." Within a year, however, fifty-five percent of the arrivals in North Carolina and seventy-two percent of the arrivals
in Arizona had moved on.[25]

While the North Carolina and Arizona projects were being
tried, the United States Catholic Conference initiated the Chicago Project to prove that newly arriving refugees could be
employed within six months and make progress toward self-
sufficiency without needing welfare. An independent assessment by the Refugee Policy Group gave the project good marks
for its work in obtaining jobs for the refugees, reducing their

dependence on public aid, finding sponsors, and reducing costs. RPG felt it was too early to arrive at definite conclusions about whether the refugees would become self-sufficient. It should be noted, however, that the refugee population was small (421), the number of employable refugees was even smaller (246), and of those employable, only 43 were Southeast Asian.[26]

ORR's placement strategies have limitations. First, most Southeast Asians are placed with their families, in what is usually an impacted area. Second, refugees have the right to move, and they do so for their own valid reasons, government placement policy notwithstanding. At the root of the secondary migration issue, aside from the irresistible pull of kin and climate, lie objective differences in the quality of resettlement. Providence, New Orleans, Houston, Minneapolis, Seattle, San Diego, and other cities all resettle refugees according to local conditions. The most certain way to diminish the incentive for migration is to improve local conditions. This means providing job training, English-language programs, health programs, and other support services. These items carry a price tag that the federal government should pay. When the government cut in half (from thirty-six to eighteen months) the time period for which states were to be reimbursed for cash and medical assistance to refugees, resettlement efforts were hurt and refugees migrated to states which had higher welfare benefits.[27]

Placement policies, even if they work, are only a small safety valve for impactment. While impactment involves high costs, it is less of a problem than it is perceived to be. When the uprooted refugee comes together with others of his ethnic community, he gains a sense of belonging, a sense of identity, a sense of not being alone. Refugees are able to help one another and to exchange information. Those members of the refugee community who are assimilating and learning to speak the new language help other refugees who are less assimilated and do not speak English. Heavy concentrations of refugees, while they may strain resources, also aid in resettlement.

Other problems of resettlement are also subject to varying

interpretations. Perhaps the thorniest set of questions deals with issues of equity: whether and, if so, to what extent refugees should receive benefits not available to the rest of the population; what sort of assistance should be given to refugees, and for how long. The questions give rise to a spectrum of answers. At one extreme are those who believe that the refugee is owed nothing other than the opportunity to enter the United States and make his own way. At the other extreme are those who hold that refugees have been subjected to particularly traumatic experiences and therefore need compensatory long-term social assistance. Resettlement policy falls somewhere between these two extremes, but even here there are significant philosophical disparities.

One middle view holds that a refugee is a capable survivor, anxious to reassert control over his own life. Resettlement aid, therefore, should consist of providing the refugee with opportunity and solving the short-term problems that inhibit his adjustment. This approach asserts that the refugee should take the earliest possible employment, even an entry-level job; resettlement aids (language, vocational upgrading, and others) should be provided while the refugee works. The opposing middle view stresses that a refugee is a disadvantaged person unable to cope with his new environment without a lengthy period of public support. This view emphasizes "front loading"—giving language lessons and providing social services first, before the refugee looks for employment. Front loading, in turn, raises ancillary questions: What programs? For whom? To what level? For how long?

The concern for equity with other segments of the population who are disadvantaged (and the desire to save federal dollars) was a major rationale in reducing from thirty-six months to eighteen months the time in which a refugee was entitled to special cash assistance. Equity was also a rationale in the 1983 arguments by HHS that there should not be a special medical-assistance program for refugees.[28] When Congress reauthorized the domestic refugee resettlement program (Refugee Assistance Extension Act of 1986), the Senate deleted a provision in the House bill that would have granted refugees "presumptive eligibility" for Medicaid during their first year in the United States.

To assist in resettlement, the State Department gives reception and placement grants to the volags to provide core services for ninety days. Core services are food, clothing, shelter, orientation, health counseling, and employment-assistance referral. The reception and placement grants are per capita and have varied over time and with various refugee groups. For example, to resettle an Indochinese, volags received $500 from 1975 to 1977, $300 in 1977, $350 in 1978, $525 in 1983, and $560 in 1985 and 1986. The agreements between the State Department and the voluntary agencies stipulate that the refugee become self-supporting as soon as feasible.

Congress, as part of a general tightening up of resettlement costs, directed the General Accounting Office to investigate the initial reception and placement grants between the State Department and the participating voluntary agencies. In 1986, the GAO found that the State Department gave only minimal attention to the way in which the volags used the grant money and the adequacy of the services provided to the refugees. The GAO suggested that performance standards be imposed on volag services and that the volags be more financially accountable. The volags found the GAO study to be flawed in a number of serious ways. Responding to the GAO report, Karl D. Zukerman of HIAS, on behalf of the volags, correctly pointed out that the GAO statistical sample was atypical and did not distinguish between Southeast Asians and other refugees, the parameters for employability were too broad, and self-sufficiency in ninety days, in many cases, was an unrealistic goal. Nonetheless, methods are now being put into operation to satisfy the GAO's criticism of accounting and fiscal-reporting requirements.[29]

For most refugees, the ninety days of core services provided by the reception and placement grants are but a start. For the refugees who need it, the Refugee Act has established a panoply of entitlements. These programs are divided into two major components: cash, medical, and supplementary income assistance, which the states or their localities provide; and language, job, and other support services, which the states provide directly or, more frequently, through contracts with service-providing organizations.

A refugee is eligible to receive cash assistance if he or his family meets the state's income and resource tests. Need is determined under the standards of Aid to Families with Dependent Children (AFDC). A refugee may qualify for AFDC or refugee cash assistance (RCA). Refugee Cash Assistance, unlike AFDC, is available regardless of family composition. Refugees who receive cash assistance or RCA are also eligible for Medicaid. Refugees not meeting the categorical requirements of Medicaid may qualify, under somewhat looser standards, for refugee medical assistance (RMA). Refugees who are aged, blind, or disabled with low or no incomes are eligible for Supplemental Security Income. Also, low-income refugees are eligible to receive food stamps on the same basis as nonrefugees.

HHS funds support-service programs are generally in proportion to the number and distribution of a state's refugee populations. The specific programs and their design—who receives what services from whom—are the responsibility of the state. In addition to the flat-payment or cost-reimbursement programs, a small matching-grant program, previously mentioned, rounds out the benefits available to refugees.

The flow of public money to private voluntary agencies for public purposes raises issues of control, accountability, and responsibility. How well do the volags spend their public (and private) dollars? Who monitors the volags? And how effective is the monitoring? By and large, both public and private monies are managed well. Volags, on the whole, probably perform better, and certainly no worse, than most federal and state programs. Because the volags are diverse, some are less efficient than others, and monitoring performance levels in a nationwide resettlement system is difficult. Over time, both the contractual language and the monitoring of the Department of State's reception and placement cooperative agreements have improved. But State, with its focus on broad foreign-policy issues, has a limited interest in and capacity for monitoring. ORR and the state bureaucracies are more administratively attuned to monitoring, and as long as no large-scale massive emergency ensues, will be able to expand and improve their monitoring activities. Overall, volags spend public money wisely and effectively, but monitoring activities should continue and be expanded.[30]

While one generally speaks of the voluntary agencies as a collective noun, they are as diverse as American life. The private voluntary agencies vary in history, experience, size, nonsectarian or denominational affiliation, resettlement philosophy, primary clientele, administrative structure (decentralized versus centralized), resettlement capacity, and institutionalized resettlement policies and arrangements. While they are heterogeneous, however, they share the common goal of successful resettlement, which they define in the same basic way as the creation of a self-reliant, economically independent client who functions in his new environment. Donald G. Hohl, the respected resettlement expert with the United States Catholic Conference, once observed that in some ways volags are like parents: they want the best for their children (refugee clients), but like parents they approach their children differently. And the results are not seen immediately, but in many cases years later.[31]

The volag is central to resettlement. Its services range from governmental and quasi-governmental functions to purely private aid activities. It links the refugee to the various public and private bureaucracies. The volag acts as, or works with, the refugee's sponsor (be it individual, family, religious congregation, or civic group). But the volag goes beyond the critical issue of sponsorship; the volag is integral to the formulation and

execution of refugee policy in general, and resettlement specifically, in general acting as the public's conscience; the private
voluntary agencies testify before Congress on which, and how
many, refugees should be permitted to enter. They also testify
on what the refugees' status and benefits should be, and for
how long those benefits should continue.

Overseas, the volags participate in the management of the
refugee camps and in preadmission screening. In this country,
they help the refugee cope with the myriad problems of adjustment and acculturation, with benefits, services, and personal problems. They instruct the refugee in the naturalization
process. And when the refugee is no longer a refugee, but a
citizen, some voluntary agencies continue to provide psychological and material help.

Each volag is concerned about preserving its own autonomy,
independence, and idiosyncratic method of operation; nonetheless, the volags work together under the aegis of the American Council for Voluntary International Action (InterAction).
InterAction's roots go back to 1943, when the American Council of Voluntary Agencies for Foreign Service, Inc., was created
as a forum for information exchange, cooperation, and joint
planning among the independent voluntary agencies. Inter-
Action is a broadly based, participatory association of over one
hundred private and voluntary agencies working in a broad
range of public policy areas, among them migration, refugee
assistance, and resettlement. Because InterAction has a large
board membership, actual operational policy is made by the
executive committee which, in turn, relies on standing committees composed of representatives of interested agencies. The
Committee on Migration and Refugee Affairs acts as the co-
ordinating mechanism for the resettlement volags. Major policy
positions of the volags generally are issued over the signature
of the chairman of the committee. Emphasizing the cooperative
nature of the committee, the chairmanship periodically rotates
among the volags.

Reflecting those ethnic differences, and sometimes perform-
ing the resettlement functions of the volags, are the private
groups known as mutual-assistance associations (MAAs),
self-help groups that have grown out of the new refugee communities. These associations perform cultural, religious, educational, professional, and social functions. Since 1975, more
than five hundred MAAs have been created within the Indochinese communities, and their number continues to grow; like
volags they vary widely in size, organizational maturity, and
effectiveness.

Both the federal and state governments recognize that the
MAAs can help their members adapt to their new homeland.
Since 1978, the federal government has encouraged the MAAs
to provide social services for refugees. The Department of Health,
Education, and Welfare established an Indochinese Mutual Assistance Division to act as a liaison with, and provide technical
assistance to, the MAAs. The Office of Refugee Resettlement,
after its formation within HHS, gave direct grants to a small
number of MAAs nationwide for a variety of services such as
orientation, counseling, employment assistance, and interpreting. An MAA incentive-grant program followed in 1982, designed to encourage the states to fund MAAs as part of their
refugee programs. The incentive-grant program has grown from
one in which states competed for grants to the present program
in which grants are allocated to the states by formula.

The MAAs have created both benefits and liabilities for the
resettlement system. One benefit is that the MAAs can make
services more readily available to specific groups, such as older
refugees. Another benefit is that, through the MAAs, refugee
leaders can make decisions about matters affecting their own
communities. But tensions have arisen when some MAAs have
been awarded competitive service contracts (sometimes because
of bonus points or other affirmative action) at the expense of
long-existing service providers. At other times, refugees have
used the MAAs in power struggles between refugee clans and

groups. Some volags fear that since ORR funds the MAAs, the MAAs might come to serve the interests of ORR. But ORR believes that the benefits outweigh the liabilities and plans to continue allocating funds to the MAAs. Nonetheless, with or without MAA incentive grants, the growth and development of ethnic community associations were inevitable.[32]

While the volag is the key to resettlement, the Office of the Coordinator for Refugee Affairs orchestrates all the agencies working with refugee admissions and resettlement. Initially created by President Carter in response to the inflow of Vietnamese boat people and Russian émigrés, the office was made the organizational centerpiece of the Refugee Act. The act gives the coordinator the rank of ambassador-at-large for his international duties. The coordinator is appointed by the president and confirmed by the Senate. The act gave the coordinator broad responsibilities for the development "of overall United States refugee admission and resettlement policy." And because Congress, in hearings on the refugee problems, had been sensitized to the strains of impactment and the concerns of the receiving communities, the act instructed the coordinator to "consult regularly with states, localities, and private nonprofit voluntary agencies concerning the sponsorship process and the intended distribution of refugees."

When the coordinator's office was being discussed, during the passage of the Refugee Act, the location of the office became a matter of concern. Some wanted to locate the office in the White House, thinking its location near the president would signify that the coordinator was responsible for both the domestic and foreign aspects of refugee policy. Others thought the proper location was the State Department. The final version of the bill, a compromise, left the location of the office up to the president. Since the passage of the act, the office has been located in the State Department, but its physical location still remains a matter of debate.

Location notwithstanding, the role of the coordinator's office depends, like many positions in the bureaucracy, not so much on the job description as on the abilities and the personality of the incumbent. Senator Dick Clark, the coordinator under Carter's directive, was concerned primarily with the international aspects of the problem of the boat people. He remained in office for less than a year and departed before the Refugee Act became law. After Clark resigned and before the next coordinator, Victor Palmieri, took office, an interagency task force was established to review the domestic resettlement process and make recommendations as to how it might be improved. Amitai Etzioni, the White House resident social scientist, suggested that the federal government not expand its role in resettlement, but that it emphasize a broader voluntary approach. Professor Etzioni wanted to go beyond the volags and include such community-based social service agencies as the Red Cross, the YMCA, and the United Way. Etzioni, in a memorandum, explained his position:

. . . the public is sick and tired of the Feds taking on more and more issues, often not solving them, at increasing costs, etc., etc. It has been the general orientation of the Carter Administration *not* to follow the Great Society—throwing millions of dollars and Feds at each problem—but to rely more on the private and voluntary sector.

Second, the refugees are *particularly well suited* for the Feds' backseat approach. It is a relatively *limited and transient* problem as compared, say, to poverty, unemployment, inflation—hence relatively easier to handle, more suitable for voluntary-private efforts.[33]

When Victor Palmieri, a lawyer and successful management specialist who had been deputy director of the (Kerner) Commission on Civil Disorders, became the first coordinator to occupy the office under the Refugee Act, Etzioni continued to press for an expanded voluntary resettlement option. Palmieri, new to the office and concerned with the Mariel emergency, rejected Etzioni's suggestions. Palmieri reasoned that the established resettlement agencies, although lacking the resources to follow the refugee cases after their initial reception, were the logical agencies to be primarily involved in resettlement because of their commitment and expertise. What they needed was a long-term funding agreement.

Responding some time later to Etzioni, Palmieri wrote:

> The difficulty with Professor Etzioni's idea, however, was not simply bad timing, it was simply a bad idea. . . . The idea of dumping the casework problem in the laps of the privately-funded community-based social service agencies was ludicrous. The suggestion that they were willing or even eager to assume this monumental burden without Federal government support and without any of the specialized infrastructure in place lacked credibility, then as it does now.
>
>   . . . More importantly, to draw the major voluntary organizations such as United Way into refugee support activity meant diverting their attention and resources from the mounting problems of blacks and other disadvantaged domestic minorities. Unprecedented numbers of refugees and migrants were saturating the secondary labor market of major urban centers at a time when the labor economy was under growing stress and tensions over jobs and housing were rising in the minority community. Congress had already mandated relatively rich welfare, Medicare, and social service benefits for refugees. For the Administration to try to mobilize voluntary sector resources customarily dedicated to minority communities on behalf of refugees was on its face not only foolish but insensitive.[34]

Palmieri did not change the pattern of resettlement. The traditional volags were not displaced, and as the numbers of refugees entering the country grew, so did federal funding and involvement. In retrospect, Palmieri's decision was wise.

When the Reagan administration took over, the office of the coordinator was not filled for over a year. Observers believed that the position remained open so long because refugees were not an administration priority. Moreover, the new coordinator had to be politically acceptable. Finally, in March 1982, H. Eugene Douglas, corporate director of international trade and government for Memorex Corporation, became the coordinator.

Douglas took office believing that an imbalance existed between the foreign and domestic aspects of refugee policy. Admission levels were exceeding resettlement capacity.[35] After a year in office, Douglas, in a prepared statement to the House Subcommittee on Refugees and International Law, outlined his priorities. First, Douglas wanted to internationalize refugee relief and resettlement. He continued:

. . . A substantial part of our international effort has been devoted to developing a process of forward planning and program improvements. These efforts have included a careful managing down of refugee admissions, modulating monthly refugee arrivals in the U.S., and improving the preparation of refugees prior to the arrival in the U.S.

Douglas then went on to address the domestic program. He unequivocally stated that "costs are too high and significant inefficiencies exist in many areas." He was aware that "the prospect of change creates substantial anxiety among state and local officials and the voluntary agencies." Stressing a recurrent theme, he emphasized that "to maintain our ability to admit refugees to this country, the costs must be lowered and the funds must be used more efficiently."[36] To this end, Douglas advocated changes in the domestic refugee program: a system of per-capita grants to generate local initiatives, incentives to reduce welfare dependency, and better accountability for public funds disbursed to the volags.

But Douglas's efforts to remake the resettlement system were marginal because of the reluctance of bureaucratic institutions to change entrenched ways, the fear that changes would diminish the powers and prerogatives of individual agencies, and sharp policy differences with advocates of liberal refugee admissions. The various actors in resettlement resisted major changes in the system. A General Accounting Office review of the operation of the coordinator's office noted a perception "that the overriding objective of the Coordinator's Office is to reduce the scope and funding of refugee programs and that the proposals made by the Coordinator's Office were predetermined to meet this objective." The GAO, in a politic understatement, reported that "the current Coordinator's relationships with State, HHS, INS, and the voluntary agencies generally have been described as less than constructive."[37] And a study by the Refugee Policy Group found that "the Coordinator tends more to create controversy than to resolve it."[38] Indeed that was so. At one point, a bipartisan group of eight senators sent a letter to President Reagan asking him to relieve Douglas of his duties. The senators cited incidents which they felt were examples of Douglas's frustrating the execution of refugee protection and resettlement policies.[39]

By the time Douglas resigned, at the end of October 1985, he had succeeded in "managing down" numbers, but had made only incremental change in tightening the resettlement system. Douglas had not achieved his major goal of domestic resettlement—a dramatic reduction in the use of public assistance programs. Federal costs had been reduced because of the declining admission rate.[40] After Douglas's resignation, Jonathan Moore, director of the Institute of Politics at the John F. Kennedy School of Government at Harvard University, became coordinator of refugee affairs in July 1986.

The coordinator deals with a working, but fragmented, system. His mandate to develop overall admission and resettlement policies is a difficult one. Policies are colored by sensitive foreign and domestic politics. Controversy is endemic to the office. The office has a small staff (historically characterized by a marked lack of continuity), limited resources, and a lack of authority. The office carries responsibilities, but no line and budgetary authority over the major departments (Justice, State, HHS) that touch on the coordinator's sphere and frequently do not act in concert.

The State Department Bureau for Refugee Programs (BRP) and the Health and Human Services ORR are both important to resettlement. But their functions, outlooks, perspectives, administrative styles, and constituents are poles apart. While the BRP administers volag reception and placement grants, its major concern, as part of the State Department, is foreign policy, of which the refugee program is considered an adjunct. The BRP predicates admissions on international needs, not on the costs of resettlement. The State Department has worked with the volags for years and has an easy symbiotic relationship with them. Until recently the State Department had no great interest in monitoring volag performance on the grants.

ORR, in contrast, is mainly concerned with domestic aspects of resettlement. ORR views admissions from the perspective of costs and the effect refugees will have on states and localities. Unlike State, with its loose style of management oversight, ORR stresses tight managerial oversight, procedural uniformity, and strict performance standards. ORR traditionally has worked with state and local officials, a working relationship that was carried over into the Refugee Act. The act, recognizing that resettlement is ultimately a local activity, required the states to draw up refugee plans and appoint state coordinators.

State coordinators administer federal refugee aid and ORR social-service grants, and supervise state and local programs. Given the diversity, location, and size of the refugee populations, state and local policies and programs vary widely.[41] Two geographical and numerical extremes are illustrative: California has a large refugee population, most of the refugees crowding together in certain communities and creating drains on resources. Vermont has a small refugee population, causing the refugees to feel isolated, while the bureaucracy, in turn, is reluctant to create special programs for a few refugees. Throughout the resettlement process, at every level—federal, state, and especially local—is the need for continuity in programs and for effective working relationships among the entities serving refugees and the refugees themselves. To achieve this continuity and coordination, mechanisms such as county or city forums, task forces, and councils have proven useful and workable.

The federal government's singular responsibility for admissions has inexorably led to a pivotal federal role in resettlement. Federal dollars, accompanied by a constantly changing complement of rules and regulations, flow from Washington, D.C., to the states and localities. All the monies and all the directives are designed to ease the refugees' successful resettlement; not only because smooth resettlement by itself is a federal goal, but also, and perhaps more importantly, because admission of refugees in the future is dependent on successful resettlement of refugees in the present. When the public perceives that the economic and social costs of resettlement are low, there is less opposition to continued admission of refugees. Conversely, when the public believes that lavish amounts of money are being spent on refugees, they resent the refugees in their midst and oppose further admissions.

Resettlement policy is driven far more by practical concerns than by pure humanitarianism. Therefore the primary goals of federal resettlement policy, the how issues, are how to reduce costs and how to avoid conflict between refugees and citizens, conflicts conceived in xenophobia and racism, and fed by competition for scarce housing, employment, and municipal services.

Coordination is critical for resettlement. Within the resettlement system, each actor—federal, state, and local agencies, vol-ags, and the refugees themselves—has his own priorities and perspective. The federal government, states, and localities aim at reducing costs and avoiding conflict. States and localities realize, however, that they will continue to pay for refugee services long after federal time-limited refugee entitlements end. And for the refugees, and the volags who work closely with them, resettlement is more than "economic self-sufficiency."

The philosophy of resettlement shared by many volags was well expressed by Wells C. Klein when he testified before the Select Commission on Immigration and Refugee Policy in 1980. Klein, executive director of the American Council for Nation-alities Service, took as his basic premise that refugees have "particular disadvantages deriving from being refugees." Ac-cordingly, the overall policy objective should be "to assist the refugee to achieve economic self-sufficiency, and a degree of social integration sufficient for him to relate productively to his new environment." The conjunction *and* in Klein's statement indicates what he believes resettlement policy objectives should be, objectives that serve the interests of both the refugee and his new community. Klein went on to state:

> Refugee resettlement is social engineering. It involves the provision of specific services, a general counseling and "help-ing" component, and assistance to the refugee in formulating, testing, and eventually adopting new attitudes and social be-havior. Resettlement takes place at the local level in the com-munity and, in large measure, results from interaction be-tween the refugee and the community.

For Klein, the volag provided "the point of reference and con-tinuity throughout the resettlement process." Resettlement was not static. "Seen as a group, refugees are not a dependent pop-ulation, but rather a population in transition."[42]

The majority of refugees do not remain on welfare. As they

move up from entry-level employment, they pay more taxes and become more self-sufficient. While most refugees find life hard for many years, the longer they remain in this country, the more likely they are to be employed. And with longer residence in an area, impactment decreases and an infusion of new life begins. The Cubans revitalized a tired Miami; the Indochinese have begun to revive parts of Chicago, Providence, and other cities where they have settled; the Russians are rejuvenating a declining Brighton Beach. Refugees are self-selective. They are survivors. While they carry with them the traumas of the past, they also carry hope and vitality for the future. America can absorb refugees, for each refugee carries with him his own absorptive capacity. Refugees, after their initial difficulties, become contributors.

"Cuban-Americans," according to Professor Thomas D. Boswell, "have made remarkable progress in their adjustment to life in the United States. . . . By almost any measure it is apparent that the Cubans are becoming rapidly assimilated into American society, although they are still readily visible as an ethnic minority."[43] Indochinese, sociologist Peter I. Rose has concluded, "are coming to be seen by many not merely as 'model minorities,' but as 'model Americans': hardworking, achievement-oriented. . . . "[44] The major barrier to rapid assimilation for the Indochinese has been language. Once that difficulty is overcome, acculturation proceeds rapidly. Researchers Andrews and Stopp have found that the Indochinese "have adapted very rapidly in comparison to other groups in the past. . . . In particular, higher education is being used to a remarkable degree to accelerate assimilation."[45]

A University of Michigan study of boat people who arrived in the United States in 1978 concluded that, despite the trauma they suffered, the parents are making steady economic progress, and their children are doing extraordinarily well in school. As a group, the children evidenced "a high level of academic achievement, whether measured by grade point average or scores on nationally standardized tests."[46] Newspapers recount Indochinese success stories: the high school students who, only a few years after arriving from refugee camps with little or no English, graduated as high school valedictorians; refugees who were recertified as doctors; the Vietnamese lawyer who, without attending an American law school, succeeded in passing the New York bar; two refugees who graduated from West Point in 1985, ten years after escaping from South Vietnam; the 1979 boat person who graduated first in his class from City College and went on to do graduate work at the Massachusetts Institute of Technology; the twelve-year-old Cambodian refugee who made it to the zone finals of the National Spelling Bee, only to fail on the word *enchilada*; the refugee who won the Westinghouse Science Talent Search; the refugee who graduated from the Air Force Academy and was named a Rhodes scholar.[47]

The Russians also are making a good adjustment. After an exhaustive study, Rita J. Simon concluded, "From many points of view—the educational and technical skills they brought with them, their labor-force participation, and the taxes they pay—the Soviet immigrants seem to be making a good economic adjustment to their new environment and are proving to be an excellent investment for native Americans. . . . After being here only a short time, they are already contributing rather than taking from the public coffers."[48]

If refugees are looked at as populations, rather than as individuals, then all are contributors, and all will ascend the ladder of transition. If the refugees themselves do not make it to the top rungs, then many of their children will. Immigration and refugee scholar Gary Rubin has pointed out perceptively that a better term than *cost* would be *investment*. "If you look not only at the long term, but also at the middle term, refugees are an asset to the community. We may have to pay for them in the beginning, but eventually, as all the research shows, they contribute considerably to the community. . . . 'Cost' doesn't seem to be the word that captures the refugee experience. 'Investment' does. . . . We have to lay out money, but we lay it out for future gains."[49]

In slightly more than two decades, the United States has resettled, largely successfully, some two million refugees—primarily Cubans, Indochinese, and in lesser numbers, Russians, East Europeans, and others from the Middle East and Africa. This is a remarkable achievement. The resettlement system has grown from a small-scale private enterprise to a complex intergovernmental bureaucracy. As with any large-scale enterprise, vigilance is needed to prevent waste, duplication, and inefficiency. The record of resettlement is a record of improvement in the face of low political priorities. As congressional oversight has tightened, and as the various entities involved in resettlement have gained experience, the managerial aspects of resettlement have improved, evincing a growing sophistication.

The volags, which became only incrementally the mechanism linking the federal government and the refugee to local settlement, remain reluctant to relinquish their individual and idiosyncratic ways, but they are learning that the receipt of public monies entails responsibility and accountability. And the federal departments that work with the volags, State and HHS, are learning, even if belatedly, to supervise and monitor.

Problems remain. Resettlement has to compete with other demands, with higher priorities such as programs in defense, space, medical research, and subsidies to powerful groups. Refugees as a pressure group have a limited constituency. Partly because of its low political priority, and partly because of its historical development, resettlement has been institutionally fragmented and plagued by discontinuities in personnel, programs, and funding.

Discontinuities abound. The Office of the Coordinator of Refugee Affairs went unfilled for many months in both the Carter and the Reagan administrations. The physical location of the coordinator's office has been in question since the office was created. Within the Department of State, there have been fre-

quent reshufflings of the administrative apparatus and personnel of refugee programs: foreign-service officers generally feel
that refugee work hampers their career advancement. The turn-
over in State Department officers assigned to refugee programs
has resulted in poor institutional memory. State has done little
contingency planning for massive refugee flows to this country.
Only recently, under congressional prodding, has State tightened its reception and placement contracts and begun to monitor volag performance.

Within HHS, the refugee apparatus developed slowly and was
subject to administrative shifts. Initially, refugee activities were
carried out by a low-level special-programs staff within the
Office of Family Assistance in the Social Security Administration, then by an HHS Refugee Task Force comprising the heads
of the principal operating components in the department, then
by an Office of Refugee Affairs, and finally by the permanent
Office of Refugee Resettlement. ORR, under the Reagan administration, has been moved from the secretary of HHS's office to
the Social Security Administration office. This administrative
shift, to some observers, was an indication that the administration was becoming less concerned with resettlement.

Changes in federal policy have often been abrupt, creating
administrative problems. At one time the program to admit
unaccompanied refugee children had a high priority; then the
numbers were reduced, and the many state programs that had
been created found themselves competing with one another for
sponsorship of the remaining several hundred eligible minors.
The regulations on cash and medical assistance, most state refugee coordinators feel, were enacted without appropriate state
consultations: federal officials consulted with representative state
coordinators on the same day that the final regulations appeared
in the federal register.

Resettlement funding reductions, some planned, others in
response to budget deficits, create uncertainty for states in refugee programing; so will a future of federal budget restraint,

particularly for low-priority programs. ORR's shifting policies, regulations, and restrictive interpretation of funding cause other uncertainties.

One change required that eighty-five percent of social service funds must be used for employment-directed services and fifteen percent for other necessary services. But as a National Association of Counties representative testified before Congress, "the eighty-five/fifteen requirement is arbitrary. It has fundamentally undermined the states' and the counties' abilities to administer the program and expedite refugee self-sufficiency and ignore the nonemployment aspect of resettlement."[50]

In a recent study, social scientists Strand and Jones found that "federal funding changes and continued uncertainty over funding levels have forced states to reconsider their refugee resettlement program designs and to increase the emphasis on employment, program coordination, and accountability. . . . The decision to limit eligibility for ORR reimbursement to eighteen months has created financial hardships for county General Assistance programs."[51]

Nor should one forget that states, local agencies, and volags are not immune to inefficiencies and poor management. Problems can also arise at the local level, where cooperation among volags and state and local governments depends on varying resources and personnel, and on administrative capabilities and receptivity to resettlement that differ among states and localities.

While better continuity and coordination would improve the delivery of services to refugees, the resettlement system works overall. Resettlement should bring two interconnected premises to mind: the national government has a responsibility for resettlement, and both government and the public should think of refugees as contributors to American society rather than as perpetually welfare-dependent clients.

Refugee admission is a federal responsibility; logically, the national government has an obligation to the states and localities that serve as host communities for the refugees. This means that impactment aid is a federal responsibility. If policy makers concentrate primarily on costs, they ignore other overriding considerations. Linking admission numbers with costs is dangerous, allowing one to assert, with faulty logic, that if the price is too high, we cannot admit refugees. Humanitarian and foreign-policy considerations should take precedence over costs. The costs of resettling refugees pale in comparison with other federal expenditures. Federal expenditures for both foreign and domestic refugee assistance are an infinitesimal part of the total budget.[52] Refugee-assistance costs of states and localities make up an equally small proportion of their total expenditures. Too often overlooked are the refugees' assets. Refugees enrich their new communities. They make permanent cultural, social, and economic contributions. Refugees, in the final analysis, bring short-term costs and long-term benefits to their receiving communities and all of the United States.

Like refugees, those who are granted asylum in this country are also eligible for resettlement assistance. And just as the admission of refugees is, to a large extent, influenced by foreign policy and by domestic costs, so too does the acceptance of asylum applicants hinge on these considerations. But while Congress and the executive together exercise control over the numbers and the costs of refugee admissions, they have far less control of the numbers of asylum seekers. The Immigration and Naturalization Service acts almost independently in deciding to approve or reject an asylum applicant. Although the Immigration Service leans strongly on the advice of the State Department, it is not accountable to the Congress, which can do no more than react to decisions that have already been rendered. If Congress has little power to influence, and no power to reverse asylum decisions, however, the courts do have that power and have, in recent years, been making use of it. As the numbers of asylum seekers grow, the courts are providing both check and balance to the authority of the Immigration Service.

4 Breaching the Gate: The Question of Asylum

Cherished values in time become the stuff of myth. Americans hold fast the conviction that the United States will not deny asylum to any individual who comes here seeking freedom. In November of 1970, a Lithuanian seaman, Simas Kudirka, sought the protection of an American vessel, but was instead surrendered to the Soviets, who beat him and forced him back to his own ship; an article of faith had been breached. Across the country, Americans demonstrated. Newspapers editorialized and a political cartoonist depicted a besmirched and weeping Statue of Liberty.[1] The House of Representatives, over an eight-day period, investigated. And President Nixon, "outraged and shocked"[2] by the event, reaffirmed the "depth and urgency of our commitment" to those seeking asylum.[3]

The Kudirka incident not only compelled Americans to reaffirm their values, it also exposed the more pragmatic concerns that regularly govern the application of those values. The ship from which Kudirka jumped was a Soviet trawler, which was moored off Martha's Vineyard together with an American Coast Guard cutter, while a meeting was taking place between Soviet officials and representatives of the U.S. fishing industry. When Kudirka attempted to defect, instructions were sought as to what to do with him. A rear admiral in the Coast Guard made the decision:

In view of the nature of present arrangements with [the Soviets] and *in the interest of not fouling up any of our arrangements as far as the fishing situation is concerned*, I think [the Soviets] should know this and if they choose to do nothing, keep him on board [the Coast Guard cutter], otherwise, put him back. . . . (Emphasis added.)[4]

The Congress saw the matter differently. Wayne L. Hays, chairman of the House subcommittee that conducted the investigation, felt that it was not fishing but foreign policy that should have determined Seaman Kudirka's fate. "Obviously," Hays observed, "this is a foreign policy decision, ultimately."[5]

In November of 1985, a Ukranian seaman, Miroslav Medved, jumped twice from his Soviet ship; Americans returned him both times to the Soviets, who forced him, screaming and kicking, onto his ship. As it was for Simas Kudirka, the American reaction was swift, and the State Department acted just as swiftly to avoid embarrassment. The department removed the seaman from the Soviet ship and gave him physical and psychiatric examinations and interviewed him in the presence of both American and Soviet officials. The State Department concluded that Medved wanted only to return to the Soviet Union. Others who had spoken with the seaman disagreed. But, in the end, Miroslav Medved was returned to his ship and to the Soviet Union.

As before, other concerns than the simple right of an individual to ask asylum clouded the air. The incident had occurred just three weeks before a scheduled summit meeting between President Reagan and Soviet leader Gorbachev. Conservative groups contended that American officials returned the sailor to avoid an ugly international incident before the meeting. The White House, on the other hand, made it known that President Reagan had, in the words of an unnamed official, "authorized the use of force to get the sailor off the ship if that was necessary."[6]

The right of asylum has been enshrined in the American ethos, like the Wizard in the land of Oz. But behind the curtain, the myth is given power and presence by the very pragmatic machinery of foreign policy. In fact, there are not one but two machineries at work. The first drives the realpolitik of fishing agreements and summit meetings; the second proclaims our unyielding opposition to the Soviet menace.

The tension between these opposing forces in our asylum policy may never be resolved. For many asylum applicants, however, it matters not which side prevails, because they serve the interests of neither side. Neither are they outspoken opponents of Communism, nor do they carry any practical weight in the world.

In December of 1972, a leaking sailboat carrying sixty-five Haitian refugees drifted onto the Florida shore. Among the refugees were twelve political prisoners who had bribed their way out of one of President-for-Life Jean-Claude Duvalier's infamous jails. Many others were family members of the escapees. One of the prisoners explained why he had come. "I was in a cell holding eight men, and one night three of the others were taken out and never seen again. We decided it was time to leave."[7] The Immigration and Naturalization Service denied the refugees asylum, ruling that the Haitians had nothing to fear from the Haitian government.[8] This time there were no outrage and no shock, no large demonstrations and no congressional investigations. Nor were there any protests, in the 1970s, when Filipino opponents of President Marcos or Iranian opponents of the Shah were likewise denied asylum.

United States asylum policy, like our refugee policy, is predisposed toward refugees from Communist countries and disinclined to admit any others. For the government, however, a single critical consideration influences every asylum decision: the fear of overwhelming numbers. That fear has led the government to engage in practices that range from the inhumane to the illegal; asylum seekers are detained in prisons, interdicted at sea, and forcibly repatriated.

In 1979, when Congress was framing the Refugee Act, the practice of denying asylum claims had become so prevalent, and the number of asylum claims granted so few, that Congress entirely overlooked the question of asylum. Only at the suggestion of the United Nations High Commissioner for Refugees were asylum provisions included in the Refugee Act.[9] These provisions seemed, at the time, to be quite generous: the attorney general, at his discretion, could grant asylum to any individual with a valid asylum claim; up to five thousand of those granted asylum would, each year, be permitted to change their status to permanent resident, a first step in attaining citizenship. Five thousand was a very generous number, since fewer than one thousand refugees received asylum each year.

Few people, in the Congress or elsewhere, were cognizant of the many Haitians and Filipinos already in the United States who were asking for asylum, because Haitian and Filipino claims were almost invariably denied.

Within weeks of the passage of the Refugee Act, however, asylum matters would be on everyone's mind, as Castro opened the port of Mariel and a flood of would-be Cuban refugees, to be joined by a smaller stream of Haitians, began to wash up on our shores. It was immediately clear that the Refugee Act, significant as it was, had dealt too perfunctorily with asylum. Over past years, the United States had become, although few recognized it as such, a country of first asylum for refugees from the Caribbean and Latin America. With the Cuban and Haitian burdens thrust on an already underfunded, understaffed, and highly inefficient Immigration and Naturalization Service, the numbers of asylum cases multiplied geometrically. By October of 1982, there were more than 140,000 asylum claims before the INS.[10]

Soon thereafter, the ascending level of violence in Central America sent hundreds of thousands of other refugees in search of safe haven. As neighboring countries became less hospitable, many of these refugees were drawn to the United States. The asylum system by now was hopelessly blocked. Spurious claims

jammed together with the most deserving, and all would take
years to decide. America no longer perceived itself as a land of
refuge; the myth had clashed with sharp reality and been shattered.

Many now saw the asylum process as a dagger pointed at
the throat of the American immigration process. In truth, asylum had become, and remains today, a double-edged sword.
On the one side, the United States has seemingly no way to
regulate the flow of asylum seekers or to place a limit on their
numbers. On the other side, the asylum seekers cannot be sure
of a fair and just hearing.

Political asylum is a response to the refugee's immediate need—
a temporary grant of safe haven until the refugee is either able
to return home or to find permanent resettlement. The United
States is obligated under international law to offer such haven
to all who require it. There can be no limit on the numbers to
whom we may grant asylum, but only five thousand asylees
each year may obtain permanent residency here. Fearing that
asylum seekers will overwhelm this country, the United States
exercises control in the only way it can, through the asylum
process itself, through the determination of who will and will
not be granted asylum, the process of judging claims.

It is here that the other side of the sword has been turned
against the asylum seeker. There is, at present, no way to ensure
that those in need of it will receive asylum or that the asylum
process will be conducted in an efficient and equitable manner.
Discrimination as discernment has become discrimination as
bias; judgment has become prejudgment.

Our refugee system does not base an award of asylum on the
merits of an individual case. The three biases that underlie our
refugee policy are the major determinants also of asylum decisions. For this reason, the preponderance of all asylum grants
are made to applicants from countries whose regimes we oppose. For the seven-year period from fiscal years 1980 through
1986, asylum was granted in 29,926 cases. But 76 percent of

the awards went to applicants from just three countries: Iran, Poland, and Nicaragua.[11] By contrast, Salvadorans, for the same period, received only 2.3 percent of all asylum grants.[12]

Although the regulations that govern the asylum process are politically neutral, they appear to have had little influence on actual practice. Ineffective or not, however, the regulations were not to the liking of Attorney General Edwin Meese, whose aides, in 1986, told the *New York Times* that Meese "found it difficult to accept the view that the refugee law and the asylum rules permitted no distinction between aliens fleeing Communist and non-Communist countries."[13] The Justice Department began drafting new rules under which an asylum seeker from a "totalitarian" country would be presumed to have a well-founded fear of persecution. Although Meese did not sign the proposed changes, shortly thereafter the INS district director in Florida, Perry Rivkind, announced that no Nicaraguans would be deported from his district, because, he said, he "would personally—not just as a Government official, but personally—have trouble sending people from a Communist country back to that country." Mr. Rivkind, however, declined to halt the deportation of Salvadorans and Guatemalans because, he observed, "Nicaragua is the only Communist regime in power in Central America."[14]

While it is possible that among certain groups there is a higher likelihood of persecution, that likelihood is not confined to groups fleeing the governments of political enemies. In the area of human rights, one cannot generalize. A look at two asylum claims should make this clear. The first asylum applicant, a college professor, was arrested for his membership in a university organization. He was imprisoned and tortured, but pressure from international human-rights groups won his release. When the professor was once again threatened, he went into hiding, then escaped to the United States.[15] The second asylum applicant, also a college professor, feared that he was going to be jailed for his activities in an antigovernment union. When

Asylum Cases Filed with INS District Directors— Approved and Denied, by Nationality, June 1983 to September 1986

Country	Approval Rate for Cases Decided	Cases Granted	Cases Denied
Total	**23.4%**	**18,823**	**61,717**
Iran	60.4%	10,728	7,005
Rumania	51.0%	424	406
Czechoslovakia	45.4%	99	119
Afghanistan	37.7%	344	567
Poland	34.0%	1,806	3,495
Hungary	31.9%	137	292
Syria	30.2%	114	263
Ethiopia	29.2%	734	1,774
Vietnam	26.0%	50	142
Uganda	25.3%	75	221
China	21.4%	84	307
Philippines	20.9%	77	291
Somalia	15.6%	74	399
Nicaragua	14.0%	2,602	15,856
Iraq	12.1%	91	655
Yugoslavia	11.0%	31	249
Cuba[a]	10.3%	221	1,906
Liberia	8.4%	20	218
Pakistan	6.5%	26	370
El Salvador	2.6%	528	19,207
Honduras	2.5%	6	234
Lebanon	2.4%	34	1,338
Haiti[b]	1.8%	30	1,631
Guatemala	.9%	14	1,461
India	.3%	1	311
Egypt	.2%	2	703
Bangladesh	.0%	0	403

a. There were 89,606 cases from Cuba pending at the end of fiscal year 1986.
b. There were 2,042 cases from Haiti pending at the end of fiscal year 1986.

Source: Immigration and Naturalization Service (INS)/U.S. Department of Justice

he was sent out of the country to repair and bring back a racing yacht, he decided not to return. Along with four other men, he sailed the yacht to the United States and asked for asylum.[16]

The first professor had been persecuted and had proof of that persecution. Among other documents, he had a letter from the authorities, sealed by them, attesting that he had been imprisoned. He also had newspaper accounts of protests made on his behalf by human-rights organizations. But the professor's asylum request was denied; he was ordered deported to the country from which he had fled—El Salvador.

The second professor advanced only a fear of persecution. Against his assertion, there was the countervailing evidence that he had been sufficiently trusted to be sent out of the country. This professor was given asylum; he was from Poland.

For refugees from the Eastern bloc, immigration authorities find it sufficient argument that the refugee's freedom—professional, artistic, personal—had in some way been curtailed. Thus we find asylum granted to a Czech sailor whose government had refused him permission to enter a transatlantic race.[17] In non-Communist countries, however, even the most extreme kinds of repression are often discounted. Asylum was denied a Haitian journalist who, for his association with opponents of the Duvalier regime, suffered three arrests, imprisonment for long periods without arraignment or trial, starvation, and beatings.[18]

What these few, selected cases demonstrate is not that a refugee's country of origin will necessarily determine whether he is given asylum, although it will weigh heavily in that decision. Rather, even this small sampling illustrates the problems that arise because there is no clear understanding of how claims for asylum are to be judged. As a rule, asylum is awarded those refugees who are our political allies, denied those who are not. The immigration authorities and refugee policymakers regard refugees as allies if they resist Communism, and strongly favor them over other refugees.[19]

Even this seeming guideline, however, bends before the over-whelming fear that permeates all asylum policy and practice—fear of opening the floodgates. The floodgates fear outweighs even foreign policy considerations and pressure from support groups. In the end, the single question most likely to influence an asylum decision is, Will a grant of asylum to this individual encourage others like him to enter the United States? Similarly, every policy and practice put into effect by the government—from forced repatriation, through interdiction and detention, to curtailment of due process—has been based on the obverse of that question, Will this policy or practice discourage others from entering the United States?

The floodgates fear arises from three roots. First, there is no ceiling on the number of individuals who can receive asylum in this country. Second, pressure from communities that have felt the impact of large numbers of refugees and asylum seekers has far outweighed pressure from support groups. Third, there is a generalized fear among the American public of hordes of uncontrolled illegal immigrants, a fear exacerbated by state-ments such as those by President Reagan, when he warns that "concerns about the prospect of hundreds of thousands of ref-ugees fleeing Communist oppression to seek entry into our country are well-founded."[20]

In fact, each time that President Reagan describes how, one by one, the dominoes will topple in Central America, the final domino is the threat of a floodtide of refugees. The president thus confirms a tenet of his administration's refugee policy: only Communist governments produce refugees. At the same time, he plays upon the floodgates fears of the American people. The fear of Communism, however, bows to the fear of opening the floodgates. Since the Soviet invasion of Afghanistan, few Af-ghanis have received asylum in this country: from a peak of 303 in 1982, the numbers declined to a mere 57 in 1985.

The fear of opening the floodgates to refugees is less urgent than it is for asylees, since geographical distance from the United

States creates a kind of protective moat. Asylum applicants, however, have already forded the moat, and when their requests for asylum are evaluated, the floodgates question assumes even greater importance than the foreign-policy considerations of the applicants' countries of origin.

An applicant for asylum first confronts the floodgates fear when he makes his application. A refugee begins with a presumption of merit; an applicant for asylum begins with a presumption of deceit. At every level of government, one hears the complaint that refugees abroad wait patiently, sometimes for years, for an opportunity to come to the United States, while asylum applicants have simply barged right in and presented themselves for immediate acceptance. The complaint, however, betrays a basic misconception of what motivates the refugee. Implicit in the complaint is the belief that the primary goal of the refugee is to better his life in the United States. In this light, refugees who await resettlement from abroad are simply one type of immigrant, as in the days when refugees were the seventh immigration preference. Asylum applicants, on the other hand, are seen as illegal entrants, trying to violate our immigration laws.

This is not to say that the floodgates fear is only xenophobic paranoia. The problem is real. A major dilemma confronting refugee policymakers is how to distinguish the legitimate asylum claim from the fraudulent. There are few guidelines. There is no basis on which an asylum officer can easily categorize an applicant and thus determine that he is, or is not, eligible for asylum. Broadly speaking, those in genuine need of asylum are found within one of three groups—defectors, the politically displaced, and the precluded. Also within those groups, however, may be found others whose origins and circumstances may be similar, but who may not meet the standards for asylum.

Defectors are those individuals who come to this country under the aegis of their own governments, but who do not wish to return to the repressive conditions from which they came. They ask for asylum on the grounds that, having denounced their governments, they would face certain persecution if returned to their countries.

Defectors are often individuals of some importance or celebrity—diplomats, artists, athletes, or high-level scientists, who, it is clear, would be punished for having asked for asylum in the United States. Unlike other asylum applicants, defectors need not prove they were singled out for persecution *prior* to their defections.

High-level defectors are also not subject to regular asylum procedures. Their applications are approved within a matter of days, and they are never detained or required to defend their claims in an immigration court. Artem V. Kulikov, a senior nuclear scientist in the Soviet Union, requested asylum on Christmas Eve of 1984.[21] By the day after Christmas, asylum had been granted. Vladimir Moraru, a Rumanian journalist, defected during the 1984 Olympic games. While he awaited an asylum decision, he stayed at the home of friends.[22] The treatment afforded low-level defectors—seamen, for example—may vary. Shortly after customs men unceremoniously returned Miroslav Medved to his ship, in the ensuing glare of media attention, two Rumanian sailors won immediate asylum.[23]

The second group of asylum seekers consists of those people who have entered the United States legally, either as students, businessmen, tourists, or workers. While in the United States, they find that conditions in their home country suddenly change, and they face certain persecution if they return; they have become politically displaced. When their documents expire, they ask that deportation be withheld and that they be given political asylum. Typical of the politically displaced are those Nicaraguans, many of them supporters of Anastasio Somoza, who, having fled the civil war in their country, had been given permission to enter the United States on a temporary basis. Following Somoza's ouster, many of the politically displaced

Nicaraguans feared a return to their country and filed for asylum; few have received it.

For this second group of asylum applicants, foreign policy is a major influence, as it was, for instance, when the Soviet military took over Poland and the American government, in 1977, ordered that Polish applicants be granted asylum automatically. Iranians have had a more checkered treatment. Although they are now the largest group to be granted asylum, both in absolute numbers and in percentages, during the Iranian hostage crisis the INS made the deportation of Iranians a top priority.

Traditionally, U.S. policymakers have considered asylum seekers to comprise these two groups—defectors and the politically displaced. These groups were undoubtedly what the framers of the Refugee Act had in mind. They present few problems. Because these asylum applicants have been, in effect, processed before they entered the country, because their numbers are limited and controlled, and because they flee either a Communist government (in the former case) or a leftist revolution (in the latter case), they receive asylum most often.

More problematic by far is the third group, problematic because its members act from the full range of motives for coming to the United States, from individual fear of persecution, through flight from generalized violence, to the simple desire to get a job or rejoin family. Despite administration pronouncements to the contrary, to know an asylum-seeker's origin is not to know his motives. Only one factor binds these individuals as a group: unlike those in the other two groups, they must travel *to* the United States to ask asylum. Genuine refugees along with economic migrants must enter the United States illegally because, in many cases, they are not permitted to apply for refugee status abroad. As a result of deliberate, calculated refugee policy, there are no refugee slots for these people—no quotas, no waiting lists, no hope of eventual admission.

The policy that forces this third group of refugees to seek

asylum in the United States is a policy of preclusion. It has probably been best expressed by Attorney General William French Smith. In explaining how an individual applies for refugee status, the attorney general wrote:

> Before the person may be granted refugee status, . . . there must be two determinations made: First, whether refugee numbers have been allocated to persons in the region of the person's nationality; and second, whether the person falls into a group or category of persons "of special humanitarian concern" as determined by Congress and the President. *If these factors are not present, the persons will not qualify for a grant of refugee status even if he meets the refugee definition in [the Refugee Act].* (Emphasis added.)[25]

Thus we have the phenomenon of bona fide refugees being precluded even from consideration for admission. Such has been the case for Western Hemisphere refugees. Despite the large numbers of refugees in the region (estimates for 1984 ran to well over half a million in Central America alone), the State Department allocated only one thousand admissions slots overall.[26] More to the point, the department reserved those one thousand places for a particular category of individual deemed to be "of compelling concern/interest"—namely, present or recently released political prisoners, or individuals who had, for at least one year, worked for the United States government. Refugees not falling into one of these two categories, even those threatened with loss of life or freedom, are barred from consideration.

Few of even those designated as refugees, moreover, will be released from their countries, a fact of which the State Department is keenly aware. In fiscal year 1985, only fifty-seven refugees entered the United States from all of the Caribbean and Latin America. All fifty-seven came from Cuba.[27] There has been a tendency to limit refugee admissions within the region to Cubans and Argentinians. A GAO report notes that in past years, there had been a refugee ceiling for Latin America and the Caribbean of up to two thousand. The report goes on, "Until recently, however, *no Central American had been admitted to the United States* as a refugee. In the first half of fiscal year 1984, ninety-three Salvadorans were admitted as refugees."[28] (Emphasis added.) Undoubtedly, the administration admitted the ninety-three Salvadorans in response to criticisms of its refugee policy. In 1985 and 1986, only three non-Cubans were processed as refugees from all of Latin America and the Caribbean.[29]

An individual in Latin America or the Caribbean who has a well-founded fear of persecution is thus precluded from the regularized channels of refugee admission. If he wants to seek safety in the United States, only one option is open to him: he must enter the country illegally and ask for asylum.

Illegal entrance, too, is forced upon him, since United States consulates will not assist asylum seekers or give them any sort of documentation. A foreign-service officer who has served in Central America put it this way:

> If you go to a consular officer and say you want political asylum in the United States, [we] have to say that we cannot give you political asylum.
>
> Then if they say they want a tourist visa, you can't give them the tourist visa because they have already told you that they want to seek political asylum.
>
> Basically, the response is that there are many neighboring countries and suggest that you cross the border to seek asylum there.[30]

Refugees in three categories then—the politically displaced, the defectors, and the precluded—may be bona fide refugees, but they are unable to seek resettlement through regular refugee processes and must ask for a grant of asylum within the United

States. Two other categories contrast these three: individuals for whom asylum may be neither the only option nor even a proper one.

The fourth class consists of those individuals who choose, for a variety of reasons, to bypass regular refugee procedures and come directly to the United States and ask for asylum. These people are frequently referred to as "line-jumpers." That is an unfortunate term that implies calculation and dishonesty, motives for some but not all members of this class. More often, they are motivated by desperation.

Take, for example, a group of Iraqi-Armenians who sought asylum in the United States. The torture, persecution, and discrimination they had suffered in Iraq, as a result of their religious and cultural differences, impelled them to flee. Most had found haven in Greece, where they lived for two years. But economic conditions in Greece were extremely harsh, with few jobs and little money, and so they arranged for a flight to New York City, where they disembarked during a refueling stop and asked for asylum.[31] Unquestionably, these Iraqi-Armenians had had a legitimate claim to refugee status. Just as unquestionably, they had already been given first asylum in Greece and were not eligible for asylum in the United States.

Many Afghanis tell stories similar to the Iraqis'. Given first asylum in neighboring countries, the Afghanis feel that with limited numbers of refugee slots available for the Middle East, they will never gain admission to the United States. So they pay for fraudulent documents to enter the United States. Arrested, they ask for political asylum.[32] One can easily empathize with these refugees who wish, finally, to be permanently settled in freedom and security. Yet it is difficult to justify giving preference to one group of refugees over others who also must wait under even more difficult conditions. Rather than line-jumpers, this group might be called the residual refugees.

The fifth class comprises not refugees at all, but impatient immigrants. These persons wish to immigrate to the United

States, but the process sometimes takes years, and they do not wish to wait. They come to the United States and, with the help of immigration attorneys, file claims for political asylum. Though the claims are patently frivolous, the lengthy appeal process will guarantee them several years, at least, in this country, during which time they may find legitimate ways to remain. The process also proves lucrative for the attorneys. These frivolous applications create two results that are, however, hardly frivolous. First, they further congest an already clogged legal system. Second, and far more insidious, they provide palpable evidence to restrictionists that our asylum system has become a playground for a few greedy attorneys and many would-be immigrants.

The asylum official in the United States, then, sees a broad spectrum of applicants. But, unlike his counterpart abroad, who determines whether refugee resettlement will be offered, the asylum officer has little concrete assistance. The INS has established specific categories of persons who are "likely targets of persecution." When a refugee can prove that he is a member of one of the recognized groups, he need not present further evidence of persecution. Asylum cases, on the other hand, must be considered individually. Membership in a persecuted group is not, for an asylum applicant, considered evidence of persecution.

Then too, the burden of proof is far heavier on the asylum applicant than on the applicant for refugee status. When interviewing a refugee, the INS official is instructed that the "bona fide refugee is not likely to have in his possession conclusive evidence of his past persecution or his fear of persecution." For this reason, the refugee's statements alone are considered sufficient proof if "they are consistent and credible in light of our knowledge of conditions and practices in the country from which refuge is sought."[33] To the asylum applicant, on the other hand, falls the burden of proving, with concrete evidence, that he has been persecuted. Nor are conditions in his country of origin considered relevant. (The Meese rules would, of course, have changed this.)

When an INS official interviews a refugee abroad, he asks questions that presume persecution. Among other questions, it is suggested that he ask: How were you mistreated? What do you think would happen to you if the police, soldiers, or government officials were to catch you? and, Are you afraid to go back?[34] The asylum applicant is asked simply, Why did you come to the United States?, a broad question to which many refugees, afraid of being found undesirable, reply, To work. It is often the case that a fearful asylum applicant will not reveal his history except after lengthy and sympathetic questioning, a process in which the asylum official has no wish to engage.

The level of documentation the asylee will need to provide will depend on the position of the United States toward human-rights abuses in his country. If the asylum applicant comes from a country in which the United States does not officially acknowledge political repression, or asserts that human rights are improving, that individual will be required to present an almost unattainable level of documentation.[35] Asylum applicants from countries with regimes we oppose, however, will need much less proof. Since the INS itself acknowledges the difficulty of a refugee's obtaining documentation of his persecution, the disparity between Communist- and non-Communist-country refugees widens again. One INS examiner explained quite simply how he reaches a decision:

"We can't make a decision solely from the evidence presented because most people can't meet the strict standards. . . . I never ask a person anything. I just look and see if the person belongs to a nationality group that everyone agrees are refugees like the Poles."[36]

Possibly the most striking difference between the two approaches is that, while asylum applicants are customarily dismissed as economic migrants, for refugees the INS allows that persecution may take economic forms.

> The fact that an applicant departed his country in search of food, medical help, or a better future does not, necessarily, go against a claim that he is unwilling to return to his country "because of persecution or a well-founded fear of persecution." Persons subject to persecution often do not flee until learning of an alternative which offers freedom and an opportunity to escape from some of the possible indices of persecution; e.g., lack of food, lack of educational and employment opportunities.[37]

In short, an applicant for asylum within the United States must meet a much more stringent standard than the refugee abroad who asks for resettlement. This disparity has been defended as necessary. Former State Department officer and now professor of law David Martin has written, "Asylum constitutes a wild card in the immigration deck. No other provision of the INA opens such a broad potential prospect of U.S. residency to aliens without the inconvenience of prescreening and selection."[38] Martin's initial assessment is valid: asylum is "a wild card." But his supporting argument has one not entirely accurate word— "inconvenience." For some categories of asylum applicants— the residual refugees and the impatient immigrants—asylum does offer a convenient option. But others—the defectors, the politically displaced—are already in this country; they cannot remove themselves and apply for admission through regular refugee channels. Nor does the final group, the precluded, have even that option. They have been denied any opportunity for prescreening and selection. Should we subject such individuals to a more stringent standard? And even if we allow that the stricter standard is necessary, should that standard not be the same for all asylum applicants?

In the end, the factor that most determines how strict a standard the asylum applicant must meet, and whether he will be admitted, is ease of entry to the United States; the more easily an asylum applicant can come to this country, the less likely he is to be admitted. Asylum applicants from Western Hemisphere countries will almost certainly be denied admission. Asylum applicants from the rest of the world are also subject to more stringent scrutiny if it is adjudged that large numbers of their group will also come to the United States. (For example, a Pole who applies for entrance as a refugee, from abroad, will have an excellent chance of being admitted; a Pole who asks for a grant of asylum, while within the United States, has only one chance in three of being admitted.) The most leniently judged will be those who have come to the United States singly (or as a single family), from an unfriendly country from which exit is difficult, for example, the Soviet Union or Iran.

Meanwhile, the numbers of asylum applications continue to multiply geometrically, a situation exacerbated by the reluctance of many in the INS to deal with asylum cases. The procedures by which, at present, an asylum determination is made also contribute to excessive delay.

An individual may request asylum in one of two ways. In many, but not all, INS districts, he may, when he first enters the country, or at any time thereafter, submit an asylum application (an I-589) to the INS district director. Or he may raise his claim during his exclusion or deportation* hearing before an immigration judge.

If the individual has filed for asylum with the district director, he is interviewed; if he raises the claim before an immigration judge, there is a hearing. In some cases, the application is sent

---

* The distinction between exclusion and deportation is specific to the United States. Technically, an alien who is intercepted at a point of entry into the United States has never entered the country and is, thus, subject to exclusion. If he is intercepted within the country, he is subject to deportation proceedings. The alien in exclusion proceedings has somewhat fewer rights than the alien in deportation.

to the State Department's Bureau of Human Rights and Humanitarian Affairs, which may issue an advisory opinion as to whether the individual has indeed a well-founded fear of persecution. The district director or the immigration judge then rules on the application.

If the district director denies asylum, the applicant is placed in deportation or exclusion status. When his hearing is scheduled, he may reassert his claim. Further appeals of the immigration judge's denial are also possible, first to the Bureau of Immigration Appeals, and then in federal court.

The many levels of appeal would seem to insure that no deserving claim of asylum will be denied. In fact, the many levels of review serve only to reinforce policy decisions made prior to any application for asylum. Every asylum decision reflects the foreign-policy goals of the administration and the Department of State. Although it has only an advisory role in determining asylum claims, the Department of State still maintains firm control over grants of asylum.

The INS freely acknowledges that its asylum officers and immigration judges are poorly prepared to adjudicate asylum claims. Fewer than two percent of INS officers have had any training at all in refugee and asylum issues, and that two percent received fewer than three hours of such instruction.[39] But each year, the Department of State produces a thick volume—the *Country Reports on Human Rights Practices*—and two thinner ones—the *Proposed Refugee Admissions and Allocations* and the *Country Reports on the World Refugee Situation*. INS officers and judges rely quite heavily on these publications to guide them in making asylum decisions.[40] And these volumes leave no doubt as to what decision should be forthcoming.

Even the most cursory survey of these publications reveals that the department's assessments of refugee-producing countries exactly mirror the foreign and military policies of the United States. Thus, in 1980, the State Department's *Country Reports on the World Refugee Situation* omitted any discussion of Chile as a refugee-producing country.[41] The 1985 *Reports* mentioned only that "twenty thousand to forty thousand Chileans have left their country since 1973 owing to political events."[42] The book does not elaborate on the "events."

Most telling is the analysis of the flow of refugees from El Salvador. The 1985 *Report* distinguishes "three groups of Salvadorans who . . . leave their country or are displaced: political refugees, people displaced by war, and persons seeking better economic opportunities." The *Report* goes on to discuss each of the groups. The first group, political refugees, have been given refugee status in other Central American countries. A number of prisoners have been resettled under an amnesty program— ninety-three in the United States. The second group, the displaced, remain in El Salvador. "The third group consists of as many as 750,000 Salvadorans (up to 500,000 in the United States and 175,000 to 250,000 elsewhere in the region) who have left El Salvador to seek employment."[43]

In short, notice has been given that any Salvadoran who attempts to enter the United States without authorization is, by definition, coming to "seek employment." These are the country reports to which the INS turns when trying to determine if an applicant's fear of persecution is well-founded.

Nor are the published reports the only source of guidance for the INS. Elliott Abrams, as an assistant secretary of state for human rights and humanitarian affairs, spoke out frequently on refugee policy. Yet, when Abrams wrote in the *New York Times* that "most Salvadorans in the United States are not refugees fleeing persecution but would-be immigrants who want to live here,"[44] no one within the INS objected that such a statement might prejudice future asylum decisions. Rather, Mr. Abrams's statement became a dictum to reject Salvadoran asylum claims.

A few years earlier, the Haitians were the target of State Department pronouncements. In 1982, Secretary Abrams told an audience in Miami that "we've made the *judgment* that Haitians are economic migrants, not fleeing persecution.'' (Emphasis added.) Mr. Abrams acknowledged that international law and treaty require the United States to consider each case individually. ''But,'' he went on, ''when you look at the overall situation in Haiti, and you've seen claims by Haitians, common sense tells you the next ten you see won't be granted.''[45] Again, no one objected.

The Refugee Act of 1980 declares that its objectives ''are to provide a permanent and systematic procedure for the admission to this country of refugees of special humanitarian concern to the United States.''[46] The word *humanitarian* was not in the original version of the act; it was added in conference.[47] It seems, however, that in execution, the word *humanitarian* has once again been dropped. The State Department speaks for the special concerns of the United States. Who in the government speaks for the humanitarian concerns of the refugee?

Humanitarian concerns are clearly not the province of the INS. Beset with budget and personnel problems, the INS has never been certain whether its role in asylum matters is that of policeman or prosecutor. The service has never seen itself as acting on behalf of the alien. Professor Atle Grahl-Madsen has succinctly characterized the perceptions of refugee authorities. After noting that immigration authorities, as civil servants, are obligated to uphold the law and, further, to protect their country's interests, Professor Grahl-Madsen isolates four fears common to immigration personnel.

The authorities are afraid that their State should come to take upon itself a burden which they feel ought to be carried by some other State.

They are afraid to give refugees a free choice of country of asylum, as this, in the opinion of the authorities, would mean license to manipulate the laws of the State.

They are afraid of the effect a given solution to the problem of refugees would have on the behaviour of asylum-seekers generally in the future; that is to say, there is a fear that by accommodating themselves to the rules, refugees would in fact get a free choice of country of asylum, and a fear that this would mean that an unproportionate number of refugees would choose just that country whose interests the authorities are there to serve.

Finally, . . . in a period of economic difficulties . . . the authorities are afraid of being criticized for admitting foreigners—refugees or no refugees—into the troubled economy.[48]

In this country, the arm of the INS that many entrants encounter first is the Border Patrol, an armed police force whose primary function is to enforce our immigration laws by preventing illegal entrance. Each district of the Border Patrol reports monthly on the numbers of "Deportable Aliens Located." Each breaks the numbers down further in two ways: by nationality of the aliens and by status. A Border Patrol agent may assign any of eleven possible entry statuses to an alien; not one specifies political asylum applicant. It can only be assumed that these would appear under the final category, other. Like any law-enforcement agency, the Border Patrol is considered effective when it is tough. The more lawbreakers it apprehends and deports, the better its performance. Few Border Patrol agents have been instructed in the intricacies of our refugee law.

At the middle levels of the INS, the degree to which personnel are familiar with the law varies. Some district directors refuse even to deal with asylum cases. When an asylum applicant voluntarily presents himself to the INS and asks for asylum, he is making an affirmative political asylum application. In some INS districts, however, such as Arizona, the district director will not accept such applications; the alien may only present his claim before the immigration judge in a deportation or exclusion hearing.

But pervading the agency is the basic law-enforcement mentality found in the Border Patrol, a mentality at odds with the application-of-justice approach that refugee decisions require. The INS sees its role primarily in black and white: one is either a U.S. citizen or an alien; an alien is either abiding by or breaking U.S. immigration law; a lawbreaker must be punished. But asylum matters are often a spectrum of grays.

When the INS denies asylum, the decision is likely to reflect prior presumptions made about particular refugee groups. These presumptions prevent the examining officer even from considering the merits of the actual case before him. Rather, responses—and denials—have become conditioned reflexes. When Haitians, for example, fled the Duvalier regime, every Haitian applicant was regarded as an economic migrant. If the Haitian refugee claimed to have been persecuted by the Tonton Macoutes (the lawless band of thugs who, at the direction of the Duvaliers, terrorized the populace), the persecution was seen as personal, not political. To the refugee's insistence that he feared reprisal if he returned, the official responded that it had been proven that there were no reprisals against returnees.[49]

Salvadorans fare no better, only differently. The INS denies that in El Salvador any civilian groups are targets of persecution. A twenty-nine-year-old Salvadoran, for example, claimed that "because he had participated in the Salvadoran teachers' union, he had been arrested and tortured with acid, and a brother had been kidnapped, tortured and decapitated." Doctors from Amnesty International corroborated his story, and the INS did not contest it.

The service, however, denied him asylum, ruling that:

> The applicant has described the suffering which he and other family members had unfortunately endured during the civil strife in El Salvador, suffering which has been similarly experienced by other groups and political factions operation [sic] in El Salvador.
>
> The problems of the applicant and his family members,

however, do not stem from persecution but from the civil strife which has torn El Salvador apart over the past five to nine years. The tragedy of El Salvador is that the suffering, the armed kidnapping and other excesses are not confined to one particular group but are endured and perpetrated by all.

For these reasons, the applicant has failed to establish that he qualifies as a refugee.[50]

Widespread civil disorder and not persecution of particular groups, the INS reasons, causes an individual to flee. Since civil disorder is not a basis for granting political asylum, few individuals from El Salvador can qualify for that status.

Nor are these presumptions found only at the lower and middle levels of the service. An INS general counsel, Maurice Inman, claimed to hold no bias in asylum matters, but told one researcher that among Haitians with whom he had spoken, all were economic migrants. Inman based his assessment on a one-hour visit in 1982 to Krome Camp in Miami. Inman spoke no Creole and had no interpreter. His conclusion: "They want material wealth, whatever that may be to them—a house, a car, a pig."[51]

Even successful asylum claims belie the rationality of the asylum process. Attorneys who represent clients from generally disfavored groups express bewilderment when certain of their clients' asylum claims are granted. These attorneys, in every area of the country, say that the few approved cases are in no way superior to the many more denied cases. Two possible explanations have been offered. One attorney believes that the most articulate refugees may sometimes be granted asylum. Others, though, see a relationship between interest by either the public or the courts and a brief spate of asylum grants.

It is important to note, however, that even positive presumptions about a group fall under the weight of large numbers. In asylum practice, numbers take precedence over any other consideration. Whether practices are initiated at the highest level of government, as was the interdiction of Haitian boats at sea, or the lowest, as has been the case with forced repatriation of Salvadorans, the basic motive is always the underlying fear that the protective dike of our immigration laws will be washed away.

That same fear is the basis for the INS practice of imprisoning asylum applicants. In actual practice, however, detention wears two faces. The first is harsh, unrelenting, and is directed toward would-be asylees; it threatens no mercy, no reprieve from an interminable punishment. The second face is benign, conciliatory; it is directed toward the community and promises protection from the burden of unwanted strangers.

From its inception, the policy of detention arose from dubious intentions. Haitians had been arriving in the United States since 1972, and the INS had imprisoned them periodically. After a time, however, they had been paroled into the community. The practice of imprisoning Haitians was ended entirely in 1977. But in 1981, in the aftermath of Mariel, the Reagan administration appointed a high-level Immigration Task Force to formulate specific policies. The Task Force recommended that all arriving Haitians be "detained" while their asylum claims were being decided, even though detention of Haitians would have little effect on overall illegal immigration. Of all the illegal entrants to the United States, Haitians constituted fewer than two percent.[52] Why, then, institute such a controversial and costly project for such admittedly limited ends? The purpose of imprisoning Haitians, as the Task Force saw it, was not to reduce the number of illegal entries, but rather to reduce the numbers of individuals asking for asylum. The Task Force, observing that "the existing apparatus for resolving asylum claims . . . was . . . stretched to its limit,"[53] decided not to expand the asylum apparatus, but rather to discourage asylum seekers. Such an ordering of goals reveals the disesteem in which the right of asylum had come to be held.

To the INS, undocumented asylum seekers were lawbreakers, and imprisonment an appropriate means of curbing their lawlessness. By 1982, the INS claimed to be detaining *all* asylum seekers, not only Haitians, who arrived without documentation.

If the threatening face turned toward asylum seekers was authentic, the protective face turned toward the community was less than genuine. To be sure, there was a good deal of posturing. In 1981, the words *detained refugee* were apt to connote, for the American public, a Cuban cutthroat, cast out from prison in his own country and planning his escape from a prison in ours. And the INS did not hesitate to play to community fears. Thus, a prison director in Big Spring, Texas, promised that when Haitian refugees were transferred to his facility, they would be kept confined and separate from the rest of the inmates.

> The Haitians are unknown people to us and to our inmates. We don't know their habits, and we don't want our inmates to be subjected to substandard ways—we don't know if they eat with their hands.
>
> And we don't want them to mess up the relationship the inmates of this institution have with the community because a lot of our inmates are involved in community activities.[54]

Three years later, in Texas, the refugees were Salvadorans and Guatemalans, the fear in the community had subsided, and the INS wore a new face. Central American refugees were now allowed to post bond; the INS district director explained that after bond had been set, if the INS learned of "information favorable to the alien" (namely that he had family in the area), the service would either lower the bond or release the individual on his own recognizance.[55] Thus, while the INS maintains a tough enforcement posture, detention, at the discretion of a district director, can become a revolving door.

In other districts, however, asylum applicants remain in prison for protracted periods of a year or more. The reason for the seeming disparity is quite simple: detention is quite costly and the numbers can, in a short time, overburden the system. INS, therefore, will release into the community those refugees that the community does not perceive as either a threat or a burden. In the heavily Hispanic Southwest, Central Americans can blend in easily, and a thriving underground economy quickly absorbs them. In southern Florida, the community resents additional newcomers, and Haitians, like the Afghanis in New York City, are kept in remove.

As if reflecting the prevailing community attitudes, the physical facilities themselves range from the abysmal to the acceptable: from Krome, in southern Florida, which squats on the edge of the Everglades, where even after a summer drought, groundwater puddles the earth, raw sewage overflows, and, in tropical heat, threatens to contaminate drinking water;[56] to Port Isabel Detention Center, in Texas, a facility that, within its double barbed-wire fence patrolled by armed guards, is clean and orderly.[57]

These are not, as the INS calls them, detention facilities, but prisons, not a temporary stage in the process of seeking asylum, but a termination of that process. INS personnel often explain that these people have a choice: they may choose to go home. Sometimes the camp residents make other choices, choices that arise not from decision but from desperation. The nonviolent riot. The hungry refuse to eat. Heads of families commit suicide.

In 1981, a group of Haitians held at Fort Allen, in Puerto Rico, gave an open letter to a *New York Times* reporter. Parts of that letter follow:

Dear Readers, Gentlemen, Civilian, and Military Authorities,
   For the last few months we have been imprisoned without knowing what outcome our fates would have.
   One day around 4 P.M., we (women) were all gathered at the sound of whistles. We spent a day and a night awaiting

our fate, after having been tagged with a plastic ID bracelet. After that we were made to parade in the nude in front of men and women. We were splashed, badly dressed. Stripped of our clothes and belongings, we were made to sit in a room where we were to spend the night. In this distress, the room was like a wake, where sad songs were being sung. At that moment, an enormous chill would run down the spine. Around 5 A.M., we were jammed into a bus which was to drive us to the airport. This is how we left Miami for Puerto Rico.

When we left Miami, we were led to believe that we were only going to Puerto Rico for a few days. And until now we have been suffering for eight months without knowing why. Each day we hear only one thing: Those who wish to return to Haiti can come give their names.

Our situation is pitiful. We have been locked up behind barbed wire from Miami to Puerto Rico. The days are always the same for us. We don't know what the date is. Sometimes we are hungry and cannot eat.

Now we cannot stand it any more. It is too much. If we have not been freed by the end of November, a good number of us are going to commit suicide. Because we have sworn to die in the United States.[58]

Four years later, at a detention camp in Laredo, Texas, administered by the Correction Corporation of America, a private, profit-making organization, Central American detainees disclosed that, after meetings with their legal representatives, the guards subjected them to strip searches. One young girl, in describing her humiliation, protested that "no one had ever looked at me there in my life, except my mother when I was born." A thirteen-year-old girl was compelled, over her pleadings and those of her mother, to remove not only her clothing but the sanitary napkin she wore. Following the examination, she "immediately broke down and cried." Her mother underwent a "feeling of intense revulsion." Weeks later, the daughter "still cries and expresses fear that it will happen again."[59]

The detention policy has achieved one of its goals. When the policy was carried to its irrevocable limit—and combined with other, equally unrelenting policies like forced repatriation and interdiction—the numbers of Haitians applying for political asylum declined. If the numbers of undecided asylum claims continued to climb, it was because other, less systematically excluded groups had entered the system. To the extent, then, that the purpose of the detention policy was to deter particular groups from seeking political asylum, it has succeeded. To the extent that the purpose of detention was to discourage frivolous applications for asylum, it has also succeeded.

But while the threat of imprisonment will deter the less deserving, at the same time, it punishes the genuine refugee. It is precisely the most desperate, those who fear persecution, who will still risk capture and imprisonment; who, once imprisoned, refuse repatriation; who languish month after month because they have no choice. The genuine refugees have, in effect, become the hostages of our asylum policy.

Nor does the policy of imprisonment necessarily even reduce the numbers. Central Americans come across an open land border and immediately disappear into the interior where they are likely never to be found. Here too, rather than encouraging genuine refugees to come forward, so that the system can gain control of numbers and flow, the system pushes refugees underground, out of sight, and out of reach of law.

Detention, in itself, is neither wrong nor ill-advised. When large numbers of individuals apply for political asylum, it is foolish to grant them full freedom of movement and employment pending resolution of their cases. To do so is only to invite economic migration in the name of asylum-seeking. What is wrong is that individuals are not being detained but immured. They are not looking toward a fair and just resolution of their asylum claims, but awaiting an inevitable deportation.

The very conditions under which they are held bespeak punishment: separation of husbands from wives and parents from children; enforced idleness, restricted movement; lack of privacy; mental and even physical humiliation. The attitudes of the imprisoning agency strengthen the message: the INS are guardians of our immigration law which the "deportable aliens" have broken.

Detention, of course, is only one aspect of a total program to reduce the number of individuals who apply for asylum. But the INS uses the threat of detention, as well, to reinforce the second aspect of the program—"voluntary repatriation." In a system rife with euphemisms, *voluntary repatriation* is surely the most reprehensible. The word *repatriation* has about it a most beneficient connotation, implying that an individual who has left his home is now enabled to return. It is, of course, repatriation for which most refugees, early in their exile, hope. They do not, however, long to be restored to the precise conditions from which they fled, else why flee in the first place. Yet every day, refugees who arrive in the United States are offered an option: they may agree to return to their homelands or, if they refuse, they will have to remain in indefinite detention. The refugees are not told that there is a third alternative—that they may ask for political asylum.

The prevalence of this practice came to the attention of the UN High Commissioner for Refugees who, in an unprecedented action, expressed concern that the United States actions toward the Salvadorans appeared "to represent a negation of its responsibilities assumed upon its adherence to the Protocol." A fact-finding mission of the UNHCR found "continuing large-scale forcible and voluntary return to El Salvador," and that "the majority of those returning are doing so voluntarily without apparently being freely advised of their asylum rights." The UNHCR further concluded that this policy had not originated at the field level of the INS, but in Washington.[60]

In 1982, a federal district court found that

Salvadorans are frequently arrested, deposited in waiting rooms, interrogated, put onto busses, and flown back to El

Salvador all in a matter of hours. Often the aliens do not understand the language in which they are addressed, much less the chain of events which has been set in motion. In this environment, "coercion" is not limited to physical force or outright threats. The courts on numerous occasions have recognized that the more subtle effects of atmosphere, setting, and the omission of certain statements or advisals may have an equally coercive effect.[61]

What Central Americans are advised of immediately, on being apprehended, is that they may return home; they are then given a departure form to sign. This practice, like the detention policy, has, within the limits of its scope, proved effective. From October 1979 to September 1983, more than two thirds of all Salvadorans were "voluntarily repatriated"; returned home without even an asylum hearing.[62]

No one knows how many of that number were forcibly repatriated, although they had, in fact, requested an asylum decision. Refugee supporters maintain that the INS routinely turns Central Americans who have entered the United States over to Mexican authorities, and that Mexico then moves them into Guatemala. The INS denies such charges.[63] Yet in 1981, the Associated Press reported that twenty-two Salvadorans, who arrived at a port of entry in California and immediately asked for asylum, were turned over by the INS to Mexican authorities.[64]

Nearly identical to forced repatriation in its intentions and in its results, but far more costly and sophisticated in its execution, is the policy of interdicting Haitian émigrés. In 1981, the United States signed an agreement with the Duvalier government in Haiti to protect our own country from undocumented entrants through the enforcement of Haiti's restrictive emigration laws. Under the agreement, which is still in force, the Coast Guard patrols the open waters off Haiti, stops and boards Haitian boats that may be carrying undocumented Haitians, and returns to

Haiti Haitians who, it suspects, intend to come to the United States. Like forced repatriation and detention, interdiction was, from its inception, intended to reduce the number of Haitian asylum claims within the judicial system and diminish the impact of Haitian refugees on southern Florida.[65] Unlike detention, however, interdiction could proceed unrestrained by considerations of law. And unlike forced repatriation, interdiction could circumvent the law without breaking it. As President Reagan's Task Force on Immigration noted in an internal report:

> Although required by U.N. Protocol and Convention to adjudicate refugee claims prior to returning a claimant to his homeland, if interdiction occurs outside of U.S. territorial waters, the determination would not be governed by the Immigration Act.[66]

In short, the would-be Haitian asylum applicant would have neither the protection nor the procedural guarantees of United States law, while the examining officer would be similarly unbound by law. Nor do the provisions of the U.N. protocol necessarily obtain. On board each Coast Guard patrol ship is an INS officer responsible for speaking to each person on board an intercepted boat and determining if that person has a well-documented claim to asylum.[67] The Haitian, then, with no legal rights and no one to advise him, lacking either an interpreter or documents (refugees rarely carry complete dossiers), ignorant and frightened, confronts an interrogating foreign authority. If, then, the obligations of the United States under the UN protocol are not met, who is to know? A *New York Times* editorial called such proceedings "walrus courts," which it defined as "kangaroo courts at sea."[68] By mid-February of 1986, 6,245 Haitians had been interdicted; not one was brought to the United States so that his asylum claim might be looked into.

If the United States, however, did not care to investigate the Haitians' asylum claims further, Haiti did. The U.S. State Department later reported that while Duvalier remained in power, "when migrants were returned to Haiti, they were individually questioned by police officials from the Permanent Commission of Inquiry, and files were created on each. This internal security organization was dissolved shortly before ex-President Duvalier's departure from Haiti."[69]

The integrity of the entire interdiction process is predicated on the good faith of an INS officer. The courts, however, have repeatedly found that the INS acts toward selected refugee groups in bad faith. Just one year before the interdiction program began, Federal Court Judge James Lawrence King, in a historic decision, declared that the Immigration Service had instituted "a systematic program designed to deport [Haitian asylum applicants] irrespective of the merits of their asylum claims." Judge King further found that the INS had deliberately denied "the constitutional, treaty, statutory, and administrative rights" of thousands of Haitians.[70] When, therefore, the deputy commissioner of the Immigration and Naturalization Service testifies that "well-trained INS officers, with years of experience in dealing with possible claims of asylum or refugee status, are part of the boarding party whenever the U.S. Coast Guard interdicts a vessel,"[71] one must wonder what values have been inculcated by the official's training and years of experience.

Interdiction makes it possible to ignore the provisions of the Refugee Act and to subvert the protections of the UN Convention and Protocol; yet the Universal Declaration of Human Rights and the Helsinki Act, to which the United States is a party, affirm the right of every individual to leave his country. Indeed, we castigate the Soviet Union and other Communist countries for not permitting the free emigration of their citizens. Once again, however, the dual standard obtains.

Asylum has become an adversary procedure. The government has directed its asylum policies essentially toward the deterrence and deportation of selected groups; the pro bono attorneys have, for their part, tried to thwart the government in its intentions and have used a number of legal strategies in the interest of buying time. The government argues that these delaying tactics merely allow the illegal alien to remain for a longer period in the United States. The pro bono attorneys insist that their strategies win the refugee a temporary reprieve from the persecution he will inevitably face on his return.

Unquestionably, the present asylum system is ineffective. The number of pending asylum cases is growing at an increasing rate. All involved in the system—whether government officials or refugee representatives—express a sense of hopelessness, of powerlessness to effect desired ends. The government accuses the attorneys of dilatory tactics; the attorneys charge the government with mala fide practices. What is really causing the delays and backlogs? Is a small group of attorneys working to bring the entire asylum system to a halt? Or is the government conspiring to eliminate public support for the refugees?

Oddly, when both sides have looked objectively at the problem of asylum backlogs, they have reached the same conclusion: the source of the problem is, to a large extent, the failure of the government to establish consistent asylum policies that accord with the Refugee Act and, further, to provide the necessary resources to carry out its policies.[72]

The INS itself conducted a systematic study of the asylum problem, and found that in October of 1982 more than 140,000 asylum claims were pending. But it placed the main responsibility for that backlog in two areas. The responsibility lay, first, "in specific actions taken by the U.S. government, primarily for foreign policy reasons, without appreciating the relationship of these policies to the new law or making the necessary administrative adjustment in INS."[73] The study gave some important examples.

The policy of the government had been, since 1977, to grant political asylum to any Polish national. The Refugee Act, passed in March of 1980, made group determinations illegal, yet the government continued in the practice for another year and a half, until September of 1981. The preference shown to Polish applicants, though in violation of the law, encouraged many Poles who were clearly not qualified for asylum to file claims.[74]

A second policy error concerned the Nicaraguans. From November of 1979 to September of 1980, the government had granted a blanket extended voluntary departure to Nicaraguan nationals. When the status ended suddenly, the INS encouraged many of the affected Nicaraguans to file asylum claims so as to avoid being deported. They were assured, many Nicaraguans have alleged, "that their petitions would not be processed because of a scarcity of resources."[75]

Another example of a confusion of government policy leading to a chaos of practice occurred during the Iranian hostage crisis. At that time, the government advised all Iranians who were in this country under other nonimmigrant statuses that their statuses would not be extended unless they first applied for political asylum. What was intended as a retaliatory measure against the Iranians worked, instead, to swell the asylum backlog.

Of the 104,968 claims pending in March of 1982, these three groups accounted for 28,520, or 27 percent. Nearly 51,000 more, or another 49 percent of all outstanding asylum claims, belonged to Mariel Cubans, who symbolize still another policy failure. In the early days of the Mariel crisis, the INS, lacking directions to the contrary, processed arriving Cubans as asylum applicants. Although they are now considered eligible for permanent residency, the INS continues to carry the Mariel Cubans in its figures for pending asylum claims.

The second area of responsibility, the INS study admits, lies with the INS itself. Each year, the INS adjudicates more than a million and a half immigration petitions. Asylum applications are difficult and time-consuming to process, but since 1983 the INS has given them no more weight than any other immigration matter when it calculates workloads. For this reason, immigration judges will postpone the more difficult asylum cases for months, or even years, while disposing of simpler adjudica-

tions.[76] District offices do no better. In the beginning of March
1982, the Los Angeles office had a backlog of nearly eleven
thousand asylum claims. During the month, it received an additional one thousand. Yet, in that same time, the office processed only forty-eight asylum claims.[77]

The asylum system is, indisputably, not working. The Reagan
administration and the Congress have proposed a number of
solutions that they believe will address the major flaws in the
system and once again enable it to function. The administration's proposals—interdiction, detention, and denial of due process—have been essentially deterrent in intention and discriminatory in practice.

The last administration goal was incorporated into the
several-times-defeated Simpson-Mazzoli bill, which sought leg-
islatively to eliminate due process rights for aliens. As Senator
Alan K. Simpson saw it, the law "provides more due process
to the person seeking asylum than it does to a U.S. citizen who
is here. . . ."[78] His solution was simple and two-pronged.

The Simpson-Mazzoli bill provided, first, for summary exclusion of an entering alien. Under present regulations, the
benefit of a doubt is extended to the alien. If the examining
officer at the point of entry has any question about the right of
the alien to enter, the alien is detained and brought before an
immigration judge for an exclusion hearing. At that hearing,
the alien has the right to counsel and the right to present evidence on his own behalf. Under the proposed bill's summary-
exclusion provision, the examining officer could immediately
bar from entry any alien who does not ask specifically for political asylum when he enters. Since few Americans are familiar
with the term political asylum, it is even more unlikely that a
great number of refugees would have been sufficiently informed, when first confronting an immigration authority, to
ask for it. The decision of the border inspector, furthermore,
would be final, subject to neither administrative nor judicial
review.

A second provision of the bill applied to those who did request political asylum. For them, there would have been a single decision, with no possibility, should that decision be faulty, of judicial review. The asylum provisions of the Simpson-Mazzoli bill proved so controversial that, in the end, they were deleted from the revised Simpson-Rodino bill, passed in 1986.

Whatever the intentions of the Simpson-Mazzoli asylum provisions (and there was some question, moreover, as to whether they would have been in violation of the UN protocol and the Immigration and Nationality Act), one must ask whether the legislation would have achieved its desired ends. Did the Simpson-Mazzoli bill address the problem or did it merely eliminate any opportunity to examine it? The essential problem is not that certain individuals abuse the system, but that the government abuses it. All of the protections that we now afford the alien—the right to be represented by counsel, to present evidence, to call witnesses, to have decisions reviewed—have been instituted so that in our present adversary system of asylum adjudication the sheer weight of the government's will does not crush the unsupported alien.

In the end, for the bona fide refugee, his asylum decision can be a life-or-death, a freedom-or-imprisonment, decision. And it is for the bona fide refugee that the protections of law must be guarded. Our refugee law was enacted so that *no individual* might be wrongfully deported. Restrictive legislation begins from an opposing premise—that no individual should be wrongfully admitted. As T. Alexander Aleinikoff has cogently argued, "We erect a high burden of proof and give full procedural protections in criminal cases because we believe it better that ten guilty people go free than one innocent person be imprisoned."[79] We can extend no less protection to the refugee.

The fault is not in our law but in ourselves. The problem will not be solved through additional legislation, but through policy reform. The Refugee Act is clear in its intentions. The government has been just as clear in its intention not to abide by that

5 The Rejected: The Remedies of Law

The 1981 Associated Press photograph showed the prow of a wooden sailboat, paint peeling, sails lowered. In the foreground were several young black men. Three sat: two had half-turned toward the camera, their faces questioning; a third, in dark profile, bent forward, elbows on knees, one hand clutching the other, head and eyes lowered. Above them, among the rigging and furled sails, rose a fourth man, left hand on hip, right hand gripping a sail, face grim and defiant. In the background, behind the four, the heads, arms, bodies of uncountable others. The caption read:

> MORE HAITIANS ARRIVE IN FLORIDA: Some of the nearly 100 Haitians who arrived Saturday in Key Biscayne wait to be interviewed by immigration officials. Some area residents who were boating nearby offered them food; others shouted "Go home!"[1]

In the next few years, the battle grew increasingly rancorous between those who believed that the U.S. should continue to make a place for the oppressed of the world and those who maintained that our liberality had been exhausted. The Haitians became a symbol, a symbol larger than their own reality.

To those who shouted "Go home!," the Haitians were an

ominous symbol. What the shouters saw was not a hundred Haitians, but millions of poor, starving, illegal aliens who came in search of livelihood, then carved out an underground economy that undermined the foundations of our American wealth. They saw would-be lawbreakers, who began by violating our immigration laws and ended by violating the peace and security of our neighborhoods. They saw cheats and schemers who had sold the watery gruel of their life savings, so that they might drink the richer milk of the American welfare system.

To those who offered food, the Haitians were also a symbol. They looked at the Haitians and saw the most recent in a centuries-long flow of people coming to the United States to work and to build. They looked at the Haitians and saw a shameful history of racist discrimination in our immigration laws. They looked at the Haitians and saw refugees in fragile boats, turned away from our southern coast, turned back to possible imprisonment and death.

The Haitians, thus, became a rallying point for both sides in the continuing refugee controversy. They stood as an emblem for those who would leave the gate open and for those who would shut it, for those who embraced diversity and for those who mistrusted it, for those who maintained that the law should dispense justice and for those who insisted that the law impose order.

Nor has this antagonism of views been confined to the American public. Many of those who make, and those who influence, refugee policy have chosen one of the opposing sides as their constituency and have acted according to what they perceive to be their mandates. The executive—the White House and the State and Justice Departments—has made its stand with the exclusionists. It has drawn support for its position from some members of the Congress and from governors of states that have received more refugees than federal assistance. One finds opponents of the official government position in Congress, but also in the social service agencies (both public and private), in civil-liberties and human-rights organizations, and in church groups.

There is, quite obviously, a disparity of power and authority between these two positions. The exclusionists have the power to formulate policy and the authority to carry it out. Refugee supporters, on the other hand, have been able only to respond to policies after they have been effected. The most successful of those responses, thus far, have been the challenges in the courts to government misconduct. A dialectical pattern has developed. The government, impelled by its fear of opening the gates to a flood of refugees, has initiated three major policies: detention, interdiction, and denial of due process. Refugee advocates, in response, have brought suit in the courts against every one of these policies and most times have won their suits.

The pattern of action and reaction, of policy and challenge, has by now become almost automatic. But the pattern began with the government's policy toward the Haitians and with the response by supporters of the Haitians to that policy. The Haitians were the first national group to seek asylum in significant numbers; they were also the first group about whom the government made a policy decision, not only to deny asylum, but also to discourage and deter those who would apply for it. Often, the courts have struck down a policy only to have it reinstituted by an executive reluctant to be impeded.

Some of these policies would later be directed toward other groups—Central Americans and Afghanis—but they would never be as singlemindedly severe as against the Haitians. Only Haitians were interdicted at sea, returned to their country *before* they had even entered ours. Only Haitian asylum seekers could not be released on bond from detention. And, the government sought to exclude Haitians by diverting large amounts of personnel, equipment, and funds, entirely disproportionate to the refugees' numbers. The Haitians, in short, were singled out for policies and practices harsher and more unrelenting than those directed at any other group of asylum seekers, policies and practices that constitute a repugnant chapter in American history, its repugnance redeemed only by the integrity of the courts. Such policies, one should note, were not confined to a single administration. They began in the 1970s, under President Carter, and continued in the 1980s, under President Reagan.

Many in the American public—blacks and others—feel that Haitians were singled out because our asylum policy was racist. That explanation is insufficient. Although racism may have influenced the severity with which, at a local level, officials carried out policies, the policies themselves arose from a complex of causes. First, for foreign policy reasons, the United States was unable to welcome refugees from a government that was allied with us and that was geopolitically critical to the containment of Castro.

The island of Haiti lies just forty miles to the southeast of Cuba, across the Windward Passage. For the two Duvaliers, père and fils, the island's strategic location was a bargaining chip. They offered undeviating support of the United States (in the OAS, Haiti voted to expel Cuba and to impose sanctions on it) and permitted the United States military to use Haitian ports and, during the Cuban missile crisis, airfields. In exchange, the United States has supplied the economic aid without which the island-nation would have sunk, and lent military support to the regime. Thus, despite successive administrations' varying attitudes toward human-rights abuses in Haiti, U.S. policy toward Haiti, for nearly thirty years, was based on the premise that if the Duvalier dictatorship were destabilized, the kind of political disorder that invites a Communist takeover would have followed. The United States, therefore, viewed with acute discomfort active opponents of the Duvalier government.

Not all Haitian asylum applicants, to be sure, were active opponents of the regime. Many more, rather than having opposed the regime, were probably its victims. Some were victimized in ways that were not recognized by law as warranting a grant of political asylum: they were deprived of livelihood, welfare, education; they were denied the rights of free speech and of assembly; they were without protection of law. But they were not persecuted, nor did they have reason to fear persecution. To these Haitians, American refugee law offered no protection.

From Haiti, however, there were as well other sorts of victims, those who had been persecuted—threatened, imprisoned, tortured—or whose families or associates had been warned, killed, or, most chillingly, "disappeared." But the U.S. denied these Haitians asylum too, for to do otherwise would have jeopardized our carefully maintained alliance with Duvalier. Rather, the United States insisted that virtually all Haitians were fleeing poverty, were "economic migrants." They shared this designation with refugees from other allied, but repressive, governments.

A second basis for exclusion, however, was particular to the Haitians. Increasingly, Americans had come to regard the federal government as utterly ineffectual in stemming the tide of illegal foreign workers. Most illegal immigration takes place across the southern border, which cannot be closed off. Even the most ambitious and costly proposals to do so must acknowledge that the attempt will, in the end, be only partially successful. The Haitian migration, on the other hand, could be stemmed.

Jean-Claude Duvalier, like his father before him, ruled absolutely. By law and through enforcement, departure from Haiti was strictly controlled. A Haitian national did not leave his country, he escaped from it—secretly, at great cost, and at greater risk. (There were, in fact, allegations that the government of Haiti received a share of all the fees paid to smugglers of Haitian émigrés.)

President Reagan's interdiction program was based on an agreement with the government of Haiti, under which American vessels are permitted to patrol Haitian waters, and sailors in the American Coast Guard may stop and board any vessels believed to transport Haitians in violation of either U.S. or Haitian immigration laws. It became, therefore, as difficult to leave Haiti as any Iron Curtain country—perhaps more difficult, since the United States pressures the government of Haiti to restrict free movement, whereas it pressures the Soviet government to permit it. Further, Haitians left Haiti from a very few ports and had to land on southern Florida's eastern shore. With sufficient resources, the United States could either interdict, or apprehend and incarcerate, the great majority of Haitian refugees. In moving toward this goal, the administration appeared to be decisive, strong, effective, acting purposefully against a pressing national problem. Thus, though many who entered the United States were unwanted, only the Haitians could be effectively barred, making their exclusion an achievable end. The administration can cite statistics to demonstrate that from the time interdiction began, Haitian entries dropped precipitously and the impact of Haitians on receiving communities was mitigated.

Although foreign-policy goals ultimately determine the refugee groups from which individuals will be given political asylum, the impact of those groups on receiving communities determines whether the government will take action against the refugee group itself. And the decision to act is based less on the size of the refugee group than on the nature of its needs.

In the mid-seventies, for example, in Dade County, Florida, by far the largest group of arrivals was the Cubans. Since Haitians were, for the most part, undocumented, no precise figures are available on the numbers of Haitians in southern Florida. The Dade County public schools, however, did keep records of the numbers of children of various nationalities who were being served by its bilingual education program, figures which indicate the relative size of each nationality. In the academic year 1974 to 1975, a total of 3,920 children enrolled in the bilingual program: 3,712 of these were Cuban, 117 were Haitian, and 91 were of other nationalities. In 1976 to 1977, Cuban children numbered 1,293, Haitian children 288, and all others 56.[2] Thus,

Haitians were but a small proportion of the total number of noncitizens requiring services.

In the seventies, however, services to Cuban immigrants were reimbursed by the federal government, while the local communities bore the growing costs of services to Haitians. Then too, the nature of these services was such as to stir ill-feelings among many in the community. Haitians came to the United States with serious health problems—most prominently tuberculosis and typhoid—and many, if not most, suffered from malnutrition. Because so few Haitians were permitted to work, they crowded together in substandard housing, with one or two wage-earners paying the rent for all the rest. This in contrast to the Cubans, who had received excellent health care in Cuba and whose compatriots here helped them find jobs and housing.

The response in Florida to the Haitian situation was predictable: some offered food, others shouted, Go home! Just as predictably, the government acquiesced to the shouters, the exclusionists. Haitians, including those who requested political asylum, were placed in jail for indefinite periods. Only when the jails became overcrowded were the Haitians released on bond.[3] Even when they won release, however, the INS refused to give them work authorizations. (In practice, then, a Haitian would be ill-advised to present himself to the INS and ask for political asylum, for he was certain to be jailed for an indefinite period, then denied the opportunity to support himself. The INS policy was actually encouraging Haitians to go underground.)

But there were also, within the community, those who responded to the Haitians on the basis of human need. The INS policy had led to near starvation within the Haitian community. Many, particularly in the county and voluntary social-service agencies, were sympathetic. The National Council of Churches was more than sympathetic; it was outraged. The council brought suit in Florida on behalf of the Haitians, asserting that they were refugees seeking asylum under the United Nations Convention on Refugees, and that, under the terms of the convention, they be released from jail and given the right to work.[4]

The Justice Department had received its first major legal challenge. By the time the case had been appealed to the Supreme Court, it had drawn a good deal of public attention. The government capitulated. While the suit was still before the court, the INS entered into an agreement with the plaintiffs to give any Haitian who had an asylum request in process the right to work.[5]

The agreement, however, was short-lived. Whether through error or design, the INS regional office in Florida broadcast the message that *any* Haitian (not only those with asylum claims pending) who presented himself to the INS office would receive employment authorization. Three thousand Haitians came out of hiding and were given formal work permits.

Though the numbers must have seemed minuscule in Washington, at about the same time reports were also being received that the Bahamas planned to expel the forty thousand Haitians who had taken refuge there, of whom a proportion could be expected to make their way to Florida. Action had to be taken and taken immediately; no legal agreement could be allowed to intervene. The INS instructed its Florida office to revoke *all* work authorizations, even those properly granted. Further, the Carter White House and the Department of Justice passed down instructions to give out no further work authorizations.[6]

A series of high-level meetings ensued over the summer of 1978, to devise a program to expel Haitians from the Miami area rapidly and without impediment, and to discourage Haitians abroad from coming to the United States. The Haitian Program, which would lead eventually to a landmark decision in American refugee law, had begun.

To the first of these meetings, the INS sent nearly a score of its highest personnel, from the commissioner and his deputy, through regional commissioners, down to staff attorneys; the State Department sent the deputy assistant secretary for refugee and migration affairs as well as others from the Bureau of Human Rights and Humanitarian Affairs. Justice sent two representatives. There were three major areas of discussion at the meeting: deterrence, detention, and the possibility of circumventing due process.

The first concern was that Haitians expelled from the Bahamas not reach the United States. A plan was formulated that foreshadowed the later Coast Guard interdiction of Haitians. Various deterrent possibilities were to be explored; among them, the State Department would ask the Bahamian government "to curtail Haitian departures to the United States." A further possibility was that the Coast Guard notify the INS of Haitian arrivals, and perhaps remove those Haitians whom the Coast Guard was able to intercept to Guantanamo Bay in Cuba. Lest there be any doubt that the plan was directed exclusively toward Haitians, it carefully stipulated that "Bahamians or any other ethnic group in boat with Haitians should be treated as any other alien, not as Haitian."[7]

Deterrence, however, was a long-range effort; immediate measures were also necessary. The White House and the Department of Justice instructed the INS commissioner that Haitians no longer be given work authorizations. Further, all Haitian males were to be incarcerated.[8] The legal agreement with the National Council of Churches seemed to have slipped from notice.

Far more insidious than deterrence, nonissuance of work permits, or detention was another action: curtailment of due process. Deterrence—now given official standing as interdiction—is both ethically devious for the United States and gravely threatening to the genuine refugee. It is ethically devious because it enables us to avoid our obligations to refugees. It is gravely threatening to genuine refugees because it prejudges their status and bars their flight to safety. But, though morally reprehensible, deterrence may not be illegal. It offends one's sense of what is right, but it may not violate the law.

Nor is a refusal to issue work permits or the detention of asylum seekers illegal. These are policy decisions, and, although the INS failed to follow the regular procedure for changing policy, it could have done so through formal regulations. Though there are many who oppose the practice of detention, and many more who oppose its inhumane application, the practice itself can be legal.

When the government, however, chose to abridge due process rights for Haitians, it made a dangerous decision—denying the individual protection from the unbridled power of government. In this case, the power of government was bent toward the unobstructed expulsion of the Haitians. Haitian political-asylum claims were to be dispensed with as rapidly as possible. Haitian asylum applicants were not to be informed of their right to claim asylum or their right to counsel. They were not to be told that they were entitled to advisory opinion of their cases by the UNHCR. Deputy Commissioner Mario Noto called for more immigration judges, more space, and asked the immigration judges to triple their "productivity." He recommended "MASH-type hearings"—hearings in which claims before an immigration judge were lumped together and heard en masse.[9]

The Department of State acquiesced in the need for haste; it could streamline its own advisory role, and the Bureau of Human Rights agreed to render advisory opinions on its backlog of 144 cases within three or four days.[10]

All of these actions were defensible because the White House and State and Justice Departments had already determined that the Haitians were not refugees but economic migrants. In a formal memorandum to his superior, INS Commissioner Leonel J. Castillo, Deputy Commissioner Noto wrote:

Few of these Haitians are bona fide refugees entitled to sanctuary and asylum from political persecution in Haiti. Instead, most are intent to remain in the U.S. solely to better their economic opportunities and way of life. Having left a poverty-stricken Haiti and rejection by the Bahamians, they seek employment opportunities offered in the United States and hopefully their asylum claims will serve to defer and defeat return.

The State Department, he asserted, supported this view, while the UNHCR was unwittingly "compounding the problem since the latter has no cognizance of the realities involved—that in the main these are economic refugees and not political. . . ." Noto himself was all too well aware of the harsh realities involved, but he failed to grasp their irony. "They will risk their lives," he wrote, "to come to the U.S. under the guise of seeking political asylum."[11]

Informal records of the planning meetings betray an urgent sense that the state of Florida was under seige. Deputy Commissioner Noto gave orders to:

ACTUALLY PAIN [*sic*] OUT THE DIMENSIONS OF THE HAITIAN THREAT. T/A's [trial attorneys] should give U.S. attorneys more data and background as to the importance of Haitian cases.— Volatile—show that these are unusual cases dealing with individuals that are threatening the community's well-being— socially and economically. [Capitals in original.][12]

One of the U.S. attorneys, Peter Nimkoff, found a number of areas of concern, in particular that the U.S. attorney's office in Miami, of which he was then chief, seemed to be entirely bent to the will of the INS. Nimkoff, wanting to reform the office, set up a series of meetings with many of the top INS personnel. Among his concerns were the work permits, detention (which directly contravened expressed INS policy), and refusal to advise Haitians of their rights and to grant them due process.

For Nimkoff, the most memorable meeting was the one with Mario Noto, which he found a "distasteful experience," very like "an audience with a little monarch." When Nimkoff gave voice to some of his concerns, Noto explained that the INS was taking these actions in order that word would get back to Haiti and discourage others from coming. Noto believed, in fact, that the INS was being quite humanitarian: they did not sink the ships at sea and let the Haitians drown.

Leonel Castillo, whom Nimkoff characterized, in contrast, as passive, shared the attorney's reservations, but said that the Justice Department had overruled him. In a subsequent meeting at the Justice Department, Nimkoff was told that the policy had been dictated by the White House and could not be discussed.[13]

The Haitian program had been initiated by White House fiat, developed in a series of high-level emergency meetings, and now was carried out by lower-level INS employees. Some of those employees were conducting Haitian asylum interviews, obtaining the information and documentation on which final asylum decisions would be made. Experts in refugee processing acknowledge that the interview is a critical aspect of the asylum process. Refugees are often fearful of questioning and unable to document their claims. The interviewer, therefore, needs skill and sensitivity if he is to elicit information from the refugee: most crucially, he must determine whether the applicant is to be believed. Yet under the INS Haitian Program, untrained airport inspectors augmented the regular interviewers.[14] The translators also played their part in the program; a lengthy statement in Creole, asserting that the individual had suffered persecution in Haiti, was reduced to a few words in the English translation, omitted entirely, or altered to the formulaic, I came to find work.

Of equal importance to the interview in political asylum cases is the assembling of evidence in support of the claim of persecution—obtaining statements from witnesses to the persecution or any written matter that would corroborate the event. This is a painstaking process usually done by attorneys or by trained paralegals; experienced attorneys say each claim can take anywhere from ten to forty hours. The INS allowed thirty to sixty minutes, establishing deadlines that attorneys could not possibly meet.

The pro bono attorneys also found themselves the objects of intimidation. If this was war, the Haitians were only the infantry. The attorneys were the general staff, and therefore the INS regarded them as far more dangerous. INS officials harassed them too, and, in the immigration courtrooms, the judges threatened them. Attacked from all sides, they could not properly represent their clients. At times, the INS strategy verged on the comical, as when attorneys were scheduled to appear simultaneously at several asylum hearings, sometimes as many as fifteen to twenty, in different buildings. One lawyer had to run between hearings, and was berated by an immigration judge for being late.[15]

The immigration judges, of course, had their own pressures to contend with. Under normal circumstances, each judge would hear some five cases a day. Under the speedup, the number increased to 100 a day, even at one point reaching 150. A single judge, forced to hear more than 100 asylum cases in a single day, can do no more than confirm a predetermination, the predetermination to deny asylum and deport.

In general, an atmosphere of hostility prevailed—in one striking example of callousness, a travel poster visible from the interview room proclaimed "New Routes to Haiti"[16]—a hostility that verged, in one instance at least, on the sinister. A Haitian marine, who had been a member of Duvalier's personal guard, testified that he saw one Tony Heider working as an INS translator in Miami. Heider was an American whom the Haitian had seen many times in the company of President-for-Life Duvalier. During the INS interview, Heider and another translator warned a group of Haitians that they would never gain admission to the United States, but would inevitably be returned to Haiti. It would go far easier for them, the translators advised, if they returned immediately and voluntarily. In succeeding days, other translators repeated the insinuations, even taking two of the Haitians to a plane and asking them to choose smoking or nonsmoking seats. Several times during the marine's lengthy incarceration, Tony Heider returned; on at least one occasion he threatened the Haitians with beatings if they did not obey his orders. Abuse dogged their detention.[17]

Nor were these isolated instances of threats, abuse, and mistreatment. In months and years to come, in courtrooms in Miami and across the country, not only Haitians, but Salvadorans, Guatemalans, and others would add their testimony, until an undeniable pattern had emerged: The INS has repeatedly tried to intimidate unwanted aliens into "voluntarily" returning home.[18]

The exact number of cases heard during the four-month period from August to November 1978 is not known—the INS failed to keep accurate records and had no computer—but is generally agreed to have been about four thousand. Four thousand Haitian asylum claims denied. That a number of these denials were wrongly made was apparent even to those who were not supporters of the Haitian cause. One INS attorney, who firmly believed that most Haitians were economic refugees, also concluded that the government was failing to grant asylum where it was warranted. The attorney observed that "some were granted asylum, but it was such a small number that you couldn't really say in any good faith that the government was granting as many cases as there were." What finally impelled the attorney to quit the INS was the realization that the INS was acting in bad faith, that the Haitians "were being treated totally unfairly."[19] Peter Nimkoff put it rather precisely when he explained his own resignation: "It is hard," he explained, "to be a policeman of laws over which you have pause."[20]

It was the issue of fairness that would, in the fall of 1978, force the government to terminate the Haitian Program. A group of pro bono attorneys, acting on behalf of the Haitian Refugee Center in Miami and the class of Haitian asylum applicants, applied for and received a temporary restraining order from the district court in southern Florida. The order enjoined the attorney general from continuing the accelerated hearings and from returning to Haiti those Haitians whose asylum claims had already been denied.[21]

Prosper Bayard's claim had been denied. Since 1957, Bayard had worked with, and befriended, opponents of the Duvalier regime. In 1962, Bayard was arrested and, though never charged or tried, was held in prison, starved and beaten, for one year and seven months. He was released and imprisoned twice more and, after the third release, in December 1977, fled to the United States, where he applied for asylum. His attorney was not allowed to participate in the asylum interview. The INS official who questioned Bayard had had no training in asylum adjudication; he had been instructed, however, to dispatch the interview with all possible speed. Although Bayard described his imprisonment, the INS sent him its standard denial, which maintained that he had failed to supply particulars.[22]

Theodore Cadet had been an active member and then a leader of a group opposing the younger Duvalier. In June of 1975, Cadet and some fifteen other members of his group were taken to Fort Dimanche, a prison, where they were tortured. Many of the group died. Cadet's family was able to secure his release by paying a bribe, after which he walked for twelve days to the Dominican Republic, then set sail for Miami and presented himself to the INS for asylum. The conditions of his asylum interview mirrored Bayard's, as did the form letter that denied him asylum.[23]

Solomon Jocelyn had been a foreman in Haiti and had led a group of peasants to reclaim the land that the Tontons Macoutes had stolen from them. For his actions, he spent seven months in prison. Upon his release, he went to the Bahamas, but left there when the Bahamian government began to deport Haitians. He came to the United States intending to ask for asylum, but friends told him he had no chance, and so he lived illegally in Miami for two years until 1978, when he heard that the INS was giving out work permits. He then went to the INS and asked for political asylum. In August, Jocelyn's work authorization was revoked and he was told to appear before an immigration judge. At his asylum interview, Jocelyn felt very strongly the hostility of the interviewer and was so upset by some of the questions that he became convinced that "the man must have been somebody that was in Duvalier's side."

Jocelyn's asylum request was denied by Acting District Director Richard Gullage not once, but twice in a three-month period, because, as the INS form letter asserted, Jocelyn had failed to support his claim with the names of witnesses or the dates on which the events had taken place. This even though appended to his file had been the exact incidents at which he was arrested, the prisons in which he had been held, and the dates of his imprisonment, as well as the names of those who had arrested him. Indeed, the file included the name of one witness who was living in Miami. When called to testify on the Jocelyn case, during the *Haitian Refugee Center* v. *Civiletti* trial, Gullage admitted that, although he had signed the denial letters, he had never reviewed the file, had, in fact, during his tenure as acting district director, made some five to six thousand asylum decisions, of which he had reviewed no more than forty.[24]

After hearings began in the class-action suit, Mr. Jocelyn's case was reviewed a third time. This time the Department of State, in an advisory opinion, recommended asylum, and the INS granted it.[25] Other cases were also, after the trial began, reviewed, and asylum granted. Had there not been, however, a temporary restraining order barring the INS from deporting Haitians, it would have been pointless for the INS to grant Jocelyn asylum; he would already have been returned to Haiti, along with more than six hundred others.

Quite abruptly, in the spring of 1980, positions had been reversed. Now the scene of the battle had shifted from the immigration courts to a federal court, and it was not the Haitians but the government which was forced to defend itself. Much of the testimony in *Haitian Refugee Center* v. *Civiletti*, which would run to thousands of pages, was intended to prove first that the government had intended to discriminate against the Haitians, and second, that the government, in carrying out its Haitian Program, had acted illegally, violating both statutory immigration law and the Immigration Service's own regulations. As witness after witness, document after document were brought forward, evidence of discrimination and illegality mounted, evidence that the government did little to refute. So remote did the Justice Department appear to be from the proceedings in Miami that at one point Judge James Lawrence King was moved to observe that "most of the defendants, the main defendants, have washed their hands of the suit . . ."[26]

If the Justice Department seemed almost to acknowledge tacitly that the INS actions had been illegal, in one area, the State Department did advance a defense. The plaintiffs were pursuing a second line of attack, this one to show that political conditions in Haiti were such as to generate refugees and that, further, if refugees were returned to Haiti after asking for political asylum in the United States, they were liable to be imprisoned, tortured, even killed. The United States was obligated by treaty (the Refugee Act had not yet been passed) not to deport any alien to a country in which his life or freedom would be threatened. Here was an area of delicate discretion.

If the State Department recommends that an individual be denied asylum, it will also deliver the opinion that such an individual is unlikely to suffer persecution on return. The same foreign policy concerns govern both recommendations. The reasoning, in fact, is faulty. The State Department believes that an allied government such as Haiti ought not to be offended. The department, therefore, takes the position that all those who flee Haiti are apolitical, are seeking to better themselves economically rather than to escape political persecution. Having denied, on this basis, asylum to Haitian asylum seekers, the department then brings its reasoning full circle and argues that the Haitians, not having been political refugees in the first place, will suffer no political reprisals should they be returned.

Time and again, when it wishes to assert that a given group cannot possibly include refugees, the government turns to studies done by the State Department, rather than to studies done by more disinterested bodies. Just such a study was the one conducted by the State Department in May of 1979, when it sent a team to Haiti to determine the fates of some six hundred returnees. Even the composition of the team cast some doubts on its impartiality: one of the investigators, an asylum officer in the Bureau of Human Rights and Humanitarian Affairs, had participated in an earlier meeting at which the government had planned its Haitian Program.

To be sure, the team conducted its study in the accepted diplomatic manner. The team asked for and received the assurances of the "highest levels" of the Haitian government that it would cooperate in the study and would not interfere in any way. Moving into the countryside, the study team inquired as to the whereabouts of individuals on their list. Twice they made radio broadcasts, asking specific individuals to come and speak with the team.

Of the six hundred names on the original list, the State Department was able to locate eighty-six and to speak with the families of eleven others. The investigators found no evidence that the returnees had been mistreated and were told by those they interviewed, "sometimes quite emphatically, that they had left for economic reasons."[27] The study team concluded that the Haitian government punished only organizers. Others were unharmed because, in the view of the Haitian government, "the typical emigrant's sale of possessions to pay for travel, combined with the embarrassment of failure to gain entry into the U.S., itself constitutes 'punishment enough.' " As to political persecution in Haiti, the team felt that because Haitian émigrés were uneducated, even illiterate, the Haitian government did not regard them as politically aware or active and therefore did not prosecute them.[28]

In Haiti, however, one did not express opposition to the ruling regime through political activity, nor did that regime regard only political activity as subversive.[29] In the 1950s, when François Duvalier took office, the lines of power were restructured so that all owed their allegiance directly to the president. In the army, officers followed not their commanders but the president himself (first François Duvalier and then his son, Jean-Claude). To counterbalance the army, the Tontons Macoutes were formed (later officially named the Volunteers for National Security, or VSN), a body whose central core comprised lawless thugs. As did the army, the Macoutes owed unswerving allegiance to no one but the president-for-life. They acted primarily as spies, reporting directly to the president on the populace and on each other. In return for their services, the Macoutes received no pay (hence the name *Volunteers*), but they were permitted to carry guns. Thus the VSN made their living prowling the countryside, offering protection in exchange for money and favors, extracting their own meager tributes from the terrified populace.

Alongside the VSN, in the rural areas, was what passed for local government: the section, or political division, which was under the control of the *chef*, usually a prominent local citizen. The *chef* controlled the area police, and he himself received only a token salary so that, like the Volunteers, he had to wring his living from the peasants. Nor was he, any more than the VSN, subject to the rule of civil courts.[30] Haiti was in many ways a police state, not a tightly controlled police state with central lines of authority, such as exist in Communist countries, but a state kept in agitated disorder by petty thieves and mercenaries.

Therefore, when the study team went into the countryside and inquired as to the whereabouts of family members, when it broadcast on the radio the names of Haitians with whom an American government mission wished to speak, it was misled if it assumed that the answers it would be given were candid.

In commenting, during the trial, on the State Department study, Stephanie Grant of Amnesty International found of greater significance than the eighty-six returnees who came forward the five hundred who did not.[31]

In other areas as well, Grant found the State Department report to be woefully credulous. The report noted that no returnees had been brought before a special Haitian tribunal, established to investigate charges of defamation of the nation. "Had the team looked more closely," Ms. Grant states, "they would have found that that tribunal has never met, has never heard a single case."[32] Secondly, the team never found out whether any of the people they interviewed had actually applied for political asylum in the United States, an act that could both predicate earlier persecution and possibly incur further persecution on return.

Finally, the State Department team had neglected to visit any of the Haitian prisons to investigate whether they held any returnees from the United States. During the *Haitian Refugee Center* v. *Civiletti* trial, former political prisoners came forward to testify that the cells of Duvalier held many who had been deported from the United States. Marc Romulus, a former prisoner who has written a book recounting his experiences, explained that the Haitian government placed returning Haitians in two categories. Those who were returned from the Bahamas or the Dominican Republic—where they had not requested political asylum—were sent only to the National Penitentiary. But those deported from the United States were consigned to Fort Dimanche, an infamous prison in which most died—of tuberculosis, malnutrition, or intestinal disorders—but from which even death provided no release. Guards removed the corpses from the cells at night and took them behind the prison to be eaten by dogs.

Romulus knew many returnees from the United States, but became close to one, a young peasant named Serge Donetius, accused of being a "traitor because he asked for asylum abroad."

Donetius died of torture for which he received no medical attention.

Romulus, himself released because of pressure from international organizations, explained that within the country, political prisoners are unknown persons. One year prior to his release, the Haitian government had responded to inquiries on his behalf by asserting that he was "unknown in Haiti."[33] In Haiti, "unknown" persons are often unknown even to their families. Michelle Bogre, a journalist, made two trips to Haiti where, using the State Department's own list of returnees, she attempted to determine their fates. She located eight families, and of these, seven did not know that their relatives had been deported from Miami.[34]

The testimony and the evidence on behalf of the plaintiffs in *Haitian Refugee Center* v. *Civiletti* were considerable. No amount of testimony or evidence in any class-action suit, however, can determine whether a single individual ought to be given political asylum. Nor was this the goal of the litigants. Rather, they intended to prove two points: first, that the Haitian refugees had been denied the rights guaranteed them under law, and second, that the government had, before the fact, prejudged their asylum claims as frivolous.

On both points, Judge James Lawrence King, a Republican appointed by President Nixon, found for the plaintiffs. In his lengthy decision, Judge King wrote, "The plaintiffs charge that they faced a transparently discriminatory program designed to deport Haitian nationals and no one else. The uncontroverted evidence proves their claim."[35]

Judge King concluded:

Those Haitians who came to the United States seeking freedom and justice did not find it. Instead, they were confronted with an Immigration and Naturalization Service determined to deport them. The decision was made among high INS officials to expel Haitians, despite whatever claims to asylum individual Haitians might have. A Program was set up to accomplish this goal. The Program resulted in wholesale violations of due process and only Haitians were effected [*sic*].

This Program, in its planning and executing, is offensive to every notion of constitutional due process and equal protection. The Haitians whose claims for asylum were rejected during the Program shall not be deported until they are given a fair chance to present their claims for political asylum.[36]

The government decided to appeal Judge King's ruling. But the same sense of urgency that had motivated the Haitian Program—and that had, to a large extent, contributed to its illegality—impelled the government once again to avoid protracted legal remedies. If compliance with the court would impede the expulsion of the Haitians, the government would have to remove the Haitians from the court's jurisdiction.

Within two months of Judge King's ruling, the White House announced that newly arriving Haitians would no longer be processed in the Miami area, but in Fort Allen, an old army base in Puerto Rico. The move could serve many goals. First, Judge King's ruling barring the deportation of Haitians did not apply outside of southern Florida. Second, there were in Puerto Rico no base of community support for the Haitians and no cadre of pro bono attorneys to assist them. The "processing" of Haitian arrivals, therefore, could proceed swiftly.

As initially announced, the plan seemed genuinely intended to bring order to the chaotic aftermath of Mariel. The White House proposed to send to the camp in Puerto Rico those Cubans and Haitians from the Mariel influx who remained without sponsors, as well as any new arrivals. Haitian supporters protested immediately that the proposal was only a smokescreen, that its true purpose was the expulsion of the Haitians. Within two months, their predictions were confirmed. By November, the plan had been changed: no Cubans, only Haitians would be sent to Fort Allen.

Now one of the strangest alliances in American refugee history was formed, an alliance that linked Puerto Rican opponents of refugees with southern Florida refugee supporters. The White House plan incensed the people of Puerto Rico. Nineteen eighty was an election year, and incumbent Jimmy Carter, because of Mariel, stood to lose the state of Florida. Many felt that the move to Puerto Rico was intended to win votes in Florida; it strained relations with the commonwealth, but Puerto Ricans do not vote in presidential elections. Thus the transfer was, at least for the moment, politically safe. The proposed movement of the refugees, however, only further exacerbated the conviction of many Puerto Ricans that Washington regards them as second-class.

Puerto Rican Governor Carlos Romero Barcero decided to fight back, and filed a suit to block construction of the camp on environmental grounds. But the White House was not to be impeded, and President Carter ordered the camp exempted from local pollution-control requirements. A complex series of suits and appeals led all the way to the Supreme Court but, by November of 1980, the way had been cleared for the transfer of the first group of Haitian refugees to Fort Allen, Puerto Rico. The fort was ready, it was announced, and so were the Marines—444 of them, "trained in combat tactics and riot control."[37] But on the morning of November 10, as the plane awaited, there were no Haitian refugees to be transferred from the Krome Avenue Camp outside Miami. Working frantically over a ten-day period, church groups and Dade County agencies had managed to find sponsors for every one of the 1,138 Haitians still remaining at the camp, the last 53 of them on the morning of the scheduled flight.[38] But that tactic would not work again: the special-entrant status would no longer apply to newly arriving Haitians, and they would have to be kept in detention until their asylum claims were decided.

In succeeding months, the INS removed a number of Haitians from Krome Camp, where they had legal representation, and took them to Puerto Rico, where they had none. No one told the Haitians of the transfer until it took place; their attorneys did not learn of it until afterward, until they appeared at Krome to speak with clients and were told that they were no longer there. Efforts to track down the refugees, even by family members, often proved futile.[39] And just as predicted, the INS quietly sent many Haitians from Puerto Rico back to Haiti. Despite assurances from the Haitian consul in Puerto Rico that no harm would come to any returnees, witnesses have affirmed that Haitians returned from Fort Allen to Haiti, like their predecessors, faced arrest, imprisonment, and beatings.[40]

By the summer of 1981, the infamous Haitian Program was being reenacted in southern Florida, once again having been planned at the highest levels of government.[41] In June, mass hearings were held. At each hearing, thirty Haitians were placed in a courtroom, from which their attorneys were excluded and to which the doors were locked. Once again, the pro bono attorneys, in this case the National Emergency Civil Liberties Committee, turned to the courts for relief, and once again a temporary restraining order was issued. The Justice Department was barred from deporting any Haitian whose case had been decided in a mass hearing. Eleven Haitians had already been deported.

The Justice Department later admitted that the hearings had been improper, although it insisted that the deportation orders issued at the hearings were legal. According to an INS spokesperson, the government made the concession to avert a protracted lawsuit.[42]

Though the mass hearings were stopped, other echoes of the Haitian Program reverberated for months. The few available attorneys were, as before, scheduled to appear in three courtrooms simultaneously. Two very well-documented asylum claims were denied, according to one attorney, because the immigration judge complained that the lawyer was hopping in and out of the courtroom.[43] From October 16 to November 19, eighty

Haitians with legal representation were ordered deported because their attorneys had not been present in the courtroom, and the refugees were unable to put forward strong evidence in support of their asylum claims. All that the terrified Haitians were able to say was that if they were sent back to Haiti, they would be killed.

Nor did the presence of a lawyer significantly influence the outcomes of the hearings. Lawyers were permitted no more than one or two minutes to talk with their clients, and continuances were consistently denied. The lawyers, in fact, felt helpless against immigration judges who acted, they felt, like prosecutors. Although the Haitian client had not yet talked with his attorney, the judge would interrogate the applicant, then declare, No prima facie case. Even at the detention camp, attorneys found that access to their clients was severely restricted, and the attorneys were guarded at all times.[44]

Finally, in a reincarnation of Fort Allen, the government once again began transferring Haitians represented by counsel in southern Florida to detention centers in such distant areas of the country as Big Spring, Texas, Lake Placid, New York, and Morgantown, Virginia, as well as to Fort Allen, Puerto Rico. Once again, refugee advocates brought suit, *Louis* v. *Nelson*, in 1981 on behalf of 2,100 Haitians held in eleven detention centers and federal penitentiaries around the country. Once again, a federal judge stepped in, this time to enjoin the INS from transferring Haitians away from their attorneys. When the Justice Department, however, was asked to provide the court with the names and locations of all the Haitians affected by the suit, the department refused to do so. To which Judge Alcee Hastings angrily responded, "The only reason geography has become an issue is that the government has made geography an issue by moving these people. The issue would not be unmanageable if the government had not made it [so] by playing this human shell game."[45]

For a second time, the government was being forced to defend

its policies and practices in court. Also for a second time, a
Justice Department attorney found himself at odds with that
department's policies. Assistant U.S. Attorney Richard Marshall, while acting as lead counsel in *Louis* v. *Nelson*, was also
working to convince the Justice Department that Haitians in
detention were entitled to receive the volunteered assistance of
some twenty-five pro bono lawyers. When persuasion failed,
Marshall, like Nimkoff before him, quit. To continue repre-
senting the government, he said, "I would have had to evis-
cerate my conscience."[46]

And, as before, the Justice Department continued to maintain
that the Haitians were fleeing poverty, not persecution. As evidence in *Louis* v. *Nelson*,[47] Justice called up not a State Department study trip, but a trip undertaken by the third-ranking
official of the Justice Department, Associate Attorney General
Rudolph Giuliani. Giuliani testified that he had been reassured
that there was no repression in Haiti. In countertestimony, Stephen Cohen, a former deputy assistant secretary of state for
human rights and a consultant to the State Department, called
the government of Haiti highly repressive and, out of court,
characterized the associate attorney general's observations as
"laughable." Cohen said, "It would be like someone in our
own government getting up to say that the Soviet Union is a
democracy."[48]

The plaintiffs in the case also tried to prove that the Haitians
were being singled out for treatment more severe than that
accorded any other group of entrants. They brought in statis-
ticians who argued that the probability of the Haitian detention
having been random, rather than selective, was one or two
chances per billion—"a statistical joke," as one expert put it.[49]

Judge Eugene Spellman, who had been called in to replace
Hastings, issued an equivocal ruling. The judge disagreed with
the government defendants and found that the due-process
guarantees of the Fifth Amendment extend even to excludable
aliens. (This finding, however, was without effect, since the

government had already admitted that the mass-asylum hearings held for ninety-six Haitians might have been improper.) The judge also found that the government policy of detention, while not illegal, had been instituted without public notification of the change in regulations. For this reason, the 1,900 Haitians in detention were to be released on parole. On the other hand, Judge Spellman found no evidence of discrimination on the part of the government. Spellman felt, rather, that the government had "intended to be fair." "The evidence shows that the detention policy was not directed at [Haitians] because they are black or Haitian, but because they were excludable aliens."[50] Both sides claimed victory in the case.

Judge Spellman's finding was open to some question. No evidence has ever shown that the Haitians were singled out because they were black. Significant evidence, however, has accrued to demonstrate that the Haitians were singled out from all other national groups. The Haitian Program was not initiated because the Haitians were black; it was instituted because they came from a country that allied itself with the United States against Castro, because they were the most easily barred of all the illegal entrants, and because the receiving community did not unequivocally welcome them.

The case was far from concluded, however. The Justice Department decided that it could not accept Judge Spellman's order to release the Haitians in detention, for to do so would encourage other illegal entrants. Detention, after all, served not only to relieve the burden on the local communities (a burden that was frequently translated into pressure for federal assistance), but, more importantly, to discourage other Haitians from coming here. Fearing a major influx of illegal entrants if it put the release order into effect, the government appealed. When the federal appeals court upheld Judge Spellman's release order, however, the Justice Department, still dissatisfied, asked that the appeals court rehear the arguments in the case. This time the government had made a tactical error. When the appeals

court had heard the arguments, it not only upheld Judge Spellman's order to release the Haitians from detention, but decided,
in contravention of Judge Spellman, that the government *had*
acted in a discriminatory manner.[51] The higher court found, in
words reminiscent of those used by Judge King, "a stark pattern
of discrimination." Judge Phillis Kravitch, one of the three appeals judges, wrote, "There was ample unrebutted evidence that
plaintiffs were denied equal protection of the laws."[52] This time
only one side could claim victory.

The Haitian detention suit, however, was not yet closed. In
1984, the entire Eleventh Circuit Court of Appeals reconsidered
the finding of its three-judge panel, and issued a decision of
sweeping implications. The court decided that arriving aliens
in exclusion status may be detained or paroled *without the protection afforded by the Constitution.* The court affirmed the right of
the executive to discriminate against arriving aliens on the basis
of their nationality; recent judicial decisions on detention, the
court felt, "would cause us to lose control of our borders."[53]

INS Commissioner Alan C. Nelson was quick to applaud the
decision as "a clear victory for the Reagan Administration. This
decision reemphasizes the nation's sovereign right to control
its borders."[54] Ira Kurzban, attorney for the Haitian plaintiffs,
mourned the court's opinion as "the Dred Scott decision for
refugees."[55] (In the Dred Scott case, the court found that black
persons had no standing under the law.)

The victory was far greater than just a victory for a Justice
Department detention policy. The Eleventh Circuit Court had
ruled for those Americans who shout, Go home! and against
the breadgivers. It had ruled in favor of the stance of exclusion
and against the hand of welcome. It had ruled that order must
take precedence over law.

When, in 1985, the Supreme Court heard the case, the court
sidestepped the issue and declined to rule on whether the Haitians are entitled to the equal protection guarantees of the Constitution. Rather, the court found that the INS regulations, which

prohibit discrimination, afford the alien sufficient protection. The Supreme Court left to the lower court the question of whether the INS had violated its own regulations.

In the past, the INS has not hesitated to breach its own asylum regulations when there was a perceived threat (perceived by the Justice Department, the White House, or even the Immigration Service itself) to the national sovereignty. At times the breach has been blatant, as with the Haitian Program. At other times the breach has been more subtle, as when, in 1982, the Justice Department sought to lay to rest the issue of discrimination. The department issued new regulations, under which *all* "inadmissible aliens"—all those without documentation—would be detained. Parole was to be "an exception to the rule . . . carefully and narrowly exercised."[56] A report issued two years later shows that the parole power had indeed been narrowly, in fact geographically, exercised: during the two-year period, no individual from Eastern Europe had been held in detention. In fact, from all Europe, only Greek nationals were detained.[57] Clearly discrimination still existed, but it was now directed against a broader spectrum than just the Haitians.

The broader spectrum included Central Americans who, beginning in 1981, arrived in significant numbers. They too were to be subject to detention, coerced departure, denial of due process. And like the Haitians, these later groups would, as a class, take their grievances to courts of law.

Congress has enacted our immigration laws to give the government the power to control our borders, to determine who will or will not be admitted to the United States. The Refugee Act, however, amended the Immigration and Nationality Act, and did so for a single and quite special purpose: to extend the protection of the United States government to those individuals who cannot enjoy the protection of their own government—to refugees.

The Refugee Act established, for refugees, an extraordinary admission procedure, entirely separate from ordinary immigra-

tion regulation. Refugees are not subject to immigration numbers; applicants for asylum may enter without documentation.
The Immigration and Naturalization Service, as a result, seems
to find itself in an uncomfortable situation. Is its role to admit
to the United States those with proper documentation? Asylum
seekers have no such documentation. Is its function to deport
those who enter the country illegally? Asylum seekers, then,
must also be deported. The INS—at the behest of the executive—has chosen to maintain its traditional role of immigration
law-enforcer and to set itself in opposition to applicants for
asylum. The INS is not the disinterested judge of the pleas of
asylum seekers, but the policeman who arrests them, the jailer
who incarcerates them, the prosecutor who proves them deportable.

The position of the INS has been most admirably summarized
in *Nuñez* v. *Boldin*. In that case, the INS argued that it had no
obligation to inform arriving aliens of their right to claim asylum
(the same position taken by the Eleventh Circuit Court). The
preliminary injunction in Nuñez observed that:

> The Immigration Service argues that the cornerstone of
> American jurisprudence is the adversary system, and that
> notifying detainees of their right to apply for asylum goes
> against the grain of that system. Our system of jurisprudence,
> however, is designed for determining the truth, with the
> premise that the truth is best arrived at by full development
> of all the issues involved. Full development of the claims of
> asylum of these fleeing people, however, must start with
> notice of that issue, lest they never have their day.[58]

The court then went on to discuss the crux of the issue:

> This Court fully appreciates the burden that may result to
> defendants due to the requirements of this order. Providing
> refuge to those facing persecution in their homeland, how-

ever, goes to the very heart of the principles and moral precepts upon which this country and its Constitution were founded. It is unavoidable that some burdens result from the protection of these principles. To let these same principles go unprotected would amount to nothing less than a sacrilege.[59]

The Supreme Court extended its protection to one of those principles by ruling, in its Cardoza-Fonseca decision of March 1987, that the government had been applying a stricter standard for asylum than was intended by the Refugee Act. The act had specified that, to be eligible for asylum, an alien need have only a "well-founded fear of persecution." The government, on the other hand, had maintained that the alien must prove a "clear probability" of persecution. The court's ruling will make it easier for an individual to apply for asylum—but not more likely that he will receive it, since the attorney general retains the discretion to grant or deny asylum.

For some years, the White House and the State and Justice Departments have stood as adversaries of the asylum seeker, maintaining a system in which many asylum seekers have been presumed guilty, rather than innocent. In response, those who felt that the asylum system was operating improperly have sought redress in the courts.

In the end, the question of the rights and obligations of the United States as opposed to the rights and obligations of the asylum seeker may never be settled in the courts. The courts, like any other social institution, tend to reflect the ethos of their times (thus Kurzban's reference to the Dred Scott decision). But as we have no better forum in which to address these questions, it is likely that litigation will remain, for the foreseeable future, a major avenue of redress of wrongs and determiner of rights.

Immigration law and the Refugee Act, however, apply to a particular kind of refugee, one who meets the narrow standard

6 The Unprotected: The Remedies of Congress

Immigration law builds a wall around a nation, then devises a number of gates through which those who wish to gain admission must pass. With the Refugee Act of 1980, Congress created a new gate of legal entry—a gate for asylum seekers. From its inception, however, the gate of asylum has been criticized for its design and for its operation.

There have been many attempts to rebuild the gate. Some people oppose its basic design; as it stands, they argue, the gate can open wide enough to admit a veritable flood of impoverished migrants. These critics prefer a more narrowly designed gate, one which admits selectively or in accord with specific foreign-policy imperatives.

A second group of critics argues that the entryway is not single, but a series of gates, each leading an asylum applicant further inward. These interior gates of review and appeal make it possible for any unwanted entrant to remain for many years, if not permanently, in the United States. These critics would like to tear down the inner gates and rebuild the asylum entrance as a revolving door, with immediate ejection of those who are found inadmissable.

A third group of critics finds the design of the gate—if less than perfect—nonetheless serviceable. Where they find fault is in the operation of the gate. They feel that it should operate in a regular and predictable manner, according to the dictates of our refugee and immigration laws and the imperatives of our treaty obligations.

While the critics wrangle, however, and press their causes in Congress and the courts, the pressure at the wall mounts as hundreds of thousands of Central Americans are driven from their homelands, yet find scant opportunity to enter the United States legally.

Other groups of Americans, no less vocal or visible than the first three, have responded to these refugees. These Americans have turned away from the gate of asylum and looked in new directions. One of these groups has proposed a bill to open a temporary gate—extended voluntary departure—which would offer safe haven until such time as violence and civil disorder have abated and the refugees are able to return home.

The controversy over entrance for asylum seekers would appear, at first, to be merely a resumption of the argument that began when the first immigrants arrived in the United States— the argument between those who would admit the newcomers and those who would bar them, over whether to admit refugees for political or for humanitarian reasons.

The familiar currents still run beneath the surface of this controversy, but the Central American refugees bring with them a phenomenon with critical portents. The political refugee, as we recognize him today—the individual who is singled out by his government for persecution—is a recurrent, but not continuing figure in history. The atrocities of the Second World War led to the present legal definition of a refugee. Prior to the war, however, there had been, and there are again today, mass movements of refugees, people who flee not because they have been singled out to be killed, but because killing is all around them, at once so random and so relentless that even those who are not killed are unable to live.

The definition of a refugee, so hard-wrested a concession of responsibility by the nations of the world, is inadequate to the present situation. The UNHCR has expressed its view this way:

The Universal Declaration of Human Rights—the modern-day Magna Carta—embodies the principle that *everyone* has the right to seek and enjoy in other countries asylum from persecution. Underlying this basic humanitarian principle is the universal conviction that every person is entitled to freedom from persecution. The vast majority of those seeking asylum today are however not persons fleeing from direct persecution or because of fear of persecution, but rather persons who have been displaced from their countries owing to severe internal upheavals or armed conflicts.[1]

In the United States, as in many other countries, no statute recognizes these people as refugees, and no agreement exists as to how, or even when, they might be protected. We have, in fact, no common term by which to call them. The United States government insists that "refugee" is a word with precise meaning in law, referring only to those who fear persecution. The UNHCR, on the other hand, applies the term *refugee* also to those who flee generalized violence. The words matter. A Salvadoran refugee in Mexico, recognized as such even by our own State Department, becomes an economic migrant as soon as he crosses the U.S. border. This is less of an anomaly than it would appear, for the State Department concedes that all individuals under the protection of the UNHCR are, by the definition of the latter organization, refugees; if they forfeit that protection, however, they also forfeit the designation.

While the State Department disputes their designation, Central Americans have been and are being displaced. Few of them have found even temporary haven. In recent years, violence and civil wars in El Salvador, Guatemala, and Nicaragua have caused hundreds of thousands to flee.

Nicaragua generated refugees in two waves. Many of those who left during Nicaragua's civil war in 1979 later returned; subsequently, the government began to forcibly relocate the Miskito Indians, driving them from their homelands, imprisoning and torturing some. The Miskitos fled to neighboring countries but, in 1985, the Nicaraguan government acknowledged its wrongdoing and a number of the Indians began to return. Others, who oppose the present government, have also fled. Nicaragua itself, at the same time that it generates refugees, has also offered asylum to refugees from neighboring El Salvador and Guatemala.

In El Salvador, violent political conflict is not a recent phenomenon. Over the past hundred years, an all-powerful oligarchy, the "fourteen families," have held most of the country's fertile farmlands in an unyielding grip. Time and again, the land-deprived peasants rose in revolt. Time and again, the army, at the bidding of the oligarchy, ruthlessly suppressed the uprising, killing tens of thousands. The combined economic power of the landowners and political power of the military seemed unassailable.

In 1979, a civilian-military junta took power and promised sweeping reforms. Within three months the civilians had resigned, leaving the government in the hands of the military, whose modest attempts at economic reform led it into direct confrontation with both the established right and the powerless left. For the right, even a modest redistribution of wealth was unthinkable; for the left, the initiated measures were insufficient. Civil war ensued. Tens of thousands were killed, many times that number left homeless. Despite the election, in 1984, of José Napoleón Duarte as president, the war continues. Killings and disappearances are fewer than in the early part of the decade, but human rights organizations, including Amnesty International, have expressed concern that such abuses continue and are now directed specifically at those who oppose the government, as well as at trade union organizers, human rights activists, and those who assist refugees. (Refugees are commonly suspected of being guerrilla supporters.)

In Guatemala, over the past thirty years, the government waged a war, not against insurgents, but against its own people. America's Watch, an organization that monitors human rights in the Western Hemisphere, called Guatemala "a nation of prisoners,"[2] a nation in which "selective violence and indeed, state terrorism, have become tools of subjugation and control."[3] Guatemala was a country so violent that no human rights organization could operate within it: all reports of massacres, disappearances, torture, and brutality had to be gleaned from the testimony of refugee survivors in other countries. Thousands of civilians were killed and millions lived in terror. Democratic elections in January 1986 brought a civilian, Vinicio Cerezo, to office, but President Cerezo very early announced an amnesty for the military. Although the violence abated somewhat, it continued in 1986, and the Guatemalan press reported more than a hundred killings each month, as well as kidnappings and disappearances.[4]

From all three countries in Central America, as in the rest of the world, there are those whose fear of persecution is founded upon their race (like the Miskito Indians), upon their membership in a particular social group (like the Indians in Guatemala), upon their political opinion (like the university students and faculty, trade unionists, and church workers in El Salvador who advocate social reform), refugees within the protocol definition. If they fail to find political asylum, it is not the definition that excludes them but the policies of the receiving country. Many others, however, run not from persecution but from military sweeps, from chemical and incendiary bombs, from forced recruitment by either the military or the insurgents, from scorched-earth policies, and from massacres of entire villages. They are refugees beyond the limits of the law, but well within the bounds of compassion.

In the United States, which did, during the Vietnam era, greatly extend the bounds of its compassion, some now argue that we have reached the limits of our compassion,[5] that our country can welcome no more. More cautiously, the administration contends that safe haven is already afforded refugees by many Central American countries and that "our programs are designed to encourage and maintain the asylum tradition" there.[6] The administration further advances that we admit few Latin American refugees because of "the hospitality and generosity with which neighboring countries accept and care for refugees."[7]

Yet a study by the Census Bureau recounts the following:

Some two thousand Mame Indians fled to Mexico [in the summer of 1981], but were refused safe haven and returned to Guatemala. Many were subsequently killed as suspected subversives by Guatemalan soldiers. . . .[8]

Salvadoran refugees in Honduras have been prevented from working and traveling freely. They are suspected of being guerrilla sympathizers and have been obliged to live in camps that are kept under military surveillance. They have lived in fear of forced repatriation to El Salvador. . . .[9]

In Costa Rica, . . . refugees have been labeled an economic burden and their presence is associated with a rise in terrorist activity. It also has been suggested that the racial purity of the Costa Rican population is being undermined. The growing anti-refugee sentiment in Costa Rica may deflect future refugee flows to other countries in the region. . . .[10]

Mexico has traditionally been a haven for political refugees, and presently has offered extended assistance and protection to Guatemalan refugees in southern border camps. However, the Mexican government opposes the establishment of permanent refugee settlements within its borders. It has argued that Salvadoran and Guatemalan refugees are taking jobs from Mexicans, and placing excess demand on social services. As a result, Salvadorans are being deported from Mexico, and rules for issuing visas have been made stricter. It is clear that refugees are considered an economic burden in Mexico. . . .[11]

Panama desires no more refugees, pleading insufficient resources.[12]

The receiving countries in Central America face a number of problems that large numbers of refugees exacerbate. Refugees place additional strain on uncertain economies while, at the same time, they compete with citizens for inadequate social services. Refugees from an unfriendly neighboring country may be feared as guerrillas or subversives, while, on the other hand, if they come from a country with which the host country has good relations, the refugees can become a diplomatic embarrassment. Finally, "rebels" or "revolutionaries" may be among the refugees, individuals whose activities are not welcome in the receiving country.[13]

Even Costa Rica, the most stable and prosperous of Central American countries, has begun to question whether it can continue to bear the burden of its refugees. Costa Rica's ambassador-designate pointed out, in a letter to the *New York Times*, that

> The number of Nicaraguans alone who have fled their homeland for Costa Rica since 1979 is conservatively put at one hundred thousand; of those, only one out of six has been formally granted refugee status. The remaining refugees, equal to almost four percent of Costa Rica's population, are scattered all over the country, competing for jobs, demanding food, shelter and health services, and claiming land as squatters.

The ambassador goes on to point out that Costa Rica bears the major responsibility for the refugees, while "neither Nicaragua nor the United States—which share responsibility for this situation—are doing enough, either to prevent Nicaraguans from fleeing their country or to help Costa Rica address the problems caused by such flight."[14]

Increasingly, the "hospitality and generosity" of our neighbors to the south is becoming strained. They can provide neither the subsistence nor the protection that are required by hundreds of thousands of refugees, many of whom, finding survival precarious in the host countries, have continued on to the United States, where they enter illegally and live the uncertain existence of undocumented aliens.

A sizable group in the Congress feels that it is the responsibility of the United States, no less than of our neighbors, to afford a temporary safe haven for the Central American refugees. They are the supporters of a bill to provide "Temporary Suspension of Deportation for El Salvador Refugees," or extended voluntary departure.[15] The bill—introduced in the House by Joseph Moakley of Massachusetts at the urging of church sanctuary groups in the representative's district, and in the Senate by Dennis DeConcini of Arizona—stipulates that Salvadoran nationals who are present in the country on the date the bill is enacted would not be deported for up to three years, during which time the president would be asked to conduct a comprehensive study of the needs of those who have been either displaced within El Salvador or driven from it as refugees into neighboring countries. The study would determine the refugees' numbers and under what conditions they live. It would also document how well they are being protected, and whether the food and medical supplies intended for them are reaching them. Finally, the study would investigate whether Salvadorans who have been deported from the United States have suffered persecution when returned. On the basis of this report, Congress would then consider how best to protect and assist the civilian victims of the Salvadoran conflict.

A measure on behalf of Guatemalan refugees has also been introduced in the House, but this resolution asks only that the attorney general grant the status of extended voluntary departure to Guatemalans in the United States.[16] Since the Justice Department opposes such a grant, the resolution, if passed, would have little effect.

DeConcini-Moakley, on the other hand, would not only establish a safe, if temporary, haven for Salvadorans in the United

States, it would also significantly alter the basis for our refugee policy.

Extended voluntary departure is not a new concept in American refugee practice. Under EVD, the government determines that conditions in a particular country are such that nationals of that country who are within the United States are temporarily unable to return home. Their departure date, therefore, is extended for given periods of time, until conditions in their country are once again stable. Since December of 1981, for example, Polish nationals have not been required to return home when their visas have expired. The departure dates have been extended, for all Poles, in six-month increments.

Unlike political asylum, EVD is not an individual but a group determination; EVD is granted not because an individual has a well-founded fear of persecution, but because of generalized conditions in a particular country. In the case of the Poles, the INS has put forth a number of reasons for their privilege, among them: "current conditions in Poland," and the "continued denial of rights to the Polish people."[17]

A further difference is that an alien has no inherent right to apply for EVD; rather, the government initiates the process. The Department of State asks the Justice Department to give extended voluntary departure to a particular group. The State Department bases its request on a balance of criteria: on the one hand are the department's policy objectives; on the other are the conditions in the foreign country—such as a breakdown of civil order or armed conflict—that make return of its nationals inadvisable. The State Department, thus, weighs both foreign policy and humanitarian interests. The Justice Department passes on the request to the INS, which must then consider its potential immigration impact.

As with refugee and asylum decisions, in a decision to grant extended voluntary departure, humanitarian considerations must confront the harder realities of foreign-policy goals. Because the executive grants EVD at its discretion and is not restrained from doing so by the Refugee Act, the State Department acknowledges freely that the most important consideration in any EVD decision is the influence that such a decision will have on foreign policy. When the question arose, for example, of whether to grant EVD to Polish nationals, the State Department was very careful that our response reinforce the position of our NATO allies toward the Polish government.[18]

A second reality, immigration impact, is the primary concern of the Justice Department. In 1983, Attorney General William French Smith opposed granting extended voluntary departure to Salvadorans because, he argued, it "undoubtedly would encourage the migration of many more such aliens. Because of the present and potential political and economic instability in other countries in close geographic proximity to the United States, any grants of conditional immigration benefits must be considered in light of its potential inducement to further influxes of illegal immigrants."[19]

Thus, although humanitarian concerns place a particular national group under consideration, foreign-policy goals served by a group and its limited numbers influence final approval. Only fifteen national groups have, since 1960, passed all three tests. At the end of 1986, nationals of four countries still benefited from a grant of extended voluntary departure: Afghanistan, Poland, Uganda, and Ethiopia.[20] Although our foreign policy makes us sympathetic to nationals of other countries as well, the fear of inviting large numbers of foreign nationals tends to weaken our protective posture. Therefore, for nationals of Lebanon,[21] Czechoslovakia, Hungary, Rumania, and Iran, as well as of Nicaragua,[22] the INS must make a case-by-case determination for EVD grants. In other words, a national of any of these countries must apply individually for permission to remain. (There would appear to be some lack of coordination between the State Department and the INS as to the case-by-case determinations. When the State Department prepared, as evidence in a civil case, a list of nationalities that have been granted EVD, it omitted the latter five countries, including only

Lebanon.[23] The INS, however, in an internal report, acknowledged that nationals of all six countries may be given individual grants of extended voluntary departure.[24])

Extended voluntary departure is not an open invitation for nationals of a particular country to sojourn in the United States. In each case, EVD applies only to those who were within the U.S. prior to a given date, usually the date on which EVD is first granted. Moreover, certain ground rules apply: EVD does not extend to those who were residents of a third country before coming here, or to those who have been convicted in a criminal court in the United States. A grant of EVD does, however, and most significantly, extend even to those who may have entered the United States illegally. (In the latter case, of course, the illegal entrant must prove that he was within the U.S. prior to the time at which EVD status began.)

It is not possible to compare the situations that prevail in the various countries whose nationals enjoy EVD. The martial rule imposed on Poland is diametrically opposed to the failure of the government in Uganda to control the military. The Soviet occupation of Afghanistan has created a set of problems utterly unlike those faced by the citizens ruled by the repressive Marxist regime in Ethiopia.

Yet, uniting all decisions to grant extended voluntary departure have been the same fixed set of biases that control political asylum decisions: the primacy of foreign-policy considerations and the concern for numbers. Since, however, EVD is not provided for in law, the government freely admits that these considerations govern its decisions. With the voice of restrictionism becoming increasingly voluble, we may also assume that a third consideration has weight, namely, the unobtrusiveness with which the newcomers can enter American society. Therefore, despite the civil war, deaths and disappearances, torture and intimidation in El Salvador and Guatemala, the State and Justice Departments deny that either Salvadorans or Guatemalans are in need of safe haven in this country.

On its face, the DeConcini-Moakley bill seems benign, intended to lay aside the passions of both sides that have befogged the issue and subject it instead to disinterested scrutiny. Yet, in two quite significant ways, the DeConcini-Moakley bill departs sharply from earlier proposals to grant EVD. In the first place, at no time in the past did Congress, rather than the State or Justice Departments, order a temporary stay of deportation for an entire national group. Frustrated by the failure of the State Department to respond over the years to requests by members of Congress or even to two sense-of-the-Congress clauses inserted in State Department authorization bills, all of which asked the department to grant EVD to Salvadorans, Congress took the initiative of proposing the legislation.

A second major departure concerns the legal status of the refugee group itself. Whenever, in the past, a nationality was granted extended voluntary departure, most members of the group had been legally admitted to the United States. The number of illegal entrants within any particular group would have been proportionately small. In the case of the Salvadorans, however, legal entrance has been all but unavailable, so the vast majority have entered illegally. Thus, EVD would not be extending a legal status, but conferring one.

Far more is symbolized in this brief bill than simply the authorization of still another GAO study. Enactment of DeConcini-Moakley would indicate that the strength of a popular movement, which demands for the Central Americans the same compassion we extend to the Southeast Asians, has made itself felt in the Congress.

Further, the bill recognizes that we can no longer respond to the world's refugees by offering permanent resettlement each year to a limited number. The numbers of refugees are too great, and the resources of receiving countries too small, for such a solution to answer all needs. In one sense, if we are going to move forward, we must take a few steps backward. If we are going to address the changing nature of refugee movements, we may no longer be able, nor will it necessarily be desirable, to offer all refugees a path to citizenship and services to support their earliest steps. Rather, DeConcini-Moakley recognizes that when the need is very great, it may be kinder to offer far less, for a shorter time, to many more.

The State and Justice Departments, not unexpectedly, unequivocally oppose the DeConcini-Moakley bill. They base their opposition on five arguments. First, Salvadorans have had a long history of migrating to the United States in search of jobs. The State Department asserts that, as early as 1979, before the present violence began, three hundred thousand Salvadorans were in the United States. And the pattern continues. In a recent poll in El Salvador, sixty-seven percent of the respondents agreed that they would come to the United States to find work if they could.

The department's second argument flows from the first. If EVD were instituted, it would act as a magnet; Salvadorans, knowing that they could now work here legally, would be drawn in even greater numbers to the United States.

If, the arguments continue, Salvadorans come to the United States in search of employment, then they have no need of protection. Those who do require such protection may apply for and receive political asylum. All others should apply to come to the United States on immigrant visas (over eight thousand were issued in 1984).

The State Department has acknowledged that there may be a middle ground between the political refugee and the immigrant, that there may be large numbers of people who have been driven from their homes and are in need of safe haven. But, the department insists, such protection has been amply provided for them within El Salvador itself and in neighboring countries. The existence of such havens only reinforces the idea that those who move further north, to the United States, do so because they are looking for work.

The final objection is procedural. The Refugee Act of 1980 put an end to the attorney general's practice of paroling in groups of refugees on the basis of their nationality. To legislate EVD for Salvadorans would be to restore the preferential treatment of parole.[25]

Laura Dietrich, deputy assistant secretary of state for human rights and humanitarian affairs, summarized the position of the State Department most eloquently. "I do not believe," she said, "that the appropriate response to the problems of poverty or violence in El Salvador is to allow any Salvadoran who wishes to simply live in America instead—any more than I think this is true for Guatemala, or Haiti, or Nicaragua, or Sri Lanka, or Afghanistan, or Iran, or Uganda, or Ethiopia, or Lebanon, or Vietnam, or Zimbabwe." Ms. Dietrich maintained that we should continue to respond to the problems of El Salvador with immigration, asylum, and refugee programs, with foreign aid, and with attempts to resolve the root conflicts.[26]

Ms. Dietrich failed to mention, however, that seven of the nationalities for which she felt EVD would not be an appropriate response—Nicaraguans, Afghanis, Iranians, Ugandans, Ethiopians, Lebanese, and Vietnamese—*have* enjoyed the privilege of extended voluntary departure; all but the Vietnamese still do, whether on a group or a case-by-case basis. Although the Refugee Act may well have ended the practice of group parole, it still exists, in modified form, as the temporary status of extended voluntary departure.

The State Department refuses to consider EVD an "appropriate response" for Salvadorans. While the department has no objection to the GAO study proposed in the DeConcini-Moakley bill, the department insists that, while the study is underway, it should continue to deport Salvadorans.[27] On this issue, as on many refugee issues, the State Department is begging the question. The State Department stands by a conclusion that the GAO study has not yet reached, namely, that existing programs and areas of safe haven adequately protect the Salvadorans and provide for their needs. Suppose, however, that the GAO study proves otherwise, concludes that existing programs are inadequate, that within El Salvador and in neighboring countries the very survival of the refugees is precarious. Suppose, further, that in the three years during which the GAO conducts the study and Congress discusses it, the INS has continued to deport Salvadorans at the 1985 rate of fifteen hundred per month.[28] Eighteen thousand each year, fifty-four thousand at the end of the three-year period returned to what we might, at that time, determine was neglect and death for many. What would, then, constitute an "appropriate response"?

The study proposed by the DeConcini-Moakley bill would offer, for the first time, a comprehensive view of the many facets of the Central American refugee problem and of the many responses to it. Even without such a study, however, pieces of the picture do exist, and the partial image that has begun to appear is sometimes at variance with that painted by the State Department.

No one disputes that a steady stream of Salvadorans has always come to the United States in search of jobs. What is in dispute is the magnitude of that migration. The State Department asserts that even prior to 1979, when the military junta took power and civil war began in El Salvador, three hundred thousand Salvadorans were in the United States, Salvadorans who had come for no other motive than to seek work. These three hundred thousand would constitute the majority of the half a million now estimated to be in this country. Though the State Department frequently advances the three hundred thousand figure, it never offers any source for the statistic. Yet in 1980, the U.S. Bureau of the Census found a total of 94,447 Salvadorans in this country, of whom 13,422 were naturalized citizens. Of the remaining 81,025, the bureau estimated, 51,150 had entered illegally.[29] Therefore, of the present population of some five hundred thousand, over eighty percent must have entered the United States *since* 1980, and only about ten percent entered illegally before that date.

As in any refugee flow, the economic and political factors

are inextricable, each both a cause and a result of the other. Yet a recent study by William Stanley, of the Massachusetts Institute of Technology, has demonstrated quite clearly that fear, rather than hunger, drove the vast majority of the Salvadorans to the United States.[30] Mr. Stanley studied the pattern of Salvadoran migration to the U.S. from 1979 through the middle of 1984. He found that the levels of Salvadoran migration to the U.S. rose sharply in 1980, remained high through 1981, and dropped off in 1982, coinciding with the precipitous rise in violence in El Salvador and its gradual diminution. As the military began its sweeps of rural areas in 1984, the number of Salvadoran arrivals once more climbed sharply, to levels approaching those of 1981. Even on a month-to-month basis, there was a strong correlation between reported violence in El Salvador and increased arrivals, after a brief interval, of Salvadorans in the United States.

Stanley also tested the influence of economic factors on the migration. He postulated that Mexicans come to the U.S. primarily in search of jobs, pushed by conditions in Mexico and pulled by opportunities in the U.S. Reasoning that Salvadorans would be subject to the same economic influences, Stanley used the Mexican migration to this country as a control variable. When Stanley compared the pattern of Salvadoran migration with the pattern of Mexican migration, he found "a dramatic difference in the patterns" of the two groups from 1980 to the beginning of 1982, the years when the death squads were at their peak.[31]

Based on his study, Stanley concluded that "since 1979, economic considerations have had a relatively minor impact on the decisions of Salvadorans to migrate to the U.S."[32] In short, "fear of political violence is an important and probably the dominant motivation of Salvadorans who have migrated to the United States since the beginning of 1979. The level of political violence in El Salvador is closely associated with the numbers of Salvadorans who come to the U.S."[33] (If economic concerns were the primary motivation for migration from Central America, then one would expect that Honduras, the poorest country in the region and, after Haiti, the poorest in the Western Hemisphere, would send forth a stream of migrants. Yet, there is no refugee flow from Honduras.)

Stanley's is the only statistical study thus far of the Salvadoran migration. Other researchers have studied the problem from the perspective of the refugees themselves. The stories the refugees tell provide a kind of gloss to the statistics, reminding us that each line on a bar chart, each number in a table represents but an aggregate of individuals.

Robert Kahn, a journalist, interviewed Salvadoran refugees in every area of the country in which they cluster. No less scrupulous in his investigation than Stanley, Kahn allowed the refugees to speak for themselves, asking them only three questions: Why did you leave El Salvador (or Guatemala)? How is life in the United States? If you could talk to the North American people, what would you tell them?[34] He neither interrupted their narrations, nor did he edit them so as to support a particular view.

The men and women Kahn interviewed were, once he had gained their confidence, quite candid in their responses. Tomás and Umberto admitted that they had come to the United States to find work. Tomás, the oldest child in a fatherless family, had been working as a dental technician in Guatemala City when relatives in Houston sent for him. Umberto could find no work in El Salvador because an eighteen-year-old who is not in the army is considered subversive. He now waits in INS detention. But of the fifty-one Central Americans interviewed, these two were the only ones who fit the economic-migrant characterization. Each of the others had left his home not in expectation, but in fear.

Many of them suffered severe losses of both income and status as a result of the relocation. Indalecio, for example, related how her father had taught in the medical school at the University of Guatemala. He also treated the Mayan Indians, and for this he was arrested and tortured. Afterward, he could no longer work as a doctor. He came to the United States and asked for asylum. His application was rejected. He tried to find work in a hospital laboratory, but was told he was overqualified. Now the former doctor earns his living cleaning floors in a movie theater.

Oscar had been a doctor in El Salvador, where he worked in a camp for displaced persons. "One day two army trucks drove to the doorway of the clinic and machinegunned the building. There were fifteen dead and wounded. I was wounded in the stomach, the head and the legs. They took me to barracks and tortured me for twenty-four days with electric shock applied to my ears, my tongue, sex organ, and the exposed bones of the bullet wounds."[35] The intervention of the Red Cross secured Oscar's release, but he could no longer work as a doctor. Now in the United States, Oscar spends his days working for CRECE, an organization that serves Central American refugees. Two or three nights a week, he works as a janitor.

Laura had been a student in El Salvador; now she cleans houses. Gabriela's husband had been a professor of philosophy at the university. Like many others, he was suspected of being a Marxist. Although Gabriela and her husband have been given political asylum, he works nights as a waiter; she works days, cleaning houses.

Finally, there are those who are not even fortunate enough to find regular work at all. Julio had been working in a restaurant in Texas, but, like the other undocumented workers, had not been paid in seven weeks. He continued to work, hoping he would eventually collect his back pay, but, in the end, the restaurant closed. Most Central Americans, when they do work, work in the most menial and poorest paid occupations: washing dishes, cleaning houses, in factories.

Francisco, a former student, described it this way:

Life here is pretty hard. First is work, then finding a place to live. And when you do find work, it's for a few days, and only pays enough to eat. Here in the United States the first thing we must do is work to eat. I have no work now. I am helped by my family, by CRECE. . . . Most of the work for refugees here is from friends. It is usually in factories, places where they pay the minimum wage, or less. I've worked painting cars. And always under the threat that they may call the INS. And always, they deduct taxes. Taxes at work, taxes when we buy things, and the tax money does not go to help us.[36]

Lita, who had spent thirty-two months in prison in El Salvador, and who still suffers from the torture she received, now works as a housekeeper in New Jersey, six days a week, for fifty dollars. "Your government," she protests, "says we are economic refugees. Look, there is war in our country. In my house, I never dreamed of coming here. I wanted to be a professor of mathematics, not to clean houses. I did not want to live as a person without a future. I have no way to help myself here, no way to help others."[37]

Francisco put it another way. "The main problem here is economics. The main problem in Salvador is politics."[38]

Harsh as the testimonies of these refugees may be, however, they can be interpreted in support of the State Department's arguments. For all the Oscars and Lauras in a refugee group, there are also Tomáses and Umbertos; among those who come for refuge, there are also those who come for work. Would not a blanket grant of extended voluntary departure simply increase the attractiveness of life in the United States for men and women whose own country offers them few opportunities? And, moreover, what of the Julios and the Franciscos, the unemployed who, if permitted to remain legally in this country, would also become eligible for its benefits? Finally, once the Salvadorans have become established in the U.S., will they not want to remain? In short, would a grant of EVD have a magnet effect?

The potential problems raised by these questions are valid, but not insurmountable. In fact, if government were to devote the same attention to administering an EVD program for Salvadorans that it now devotes to excluding them, we might find that certain problems would become far more manageable than they are at present.

EVD is *not* an open invitation to enter the United States. A rather simple administrative procedure can insure that it does not become one. EVD would apply to all those who are within the country on the date that the bill is enacted. If the INS were to require all Salvadorans to register at their local INS office within a given period from that date (say, thirty days), it could achieve two goals. First, the INS would have an accurate record of all Salvadorans in the United States on that date, and of their locations. Second, it could divert elsewhere much of the personnel and monies that are now earmarked for the arrest, detention, and deportation of Salvadorans.

The DeConcini-Moakley bill would not draw greater numbers of Salvadorans to the United States. Those who arrive after the enactment date would not find protection; and for them the bill would offer no enticements. The INS, however, remains adamantly opposed to a grant of EVD. In the words of William P. Joyce, associate general counsel for the INS, "We do not like EVD at all. It screws up the immigration laws."[39]

EVD need not "screw up" the immigration laws. Certain essential safeguards, however, would assure that the Salvadorans comply with the regulations. Most important is that the Salvadorans must be guaranteed the confidentiality of their registration. At present, many of the refugees do not apply for political asylum because their names might be turned over to the Salvadoran authorities and inquiries about them might be made in El Salvador; they fear for the safety of family and associates. The assistance of Central American support groups (of which there are many all across the country) would also prove invaluable. Such groups could publicize the registration dates and locations within the Salvadoran community, could provide translators, and could act as advisors to the refugees.

There are no data on the potential costs that Salvadoran refugees would cause to states and municipalities. Many localities, however, are already bearing such costs. Major cities, such as New York and Los Angeles, have announced that they will offer services to all who require them, regardless of their immigration status. The Commonwealth of Massachusetts will not deny its services or benefits on the basis of citizenship. Further, Massachusetts has formed a public agency to provide legal assistance to undocumented aliens—primarily Salvadorans and Guatemalans—who want to obtain political asylum or a stay of deportation.[40] Cities across the country, from San Francisco to Takoma Park, a suburb of Washington, D.C., and two states, New Mexico and New York, have declared themselves sanctuaries.[41] While the costs, therefore, would not increase, revenues possibly could. Under EVD, the Salvadorans would be entitled to work authorizations, enabling more of them to find legitimate employment and requiring more of them to contribute to the system.

The final question is the one least susceptible of solution. Once established here, would the Salvadorans not find it less desirable to return? To some extent, the answer must be yes. But when their legal status expires, Salvadorans who do not return would once more become undocumented entrants, without work authorization, subject to arrest and deportation. Their lives would be far from comfortable. It is likely that most would prefer to go home. Certainly the pattern observed for other Latin American countries should be instructive. Countries such as Bolivia, Uruguay, and Argentina, as they have seen political changes, also have seen the return of their exiles. If the forces of violence, repression, and persecution push waves of refugees from a country, then the attractions of peace, freedom, and fulfillment would surely pull them back.

If EVD is properly administered, and registration before a certain date is required, it will not lure anyone to this country. While the grant of EVD remains in effect, it will provide protection for those who are entitled to it. When the status is withdrawn, so will that protection be, and with it much of the advantage of remaining in the United States. An individual whose extended voluntary departure status has expired returns to the precarious existence of any illegal entrant.

The government maintains, however, that neither of these extremes—neither the protection of extended voluntary departure nor the precariousness of illegality—is necessary. Rather, it argues, Salvadorans have available to them three other options, which together address all legitimate needs: Salvadorans may apply for refugee status, or an immigrant visa, or, within the United States, for political asylum. Each of these avenues exists, but none responds to the problem.

Refugee status for Central Americans, as we have seen, is reserved only for political prisoners or for employees of the U.S. government. The numbers, even within those groups, given refugee status are minuscule. In fiscal years 1985 and 1986, from all of Latin America, three refugees were admitted from Nicaragua, 1,865 from Cuba. Immigration visas, though available in larger numbers, are allotted to close relatives of U.S. citizens or to those with job skills needed in this country. Far more significant, either refugee status or immigration visas are given to people who wish to leave their countries permanently, who plan to become Americans. The great majority of Salvadorans are asking not for permanent resettlement but for temporary protection.

· What, then, of the final option, political asylum? For most Salvadorans, it is as unattainable a goal as refugee status. They are as thoroughly precluded from one as from the other. Most Salvadorans never apply at all. Between June of 1983 and September of 1986, some 19,207 Salvadorans did ask for political asylum; 528 were granted it, an approval rate of 2.6 percent.[42]

Leonel Gomez was one of the few fortunate Salvadorans to be granted asylum. While in El Salvador, Gomez and Raul Fuviera uncovered a forty-million-dollar corruption scheme and denounced the colonel responsible, in the press, on television, and in the courts. There were eight assassination attempts against the two whistle-blowers. Gomez escaped with his life. Fuviera did not; together with two North American advisors, he was shot to death. Gomez's case was well-known to the American government; yet, when he applied for asylum here, for more than a year and a half, the State Department told Gomez that "they had lost [his] application. They said they knew exactly where it was but that it was lost." Even after the department granted him asylum, it remained uneasy about the decision. "Every time I said something about U.S. policy," Gomez recounted, "I was told in informal ways by junior officers at the State Department, that I was putting my legal status in this country in jeopardy."[43]

A less well-known Salvadoran who applies for asylum has small hope of success. In April of 1985, an American television journalist traveled to El Salvador to complete his research for a series on Central American refugees. David Patterson interviewed officials at all levels and also went to observe, firsthand, the conditions from which the Central Americans had fled. In one village, he arrived unannounced at the house in which a refugee couple had lived. The young boy who answered the door volunteered that the previous occupant had left because "he got an anonymous note that they were going to kill him." When pressed about the note, the boy explained that the former occupant had worked for ISTA, the Salvadoran Agrarian Reform Institute, and that "in that time it was the practice that anonymous notes were given, threatening people that if they did not leave the country they were going to die. But the people did not know who sent them. And then they had to leave the country."[44] Patterson, who had gone to the refugee's home without his knowledge, videotaped the interview and showed it as part of his documentary series. The reporter's affidavit was submitted to the INS together with the Salvadoran's request for asylum.

A few days later, the INS district director sent a form letter that denied asylum because the individual had "failed to establish a well-founded fear of persecution upon return to El Salvador," and, moreover, had based his claim "entirely on unsupported subjective statements," and had "failed to submit any additional evidence."[45]

If, at times, the standard set for Salvadoran asylum seekers seems higher than that set for others, at other times, the standard seems even stricter than that set forth in either the UN protocol or the Refugee Act. In one area of the country, immigration attorneys assert that the judge denies asylum because of the failure of the Salvadoran to show that he *has been persecuted*. The claimant must prove, to the satisfaction of the judge, not that he has a well-founded fear of persecution, but that such persecution has already taken place.[46]

Even the most liberal construction, however, of the basis for an asylum claim demands of Central Americans what most cannot provide and offers them what many do not want. While some Central Americans have been singled out for persecution, most have been caught between contending forces. No orders have been issued for their arrest; their names appear on no death lists. But their villages have been bombed, they have been raped and tortured, their closest family have "disappeared." They seek not political asylum, but apolitical refuge. They need not to become United States citizens, but only to remain here until it is safe for them to return to their homes. They require the temporary safe haven of a grant of extended voluntary departure.

If the government insists that Salvadorans prove that they were singled out for persecution before they came to this country, by the same reasoning, it asserts that deportation need not be withheld because Salvadorans will not be singled out for persecution if they are returned. The fear of violence, it is argued, is generalized, not specific. Once again, a straw man has been bested.

The straw man has even been invested with all the trappings

of a government study. As in Haiti, the State Department conducted its own investigation into the fates of 482 Salvadorans who had been deported from the United States and was able to confirm only one death. The department "found no evidence of mistreatment" of those returned.

As with its study of Haitian returnees, the State Department's methods were far from impeccable. The department, in fact, is itself responsible for casting the most glaring light of doubt on its findings. The report concedes that "of the 482 people on the list, 73 were not interviewed, because it was *too dangerous to travel to their homes*. These people lived in conflictive zones, classified as areas of active fighting." [Emphasis added.][47] Therefore, although it may be unsafe to live in certain areas of El Salvador, the law permits us to return people to these areas, since they will have to confront only generalized violence, not particular persecution.

In any event, the fate of the returnees is of less than pressing concern for the State Department. The *Washington Monthly* quoted then Assistant Secretary Elliott Abrams as saying, in reference to the study, "Given the pressures on the embassy, all the things it has to do, it's a question of how much time they should spend on something that we think is ridiculous."[48]

The American Civil Liberties Union (ACLU) did not consider such labors ridiculous, and embarked on its own study of Salvadorans deported by the INS. Despite the difficulties of tracing these individuals, the ACLU came up with a preliminary list of individuals who had been persecuted when returned; the State Department soon confirmed seven of the cases, among them "three deaths, two violent disappearances, one capture and one unknown fate."[49] As the ACLU observes, however, "The scale of the misery that this preliminary finding reflects is not adequately conveyed by the mere number or by the solidity of the evidence. It is better conveyed by a description of the circumstances of one such incident, which indicate that one of the persons among the seven confirmed cases violently disappeared along with six members of his family, all but one of them children aged from eighteen months to sixteen years old."[50]

Even if one concedes, however, that the violence in El Salvador and Guatemala forces many from their countries, and for the time being makes their return impossible, do not neighboring countries offer them safe haven? And by choosing not to remain in these countries, but to continue on to the U.S., do they not prove that they are economic migrants in pursuit of jobs?

In Central America, wars are not fought only between soldiers, and military raids do not respect borders. Refugees who flee the country are suspected of opposing the government and, therefore, of supporting the guerrillas. Even in flight, there is no safety. Yvonne Dilling was a volunteer in the refugee camps in Honduras when hundreds of refugees from El Salvador, in escape from a military bombing attack, attempted to cross the Lempa River to safety in Honduras. Many of the Salvadorans were unable to swim, and Dilling was carrying babies and young children across the river when she heard the sound of a helicopter.

> The helicopter first swooped down low on the Salvadoran side and started machine-gunning the shoreline. Then it went off down the river, gained height, turned around, swooped down, and fired at the Honduran side. It kept turning, up one side and down the other. . . .
>
> But all of a sudden, miraculously, the helicopter flew off. Not a single person had been directly hit. . . .
>
> I had made maybe ten trips across when we heard the helicopter return. This time I was caught on the Salvadoran side. At the sound of the dadadada, we all started running again. But this side didn't have nearly as many places in which to hide. The only cover available were trees and bushes. So Padre Ramon and I rushed under a tree, like the hundreds of others seeking cover under any bush they could find. I

thought, This is crazy. We are not protected whatsoever. . . .

The helicopter made swoop after swoop. This time, several people had remained in the river. Instead of running up the bank, they had jumped into the water and were hanging onto the ledge of lava rock. Each time the helicopter made a swoop, they ducked under the water. The soldier in the helicopter was incredibly intent on killing people. Over and over again he lay a path of machine gun fire only a foot away from the people in the water. Once he swooped so low that he almost touched the tree tops above us. One little boy was killed. I saw him jump into the water with an arc of bullet holes in his back. He was flailing his arms, still trying to swim while blood was streaming all across his back. Then the water carried him downstream.

Suddenly a bomb exploded within six yards of us. No one was hit, but the air blast covered us with dirt, flying debris, leaves, twigs, and stones. Ramon next to me said, "She is bleeding. I think she must have been killed." He was referring to an older woman on the other side of him who was holding a baby—probably her grandchild. A few minutes later he reached over to take the baby. The woman was dead.

The assault probably lasted twenty minutes, although it seemed like we spent hours under that tree. We could see the soldier leaning out the open helicopter door during a swoop, straining to see where the people were. Then the helicopter rose, made a big turn, gained height and speed, and came back down to fire over the same ground.[51]

The camp that evening held three thousand refugees.

The massacre at the Lempa River was not an isolated instance. Observers in refugee camps in Honduras have reported that both the Salvadoran and the Honduran military harass the refugees, regarding them all as guerrillas. Accusations have frequently been leveled that Honduran security forces arrest the Salvadoran refugees and turn them over to Salvadoran authorities. One group of observers was visiting the La Virtud camp in Honduras, when the cry went out that ORDEN (the Salvadoran right-wing death squad) was removing people. On the road out of the camp, the observers found twelve men armed with M-16s, leading some twenty refugees, their hands bound behind their backs. One of the twenty was a woman, eight months pregnant. Only the threats of the observers that they were from the United States and that they would make the kidnapping known to the world press won the release of the refugees. But when the group returned to the camp, they found the scene being repeated with ten other refugees.

In their testimony before the House of Representatives, the observers asserted that:

> There is unquestionably a campaign of harassment, intim-idation, and murder now being carried on by the Salvadoran National Guard and ORDEN against the Salvadoran refugees in Honduras. This campaign is being waged with the full collaboration of the Honduran armed forces, who together with the Salvadoran armed forces are themselves terrorizing refugees, international relief workers, and Honduran citizens who provide assistance to the refugees.[52]

Although it is frequently argued that such attacks no longer occur, in July of 1986, witnesses reported that at least twenty-seven Nicaraguan Indian refugees were kidnapped, over a period of weeks, from camps in Honduras. American-backed guerrillas were accused of having seized the refugees to silence criticism of the guerrillas and to conscript additional men. In-ternational relief agencies expressed their concern for the safety of the refugees to the American embassy.[53]

Similar atrocities have occurred in other countries of refuge. The UNHCR reported that in April of 1984, "unidentified armed men" completely destroyed the El Chupadero camp in Mexico,

near the Guatemalan border. The attackers killed six Guatemalan refugees, wounded six others.[54]

These are but a few of the raids carried out on refugee camps,
some well-documented, many more unwitnessed by any but
the refugees themselves.[55] A less dramatic, but more pernicious
problem is forced repatriation. Guatemalan refugees in Mexico
are sent back to their country. Salvadorans in Mexico are sent
not to El Salvador, but to Guatemala. The host government, in
short, offers protection either from military incursion or from
refoulement (return to a country in which one may be persecuted) at its discretion.[56]

So too are the refugee's freedom and level of subsistence
ungoverned by any constant standard. Honduras, for example,
welcomes Miskito Indians and gives them the rights to move
about freely, to work, and to resettle permanently. Honduras
confines Salvadorans and Guatemalans, on the other hand, to
guarded refugee camps. Mexico, which has the largest number
of refugees, considers Guatemalans to be refugees, but not Salvadorans. Thus, Guatemalans are eligible for some assistance,
Salvadorans get none.[57] For most Central Americans, protection
is not a certainty.

If the political position of the Central American refugees is
precarious, their economic position is even more so. The receiving countries of the region—Honduras, Costa Rica, Nicaragua, and Mexico—for the past several years have been re-
considering and even reversing the generous asylum policies of
the past. While the economies of these countries dwindle, the
numbers of refugees swell. As conditions deteriorate in host
countries, moreover, the citizens of those countries become
increasingly dissatisfied and, it is feared, the presence of politically dissident refugees could threaten the existing political
order.

International organizations care for only a small proportion
of all the refugees. And such care is, at best, minimal. The
UNHCR, for example, estimated that it assisted over one hundred

thousand refugees in the region in 1985. Its budget for that year was $25 million, or less than $250 per refugee.[58] Most of the refugees try to support themselves, after some fashion, but in countries which export large numbers of their own labor forces, foreign workers cannot be welcome.

Many Central Americans, persecuted in their own countries and pursued abroad, forced either to live in closed, guarded camps or without protection as foreign migrants, continue their journey north and illegally enter the United States. It is the very desire of these refugees to achieve independence, to regain a measure of self-respect, that leads the Department of State to its conclusion that they are not refugees at all but "illegal immigrants."[59] Genuine refugees, the department feels, are those who remain under the protection of the UNHCR; all others, when they strike out on their own, forfeit that status. There is, however, a single criterion by which one is judged to be a refugee: the reason for which one left one's country of origin. The refugee has been *driven* from his country. If, subsequently, he is *drawn* by more stable conditions elsewhere, this in no way negates his statelessness, his inability, if only temporarily, to return in safety to his homeland.

Among those who work with refugees, it is a truism that as a group they are highly motivated, adaptable, and possess a strong will to survive. These very qualities—particularly the will to live—drive them forth. Central American refugees, in common with all other refugees, possess these characteristics, but that which insures the survival of the refugee can threaten the stability of the receiving country. According to the State Department, a refugee who is not subject to regulation, to control, ceases to be a refugee. The department follows an interesting line of reasoning: ". . . most of those who come to the United States are not the women, children, and older persons who make up the bulk of the refugee groups receiving assistance in the region, but, rather, young, unaccompanied male migrants primarily motivated by a search for jobs."[60]

It would be just as easy to look at the population of the refugee camps and make a different assertion: only those who are unable to provide for themselves remain within the care of the UNHCR. Strong, proud, independent, those who can continue on toward some measure of independence do so. Along their way, they discover that a person whom one agency will protect, another agency will deport; a refugee in one country is an economic migrant in another.

The DeConcini-Moakley bill is a less-than-perfect response to the Central American refugees. It leaves many questions unanswered. If, for example, the violence continues in El Salvador, how do we provide for those who are forced from their country and into ours *after* the date on which the bill is enacted? And what of refugees from Guatemala? From other countries that now, or may in the near future, generate refugee flows? But if it is flawed, DeConcini-Moakley does force us to recognize the problems and, one hopes, to turn our attention to possible solutions.

In Southeast Asia, the United States has recognized that pressures on first-asylum countries can build to levels at which not only the welfare of the refugees, but also the stability of the host countries is at risk. We have, thus, assured the receiving countries of Southeast Asia that we will share the burden with them, accepting substantial numbers of first-asylum refugees for resettlement. Such has not been the case in Central America, where, we maintain, the burden under which the asylum countries stagger is, although heavy, nonetheless for them a welcome one. One wonders how long it will be before they look northward and wonder whether for us the burden might be, if less welcome, at least somewhat lighter.

The case of the Central American refugee deserves a more considered response from the United States than it has so far received, not only for the sakes of the refugees themselves, but because the problems with which they confront us portend the refugee problems of the future. If, as the United Nations has opined, tomorrow's refugees will more likely be fleeing generalized violence than persecution, then we must begin today to prepare for that eventuality. A refugee policy that extends protection only to those who flee particular persecution and rejects those who flee political unrest, that offers only permanent resettlement but not temporary haven, that can plan for refugee movements on the other side of the globe, but ignores those at our very threshold, is destined to be overtaken, perhaps even overwhelmed and unraveled, before the end of the decade.

The question that policymakers should be asking now is not how to prevent mass movements of refugees into our country. The questions, rather, are much broader and not susceptible of unilateral solution by any one country. We should be asking what our obligation is to the victims of generalized violence. Should we offer temporary protection? If so, to whom? And how do we offer it? What is our obligation to our neighbors in the hemisphere? To the rest of the world? And what is the obligation of other refugee-receiving countries toward us?

It is no longer possible to shut and barricade the gate. The pressures from without will only lead to the collapse of the entire wall.

While the Congress deliberates whether to grant extended voluntary departure to Salvadorans and Guatemalans, years pass and the INS continues to deny them asylum. Some Americans have decided that they cannot temporize while human lives hang in the balance. They have chosen, instead, to create an institution that they call sanctuary—a kind of underground asylum system, with its own screening, admissions, and resettlement. Sanctuary is illegal according to the strictures of statutory law, but quite in accord with what its supporters feel to be the precepts of moral law. Small as the sanctuary movement is, many in the American public have received it with no small measure of sympathy; others regard the movement as more of a threat than the Central American refugees.

7 The Unprotected: The Remedies of Conscience

The sanctuary movement had its beginnings during another perceived threat to American refugee law—the Mariel crisis. With all attention turned, in the spring of 1980, to the Cubans and Haitians arriving in Florida, few Americans noticed a second movement of refugees—from Central America—at our southern border. Suddenly, in July of 1980, as the American welcome for the Cuban freedom-seekers had become hostility toward Castro's undesirables, a single, small tragedy elsewhere in the country commanded our compassion. In the Arizona desert, a *coyote*—a smuggler of aliens—having collected his fees from twenty-six Salvadorans, abandoned them without water in the Arizona desert, just outside of Tucson. Half the Salvadorans died. The survivors, when Border Patrol officers found them, reported that they had drunk aftershave, deodorant, even their own urine in their efforts to stay alive.[1]

Churches in Tucson took in the refugees, who were in need of medical and emotional assistance. Church members were horrified by the stories they now heard from the refugees, stories of the conditions that had forced them into flight. When the survivors were arrested and the process of deportation initiated, churches in the Tucson area rallied to their support, raising the bond money to obtain release of the Salvadorans and providing the legal assistance that would enable them to plead their cases for political asylum. The thirteen survivors of the desert ordeal were the catalyst, bringing together many of the churches in Tucson in an organized response to the growing numbers of refugees.[2]

However irritating to the INS the activities of the religious community might have been, those activities were all legal. Not so, however, the actions that the INS now began to take. As it had been with the Haitians in South Florida, the INS was now bent on deporting the Central Americans as swiftly as possible. It began curtailing the right of detainees to due process, including their right to speak with legal representatives. Then in May of 1981, the INS tried to restrict Jim Corbett.

Jim Corbett is a series of anomalies: he is a Quaker and an "unbeliever"; with a graduate degree in philosophy from Harvard, he worked for three decades as a rancher in the Sonora Desert, until arthritis crippled him. Corbett is tough and contentious and brilliant and moral.

While he was at the Nogales jail, interviewing a Salvadoran, and having him sign the G-28 form that named Corbett as his legal representative, Corbett learned of other Salvadorans in detention and left the jail to obtain more G-28s. When he returned, Corbett was told that all the Salvadorans had moved; the INS refused to tell him where they were.[3] After some inquiries, Corbett discovered that paralegals were being afforded the same evasive treatment at El Centro, an INS detention center four hours away in southern California.

Now, as quickly as the Salvadorans could be bonded out to await their asylum hearings, Jim Corbett began bringing them to his two-room former garage. Soon Corbett's garage was packed with more than twenty refugees, but there were many others, still in detention, who would shortly be deported to El Salvador. Corbett is equally at home on both sides of the border and, along with visiting American jails and detention camps, Corbett had also been visiting Mexican jails. There he found Salvadorans with strong asylum cases who, when they had tried to ask for asylum at the U.S. border, had simply been turned over to Mexican authorities, to be incarcerated and taken back to El Salvador.[4]

For Corbett, the dictates of his faith had come into conflict with the practices of his government. To close his eyes to those practices, or even simply to protest them, however volubly, was impossible. He wrote, "We can take our stand with the oppressed, or we can take our stand with organized oppression. We can serve the Kingdom, or we can serve the kingdoms of this world—but we cannot do both." He concluded, "When the government itself sponsors the crucifixion of entire peoples and then makes it a felony to shelter those seeking refuge, law-abiding protest merely trains us to live with atrocity."[5]

Corbett had decided that he would no longer tolerate the atrocities; no longer could he shelter within the law while undocumented refugees found no shelter. Calling upon his extensive knowledge of the desert, and of how to survive in it, Corbett became a *coyote*, an unpaid *coyote* for Central American refugees.

But Corbett needed help, and he turned for that help to John Fife, pastor of Southside Presbyterian Church in Tucson. Both Fife's own background and the background of his church and the congregation led them to join with Corbett in his "sanctuary" plan. While John Fife was still a seminarian, his professors, some of whom came from Eastern Europe, drove home to him that the church had failed in its responsibilities during the Holocaust. They told Fife repeatedly that the church must never allow that tragedy to recur. He had tried in every way he knew to fulfill the obligations of the church toward the refugees of the eighties—the Salvadorans and Guatemalans. The ways he knew were legal ways—the community had spent over one million dollars just on bond money—but these ways had failed. When Jim Corbett began bringing undocumented refugees across the border, Fife decided to assist him. He turned to his congregation for their support and commitment. The congregation, too, had a history that impelled them to the task.

Southside Presbyterian has an ideal location, a block from the main highway, close to downtown, yet isolated. The congregation began as an Indian mission church early in the century. Later, the church hired a Hispanic pastor, then a black, and finally Fife. With each new pastor, another ethnic element joined the congregation. The newest members are the refugees in sanctuary, who, Fife feels, "bring the Christian faith to the Christian congregation." In recent years, three members of the congregation have gone to Central America to live there with Central American church people whose lives are at risk, who have received death notices. They hope that the presence of North Americans will help to protect the Central American, will deter the security forces. Southside Presbyterian has not only brought refugees under the aegis of the church, it has sent the sanctuary of the church to the refugees.[6]

Other churches—in California, Washington, D.C., Ohio, and New York—quickly joined Southside in its intention. Together, the one hundred or so churches formed a network to offer to Central American refugees sanctuary, legal assistance, and support, and to lobby in Washington for a halt to the deportations. On March 24, 1982, the second anniversary of the assassination of Salvadoran Archbishop Oscar Romero, across the country churches that had joined the movement made formal and public announcements of their decisions.

Each congregation that has joined the sanctuary movement has done so in its own way and for its own reasons. Joseph Weizenbaum, rabbi of a Reform Jewish congregation in Tucson that has declared sanctuary, first identified with the Salvadorans because his own father had been an undocumented entrant, a stowaway on a ship who had been detained and was about to be deported when a relative intervened. Weizenbaum, too, carries the weight of Holocaust in his memory. Other relatives perished. He believes that " 'We will not forget,' 'Never again' only mean something if we serve the living, not the dead." Weizenbaum says, "It is the same drama in the 1980s. The Jews

now are the Guatemalans and Salvadorans. The U.S. government acts in such a way that they die." And though not of the
same faith as the refugees, it is Weizenbaum's Jewish faith, he
says, that instructs him to "know the heart of the stranger."[7]

Each congregation decides alone, and after lengthy study and
discussion, whether to offer support to the sanctuary movement, but in a very short time after the network of churches
had made its public declarations, increasing numbers of people
began to inquire how their congregations might also participate.
The Tucson office, staffed by volunteers, was unable to conduct
such outreach work, and so it turned for help to the Chicago
Religious Task Force on Central America (CRTFCA).

The Chicago Religious Task Force was formed at about the
same time as the Tucson Ecumenical Council Task Force, in
1981. Like its Tucson counterpart, it was responding to a sudden
revelation of atrocities being committed in El Salvador. But
Tucson was on the border and the revelations there came from
the refugees themselves. Chicago's witnesses were church people—missionaries, nuns, priests—who had seen their churches
attacked, parishioners and churchworkers slaughtered. The gal-
vanizing event for the Chicago group was the killing, in December of 1980, of four American churchwomen.[8] Thus, while
Tucson faced the reality of the refugees each day, Chicago was
more remote, both in distance and in approach. While Tucson
took on the task of immediate assistance to Central Americans,
Chicago addressed itself to long-term changes in United States
policy toward Central America.

Because its work was with opinion, and not with people,
Chicago could be combative, even shocking. Certain that it
would be fruitless to try to influence or even educate policymakers, the Chicago group opted for the dramatic, if ineffectual,
gesture: the planting of white crosses bearing the names of
Salvadoran dead on a campus where President Reagan was to
appear; coloring of the Chicago River with red (biodegradable)
dye, to symbolize the bloodshed in Central America.[9]

While Jim Corbett was escorting a refugee family to sanctuary in a church in Chicago, he asked the Chicago Religious Task Force if it would act as a liaison to the churches across the country that wanted to know more about sanctuary. Chicago was reluctant at first, feeling that its energies were best directed to political action, but in the end, Corbett prevailed. In Corbett's words, "The contrasting styles, perspectives, and functions of the Tucson refugee support groups and the Chicago Religious Task Force complemented and reinforced each other. The sanctuary movement bloomed."[10]

Indeed, the movement has bloomed. By March of 1987, the number of declared sanctuaries had grown to three hundred and seventy-nine. Most of these declarations were by congregations, universities and community groups; there were also twenty-two city councils, twenty-eight national bodies (many of those religious), and two states, New Mexico and New York.

As the movement grew, however, its two branches grew further apart. Separating Chicago and Tucson was the critical question of whether sanctuary was essentially a religious-humanitarian, or a political-activist movement. The two factions remain true to their origins. The Tucson group still sees, as primary, the needs of the refugees. Jim Corbett's goal is to make the refugee laws work. He does not want to provoke a confrontation between church and state in which "the refugee laws get ground up in between." Instead, he prefers to look for "possibilities." Corbett does not have a platform. Rather, he begins with the refugees themselves, working to give them every possible choice. In Arizona, for example, the INS does not permit newly arrived refugees to file affirmatively, to file an application for political asylum as soon as they enter the country. Instead, they must wait in detention for their deportation hearings and then apply before an immigration judge. With the option of affirmative filing closed, few refugees will voluntarily turn themselves over to the INS to be incarcerated. Instead, they try to avoid being caught. One of Corbett's goals is to persuade the district director of the INS to reinstate affirmative filing.[11] The Tucson people say with great conviction that if Congress would pass bills awarding extended voluntary departure to Salvadorans and Guatemalans, their movement would disappear entirely.

Chicago, on the other hand, will persist in its fight until the United States withdraws from Central America. "It was the moral claim of the martyred church of Central America, even more than the presence of refugees in our midst," they assert, "that propelled the CRTFCA into the sanctuary movement."[12] For Chicago, there can be no accommodation. They see any compromise as a flight from reform; they say energies and attention directed to the problems of refugees in the United States necessarily deflect the attack on root problems in Central America. The district director of INS in Chicago asked Joseph Cardinal Bernadin for help in documenting the asylum claims of undocumented persons. He suggested that their names be submitted to the cardinal, who would then ask church officials in Central America to supply corroborating evidence of the individual's persecution. The CRTFCA branded the proposal "collaboration" with the "enemy" which would, additionally, lend credibility to United States policies in Central America.[13] Chicago, thus, stresses confrontation with the government; Tucson, cooperation whenever possible, evasion when not.

It is common, even within the movement, to speak of Tucson and Chicago, but each name represents a much larger geographic area than is indicated. Included within the Tucson designation are all the states that border Mexico—Texas, New Mexico, California, as well as Arizona—the states that actually provide "first asylum" to the refugees. Chicago refers to the inland locations that offer sanctuary along an underground railroad. At least once, differences between the two factions have threatened to sunder the movement, but, in part because they need to present a common defense against the assaults of the Justice Department, they have remained together.

Just as there are two factions within the movement, there

are two types of sanctuary: public and what might be called protective sanctuary. The former serves political ends, the latter, humanitarian. Of every twenty refugees the sanctuary movement helps, only one will go into public sanctuary, to tell his story to the American people. The other nineteen, although the movement will help them, will remain in hiding. Jim Corbett, for example, never raises the issue of sanctuary with a refugee whom he is assisting because, Corbett explains, he does not want the refugee to feel that to get help he must make his case public.[14] The Tucson Refugee Support Group declares that it will "aid refugees according to our estimate of their level of need, regardless of their political usefulness or whether they wish to go into public sanctuary." Reinforcing its position that its primary goal is assistance to the refugees, not defiance of United States policy, is the admonition to participants that "if Salvadorans or Guatemalans can survive where they are, please do not encourage them to come to the United States."[15] Not the refugee's political usefulness, but his need determines the Tucson Refugee Support Group's response.

The needs of the refugees can be very great, far greater than the few people working in the movement can respond to. The sanctuary leaders, therefore, screen all refugees so that they may provide assistance to those with the greatest need, those who run a greater than average risk of being murdered, tortured, violated in some way if they are returned home. In short, the sanctuary workers look for precisely those refugees who meet the standard of persecution set forth in the UN protocol.

One of the ironies of the sanctuary movement is that, from initial screening, through "admission," "reception," and "resettlement," it functions as a kind of shadow refugee program. In an exact parallel to the recommendations of the UN, and of the INS for overseas processing of approved refugee groups, sanctuary workers do not demand that the refugee provide documentation. They look, instead, for a credible story, remaining alert for possible indications of falsehood. In many cases, however, the refugees are able to present documentation, either from the UNHCR in Mexico City or letters obtained from the International Red Cross when they were released from prison. Corbett insists that nearly all of the refugees actually in sanctuary do have proof of their imprisonment or torture. He tells of one refugee in Rochester whose eardrums were damaged while he was in Mariona prison, in San Salvador, where electrodes were placed in his ears as a form of torture. A woman in Seattle was held, tortured, and raped; some of her children were killed. Both refugees have documentation.[16]

The first step, therefore, in the sanctuary process, as in the official process, is to determine which refugees will be "resettled" in the United States. Where officially recognized refugees are often flown to refugee processing centers and then to the United States, sanctuary refugees travel to a series of safe houses, then are met in the United States, not at a port of entry by an INS official, but in the desert by a sanctuary worker who helps him avoid the INS. Within the United States, the "resettlement agency" is an individual congregation, which uses its own resources to meet the immediate needs of the refugee. In private sanctuary, just as in public resettlement, the goal is the self-sufficiency of the refugee, but in sanctuary, most times this means easing the refugee into the underground community.

The most serious obstacle to the successful resettlement of the sanctuary refugees is that many of them suffer from what therapists have come to call "on-going stress syndrome." The stress is not, as for other refugees, posttraumatic, but ongoing: they remain hunted people. And haunted.

Just such a hunted person was a Guatemalan woman in sanctuary in Tucson. The daughter of a skilled craftsman, and married at fifteen, she had never left the Guatemala City area until, at thirty, she was forced to run. Her husband, who had kept the books for a union, was arrested and tortured, but would not reveal where the books were kept, so the authorities came after the woman. She went into hiding in Guatemala City, but kept searching for her husband in hospitals, in morgues. Several times she was nearly caught. Finally, she fled to Mexico City, but there she was caught by Mexican immigration and dumped in jail for several days, where she was repeatedly raped, then left at the Guatemalan border. Badly injured, she returned to hiding until she was able to travel north once again. This time, she was taken into the home of a sanctuary worker, a widow with grown children (most of the actual work of the movement is done by women) to whom she became a surrogate daughter. On the night that the INS came to arrest her, the young woman was not at home, and so managed to avoid capture, but she had to go underground once again, convinced that she is being hunted. She is. She is also being given psychotherapy.

Because most of the Central American refugees are like the Guatemalan woman, in their fears either for themselves or for family members left behind, very few go into public sanctuary. Also, because not only Salvadorans and Guatemalans, but also Nicaraguans lack safe haven, many within the sanctuary movement have been helping those refugees as well. The weight of the work of the movement, then, is humanitarian, not political. Public sanctuary, in which the refugee goes before the American people to speak out against U.S. policy in Central America, is but one aspect of the movement.

Not every refugee wants or is even fit to enter public sanctuary. There would seem to be a contradiction between the condition of being a refugee and the characteristics required for public sanctuary. A refugee is the victim of persecution—imprisonment, torture, rape; he may have witnessed the barbaric mutilation and killing of neighbors and family. To speak at all of what he has witnessed is difficult; to speak out in public impossible. Still others, because they escaped the most brutal punishments, fear reprisals against family or co-workers left behind. They too are afraid to speak. To become a refugee in public sanctuary is to devote oneself to a new calling, a calling that requires prodigious amounts of emotional and physical strength.

When a refugee is brought across the border, he is never asked about public sanctuary. Some, however, have heard of the work and want to participate. For those refugees, a second screening process takes place. For some time Sister Darlene Nicgorski, who is affiliated with the CRTF, decided who was suitable to be placed in the underground railroad, to arrive finally at a receiving congregation somewhere in the country.

Sister Darlene, a Maryknoll nun, has a strong kinship with the refugees. She tells her story flatly, seemingly without emotion. She had gone with her order to Guatemala and was working with the Indians there, teaching them hygiene and literacy, the latter an activity not approved by the government, when, on July 1, 1981, their priest was murdered, shot. This was a warning to the nuns, and they closed their school. Sister Darlene went to a refugee camp in Honduras, and there she heard other refugees tell their terrible stories. Forced by illness to return to the United States, Sister Darlene here learned of the sanctuary movement and shortly thereafter joined the Chicago Religious Task Force. Until her later arrest and trial with the other Arizona sanctuary leaders, she worked full-time out of Tucson.[17]

The sanctuary movement functions, then, on three levels. On the immediate level, it tries to assist individual refugees and to shield them from deportation. On a more distant level, the movement is working to influence American refugee policies and the practices of the INS. The bill to grant EVD to Salvadorans, for example, was introduced into the Congress at the urging of the sanctuary movement. Finally, for the long term, they are pressuring for a change in United States policies in Central America, since such changes will help to relieve some of the causes of the refugee problem.

Probably the most widespread and basic criticism leveled against the sanctuary movement is that its position on Central America is a political position and therefore belies the claim of the movement that it is humanitarian. Chicago replies to this quite cogently that it is moral blindness to assist only the refugees in our midst, while closing our eyes to what caused them—and hundreds of thousands whom we will never see—to become refugees. One may argue, as Chicago does, that the United States is the major cause of repression and civil war in Central America, or one may believe, as others do, that there is a confluence of causes, of which United States foreign policy is only one. Nevertheless, the point is well taken. It is not enough to administer first aid while the building continues to burn and many are struggling to escape.

The sanctuary movement has given rise to some vocal opposition, opposition of two kinds. There are those in the American public who feel that no matter how compelling the reason, the law must not be broken. There are also those who argue that the reasons have no compulsion, that the actual foundation of the movement is not compassion for refugees but an attempt to subvert our foreign policy, perhaps even our democratic system.

The law-abiding come from every segment of the American public. There is, for example, the woman who served as foreman of the jury that found eleven church workers in Tucson guilty of smuggling aliens. A devout Christian who each day during the trial read the Bible for guidance, Catherine Shaeffer found her guidance in the dictum, "Render therefore unto Caesar the things which are Caesar's, and unto God the things that are God's." She interprets that sentence to mean, "You can protest your lot on this earth, but in the end, you have to respect your government and its laws."[18] A few years earlier, the archbishop of Minneapolis-St. Paul, John R. Roach—at the time the president of the National Conference of Catholic Bishops—was less fatalistic, but equally respectful of the law. He argued that "we make progress by changing laws and not breaking them."[19]

The sanctuary participants are not willing breakers of the law. As individuals, they are most striking for their solidity; taken together, they might very well have assembled for a town meeting or a high-school fundraiser. They are law-abiding people.

A. Bates Butler, III, is not only law-abiding, but law-enforcing. His father had been lawyer and judge and a special agent of the FBI for twenty-one years. Butler himself served in the U.S. Capitol Police while attending law school, and later served as county and then U.S. attorney in Arizona, during which time he prosecuted alien smuggling cases and directed the prosecution of hundreds of others. When his church was asked if it would support the sanctuary movement, he and his father felt they could not engage in civil disobedience. Both Butlers, father and son, have since changed their minds and now support sanctuary. Although Butler does not "like to advocate positions of civil disobedience," he believes that "as Christians we have a higher responsibility. We need to see that our government follows the law."[20]

But for the second group of opponents, all questions of law and lawbreaking are immaterial. They see a far greater danger in sanctuary's challenge to United States foreign policy in Central America. These opponents insist that the humanitarian issues are no more than a smokescreen, that there is no reason, other than economic opportunism, for Salvadorans to come to the United States, there being no longer any danger in El Salvador to civilians, thanks to "the success of U.S. military training and human-rights policies."[21] The only violence in El Salvador, they contend, is that fomented by the leftist insurgents, whose cause the sanctuary movement espouses. Sanctuary is, in the words of the Institute on Religion and Democracy (a conservative Christian group), "primarily a means to undermine U.S. opposition to Marxist-Leninist movements in Central America."[22]

These attacks on sanctuary respond solely to the publications of the Chicago Religious Task Force, publications that are significantly more strident in tone than are the positions of most people in the movement. Moreover, even the CRTF, while it would like to see a restructuring of the social order in the United States, does not advocate or even contemplate a revolution in this country. Yet one writer has extrapolated from the former a committment to the latter. Rael Jean Isaac writes, "To the movement's leaders, sanctuary is ultimately a way to create revolution in *this* country: to raise the consciousness of the average church member, radicalize him, and prepare him to form Christian base communities on the Latin model, which will then lead to the overthrow of the established order."[23]

Even those critics who stop short of accusing the movement of fomenting revolution, however, are angered by the movement's opposition to a foreign policy whose avowed goal is to stop the spread of Communism. Not least among the angry is the Reagan administration. An assistant secretary of state, William H. Ball, III, in a letter to all the members of Congress, declared that the sanctuary movement "*is disturbing*," because it opposes "U.S. intervention in Central America."[24] And it was probably the threat to foreign policy, rather than to our refugee laws, that led the Justice Department to investigate secretly, arrest, and then try the leaders of the sanctuary movement.

If the movement was to be stopped, it would have to be through the prosecution and eventual sentencing of its leaders. The leaders of the sanctuary movement, however, could not be arrested or arraigned for their beliefs. But if their speech was protected, their actions—even humanitarian actions—were not. The smuggling of aliens into the United States is not an act protected by the Constitution.

The first arrests of sanctuary leaders took place in Texas, in February of 1984. In San Benito, Texas, just a few miles from the Rio Grande River that separates Mexico from the United States, Central Americans were being housed in a simple, white-frame building named for the martyred Salvadoran archbishop. Although no one attempted to disguise its function, Casa Oscar Romero was not, strictly speaking, a public sanctuary. Its primary function was to offer shelter to the Central American refugees, rather than to spirit them out of the valley.[25] Hal Boldin, the INS district director in Harlingen, Texas, made a clear distinction between the sanctuary movement, which to him was a euphemism for the illegal transportation of aliens, and the giving of shelter to those same aliens. To Boldin, a letter-of-the-law man, transporting aliens was a violation of the law, sheltering them was not.[26] (Harboring aliens can be a crime, if the intention is to keep them out of reach of the government.)

Thus, when Stacey Merkt, a volunteer at Casa Romero, was arrested, it was for the crime of transporting aliens, two Salvadorans whom she was taking to San Antonio to apply for political asylum. (She had decided that they ought not to apply for asylum locally because the INS office there had begun to arrest and deport Salvadorans who asked for asylum.) During the months of her trial and subsequent conviction and probationary sentence, Stacey Merkt became a representation of the sanctuary movement, her face instantly recognizable to any reader of newspapers or watcher of television.

In April, Jack Elder, the former high school teacher who ran Casa Romero, was also arrested on charges of transporting illegal aliens. He, however, was arrested not in the act, but subsequently, and in Casa Romero proper. The refugees in shelter there were not arrested, and Casa Romero continued to operate. One month earlier, Philip Conger, who worked for the sanctuary movement in Arizona, was also arrested, but his charges were dropped on a technicality.

The three arrests were only a foreshadowing of the government's larger intentions. Even as the INS was proclaiming that it was not "going to go out and bust down the doors of churches,"[27] the service was crawling into those churches through open windows. Four undercover agents of the INS were working within the sanctuary movement, all the while wearing concealed tape recorders and accumulating the evidence that ten months later would result in the arrests and indictments of sixteen members of the movement, and the naming of twenty others as co-conspirators.

The undercover investigation, code-named "Operation So-journer," used convicted smugglers of undocumented workers who traded jail sentences for work as informers for the INS. It was not difficult for Jesús Cruz and Salomón Graham to infiltrate the movement. They offered to help and their offers were accepted. In no time, Jesús Cruz had become a trusted worker in the movement, attending Bible sessions and planning meetings, working on both sides of the border to bring refugees to safety.

For some time, Cruz lived in the house of María del Socorro de Aguilar, a sixty-year-old widowed grandmother and a Mexican citizen, whose comfortably furnished home at the top of a steep, unpaved hill in Nogales, Mexico, had been the last shelter for many Central Americans before they crossed the border. Cruz spent so much time with Socorro that people began to joke that he ought to marry her. Instead, he turned over to the INS the tapes that led to her arrest. Jesús Cruz was everywhere, and with him went his tape recorder. He was in the Sacred Heart Church, in Nogales, Arizona, when he heard a Salvadoran woman tell how her daughters had been raped by men of the Salvadoran army; the six-year-old died. He heard another woman tell of the telephone call she received one day, instructing her to pick up her children at school. The army had gone to the school in search of two guerrillas. The woman found her three children in a pile with sixty others, all of them dead.[28]

When the informers had finished their work, they had one hundred hours of tapes, forty thousand pages of transcript evidence. The tapes, however, would not be presented in court. One possible reason for the government's decision not to use the tapes might have been that the recordings were made without a warrant. (An undercover agent needs no warrant, but he must obtain one before he uses any sort of recording device.[29]) In one of the tortuous twists of the case, it was the defense lawyers, rather than the prosecution, who might have benefitted from the publication of the tapes; on them was much testimony on conditions in Central America, testimony that corroborated the stories Jesús Cruz had heard.

Operation Sojourner was an expensive (one estimate has placed the cost at $3.5 million), elaborate (the sixty arrests were made simultaneously in cities as far from Tucson as Seattle and Rochester), and time-consuming (the investigation took ten months; the trial itself would drag on for more than seven months) operation to stop what the government characterized as an alien-smuggling ring that, by any standards, had brought in a very small number of aliens.

The government's announcement of its purpose was as disingenuous as its investigation. No one, even in the government, seriously believed that a group of clergymen, nuns, and church workers had banded together for the sole purpose of running in undocumented workers. It was not immigration policy, but foreign policy that had to be defended. The government meant the sanctuary trial to be a political trial, a trial not to punish lawbreakers but to silence dissenting opinion. The sanctuary movement was leading the voice of opposition, in the Congress, in the news media, in the churches and public forums. The sanctuary trial was meant to affirm administration policy, and its impact was meant to be felt by many more people than the defendants. In furtherance of this end, the government could not allow the challenge to foreign policy to be raised anew in the courtroom.

The defenses permitted the sanctuary workers were severely restricted. Judge Earl H. Carroll did not permit the defendants to testify on conditions in Central America, or on the political situation there. He did not permit them to introduce evidence that the United States had violated international law regarding the protection of refugees. The judge did not permit them to present evidence that the government had violated the Refugee Act of 1980. Nor, finally, did he permit them to argue, in their own behalf, that they had acted according to the moral dictates of their religions.

That the indicted church workers were not permitted even to discuss their religious motivations was, perhaps, the most critical suppression. In the earlier trial of Jack Elder in Texas, Judge Hayden Head, Jr., had found that Elder's motives did arise from the practice of his religion. The judge ruled:

> There is arguably a basis in Catholicism to demonstrate the activity charged in the indictment could fall within the religious beliefs of a seriously committed and practicing Catholic. This court rules they can.[30]

But Judge Head found further that the need of government to enforce its immigration laws carried greater weight than did Elder's religious obligations. This was the heart of the issue: the conflict between the demands of individual conscience and the necessity for government control.

In the Tucson trial, with all lines of defense closed to them, the attorneys for the defendants rested their case without calling a single witness. All the church workers were found guilty. The government seemed to have triumphed; in reality, it had misjudged. Throughout the many months of the trial, the movement had to redirect a considerable part of its energies and resources from the protection of refugees to its own protection. Nevertheless, during that same period, public support for sanctuary increased. Just two weeks into the trial, the general assembly of the Union of American Hebrew Congregations voted to urge its nearly eight hundred constituent congregations to support the movement, despite "serious legal implications of some forms of sanctuary."[31] In June of 1986, as the trial drew to a close, New York State joined New Mexico and became "a region of sanctuary for Guatemalan and Salvadoran refugees,"[32] a mere gesture, perhaps, but one laden with symbolic significance.

The most significant gesture of all came from Amnesty International, the Nobel prize–winning organization that works to free political prisoners and prisoners of conscience. Amnesty International took the position that, although the United States had the right to enforce its immigration laws, when it returned Salvadorans and Guatemalans to their countries—where, Amnesty felt, they risked "death, 'disappearance,' torture, and imprisonment"—the United States was not complying with its international treaty obligations. Amnesty International concluded that the sanctuary defendants had been "convicted of violating laws which, in their current practice, directly facilitate the violation of human rights to which the organization is opposed." Were they sentenced to prison, Amnesty International intended to "adopt [the defendants] as 'Prisoners of Conscience' and . . . campaign for their unconditional release."[33] A few months thereafter, Stacey Merkt, the young woman in Texas whose first sentence had been suspended, was arrested and convicted a second time. This sentence was not suspended and, on February 25, 1987, Amnesty International adopted Stacey Merkt as a prisoner of conscience, declaring that "when she assisted the Salvadorans those refugees could have been in danger of human rights violations . . . including arbitrary seizure, torture, 'disappearance,' and extrajudicial execution, if returned to their country of origin."[34]

The defendants in the Tucson trial were not sentenced to prison. Judge Carroll, who had, throughout the trial, shown no sympathy for the defendants or for their arguments, declined to impose prison terms on any of the convicted church workers. He gave all suspended sentences.

As a political trial, the trial of the sanctuary workers had failed, because the movement they represented is more than a political movement. To be sure there are, within the movement, those who respond to the government's equation of foreign policy with refugee policy by offering protection only to those refugees who *oppose* U.S. foreign policy in Central America. But they are not the entire movement, and their position is not accepted by the entire movement.

The Covenant of Sanctuary, which all participating bodies sign, ascribes no political responsibility for what it calls "the vicious and devastating wars in Central America." But it does place a religious responsibility upon its signers, who must affirm the belief "that communities of faith are now being called again to obey God by providing sanctuary to the refugees among us." Nor do the covenant communities attempt to hide behind a veil of religious immunity, but rather "recognize that legal consequences may result from our actions."

Precisely because every individual in the sanctuary movement has accepted the possible "legal consequences," and has decided that those consequences are of secondary importance, the arrests and trials did not intimidate the leaders or slow the momentum of the movement. After his arrest, Father Antonio Clark expressed concern not for himself, but for the refugees. "We have to be more careful now," he said, "not because we might go to jail, but because the refugees might get hurt. How are we going to help them if our avenues get cut off?"[35]

In subsequent months, the movement's leaders discovered that there were many others willing to help the refugees. And even beyond the participating communities, the American public was becoming increasingly knowledgeable about the movement and its work. The concept of sanctuary, which five years earlier had been foreign even to those who worked with refugees, had now entered the common vocabulary. And sanctuary, and the values it upheld, was becoming a force to counter the pressures of restrictionism.

By 1986, the sanctuary movement had won some small victories. Support in the Congress for a bill to grant extended voluntary departure to Salvadorans was increasing. Its cosponsors (170 in the House and 26 in the Senate) included members of both parties, some of whom supported United States policies in Central America. Cities across the country, and two states, had declared themselves sanctuary sites—a gesture with more symbolism than strength, since neither cities nor states enforce immigration laws—but an important gesture nonetheless. The declaration of sanctuary by a political entity is an act of defiance, an assertion that local officials and voters oppose federal refugee policies.

Some cities have found that their defiance quickly becomes not only symbolic, but real. As the Rochester, New York, city council prepared to vote on whether to become a sanctuary city, the INS stepped in to arrest a Salvadoran who, with his family, had been in sanctuary in a local church for the past two years. Alejandro Gomez, who had been imprisoned without charges in El Salvador, had applied for political asylum and was free on three thousand dollars bail, when he was once again arrested and his bail raised to fifty thousand dollars. The INS explained that it had information that Gomez was a national-security risk. The Rochester Sanctuary Committee said the arrest was an attempt to defeat the sanctuary vote. Nevertheless, it raised the bond money, and Gomez was released.[36] The city council, voting to declare Rochester a sanctuary, was not intimidated, but the Gomez family was. Shortly before their scheduled deportation hearing, the Gomezes left the country. A note written by Mrs. Gomez explained that they no longer had faith that asylum would be granted, and they feared for the lives of their children if they were deported.[37]

Other asylum applicants have been more fortunate. While the sanctuary trial was in progress in Phoenix, Arizona, attorneys there reported an increase in the number of asylum requests granted. From December of 1985 through May of 1986, twenty-six of fifty-three Central American asylum applications were granted, a far higher percentage than the overall rate for the country, and many times higher than the usual 14 percent for Nicaraguans, 2.6 percent for Salvadorans, and 0.9 percent for Guatemalans.[38]

If sanctuary cities are symbolic, and asylum decisions capricious, a bold initiative being taken in southern Texas may be of very real benefit to refugees. Lisa Brodyaga, an immigration attorney, has established a refugee camp in the Rio Grande valley and applied to the United Nations High Commission on Refugees, in Geneva, for both recognition and assistance. The Refugio del Rio Grande, Brodyaga explains, "will accept refugees without regard for nationality, based on the accepted international definitions." The Refugio, which will offer legal and social services to refugees, as well as medical and educational services, will "stay within even the most restrictive parameters of the law as interpreted by the U.S. Government."[39]

In a very real sense, sanctuary is growing beyond itself, beyond the few who help fleeing refugees to enter the country, beyond the handful of churches that actively shelter them, beyond the much larger number of churches and cities and states that offer support, to the still larger, if uncounted, number of Americans who believe that what the sanctuary movement stands for is, if legally wrong, morally right. Against such conviction, political trials are ineffective.

Sanctuary is becoming an effective voice for the reform of refugee policy. No other remedy—not oversight by the Congress, not injunctions by the courts—has so far effected any basic change in the philosophy and direction of our refugee policy. But the refugee policymakers are sensitive to pressures from the public. Historically, public pressures have usually been restrictionist. Sanctuary gives a voice to the admissionists.

The Refugee Act of 1980 was predicated on a fundamental premise, that the needs of the refugees, unlike those of immigrants, require an immediate response. An immigrant can wait, a refugee cannot. Yet, in the years since the act was passed, our refugee policy has become increasingly mired in the unresponsive attitudes that had previously been our practice. There are those who criticize the politicization of our refugee policy, but insist that, rather than break the law, one should work to change that policy. Without such extreme challenges as the sanctuary movement, policy and practice would be highly unlikely ever to change. Indeed, the Justice Department shows every indication of becoming *less* responsive to the needs of asylum seekers in the United States, while overseas, the avowed goal is to "manage down" the numbers of refugees we accept for resettlement. Only pressure from the American public, the kind of pressure that sanctuary is now creating, will succeed in changing policy.

One segment of the sanctuary movement has taken on a political cast because our refugee policy itself is suffused with politics. As long as there is a marked (and even at times avowed) preference for refugees from countries whose regimes we oppose, as long as the asylum claims of refugees from all other countries are dismissed as the simple desire for economic betterment, as long as the refugee system selects politically, some supporters of the rejected will inevitably respond politically. Had the refugee system been depoliticized from the outset, it is unlikely that the sanctuary movement would ever have come into being.

The sanctuary movement forces us to address, as well, a far larger problem, the problem of preventing refugee flows. Sanctuary demands that we do so not by creating barriers to entrance, but by eliminating or reducing the conditions that create refugees. For too long now, we have hidden behind the pretense that only Communist countries produce refugees. When large numbers of people flee from right-wing countries, we say that the cause of their flight is economic. Therefore, we send military support to opponents of the Communist governments and economic support to the right-wing governments. Neither solution has been effective in preventing refugee flows. Our refugee response has been simplistic. Economic hardship is a fact under Communist regimes and motivates many to flee who have never felt persecution. Conversely, right-wing governments with no tradition of democracy are often ruthless, and even "centrist" governments, when their position is unstable, can close their eyes to the human rights of their citizens. Sanctuary forces us to recognize that we, as a nation, have a responsibility not only to those who have been terrorized and uprooted by enemy governments, but also to those who have been terrorized and uprooted by allied governments. At its best, sanctuary does not see the world in red and white, allies and enemies, they and we. Rather, the sanctuary movement demands that we reexamine our motives and our actions toward all refugees.

A reexamination of our refugee policy is called for, but it is necessary to go beyond reexamination to reform. The principles and goals of the Refugee Act have not been well-served by the policies and practices of the present system. Substantive changes must be made.

8 Reflections and Recommendations

Early in the Second World War, it was still possible for Hitler's unwanted to leave Germany. But the right to emigrate is meaningless without the complementary right to be received. The United States responded to the émigrés, as did most other countries, by creating barriers to their entrance.

A ship carrying refugees stopped in Norfolk, Virginia, to refuel before returning to Europe. A delegation of Americans appealed to Cordell Hull, then secretary of state, to grant safe haven to the desperate passengers. Hull listened, then swung around in his chair, pointed to the American flag behind him, and said, "I took an oath to protect the flag and obey the laws of my country and you are asking me to break those laws."[1]

Hull was wrong. America could have admitted those refugees, and many more, without violation, or even alteration, of the Immigration Act. By bureaucratic means, the policy could have been softened. We could have softened our policy, but we lacked the will to do so. Rather than loosen its visa requirements, the State Department tightened them, making admission exceedingly difficult. The department felt its policy was justified because it was "essential to take every precaution at this time to safeguard the best interests of the United States."[2]

It was not, at that time, or in the years that followed, in the interests of the United States to admit refugees on the basis of their need. Instead, we admitted them on the basis of our foreign-policy needs.

In the 1960s, we admitted Cubans for foreign-policy reasons. In the 1970s, our foreign-policy needs coincided with the guilt we felt toward our Southeast Asian allies, and we began a large-scale program to admit Southeast Asians as refugees. Out of this influx of refugees arose the Refugee Act of 1980, which gave legal standing to a moral obligation. The act provided for the admission to the United States of individuals who have a well-founded fear of persecution in their homelands. To those who had lost the protection of their own governments, we offered the aegis of ours.

Yet the Refugee Act in no way changed our admissions policy. We continued to admit those whom we would admit, and to turn away all others. Like the group that pleaded for Hitler's victims, other groups have pleaded for admission of the persecuted, those who fear for their lives. Like Cordell Hull, other government spokesmen have draped their refusals in the flag of law.

We have a just and equitable refugee law. Those who plead on behalf of the desperate have been accused of wanting to expand the law, to stretch it beyond what our elected and appointed officials have sworn to uphold. This is untrue. The law is just and it is equitable; it is the application of the law that is unjust and inequitable.

There have been demands that the Refugee Act be revised. These demands come not from the admissionists, but from the restrictionists, who wish to see the law narrowed and limited. They base their demands on three arguments. First, they insist, Americans have done enough. There is a limit to our compassion, to our capacity to help, and we have reached it. Second, the numbers of unfortunates in the world far exceed our capacity to absorb them. Third, we did not cause the problems and have no obligation to the victims. In counterpoint, some of the admissionists say that our foreign policy caused some of the problems and we are, therefore, obligated to the victims.

But admission of refugees is not a question of charity, or of numbers. It is not even a question of obligation. It is a question of responsibility.

We are responsible not only for those who fight with us against Communism. We are responsible not only for those whose homelands have been destroyed as a result of our intervention. We are responsible, as we were decades ago, because we are morally—and legally—obligated to protect human life.

America was not responsible for the Holocaust; America was responsible for its victims. During the Vietnam War, Rabbi Abraham Joshua Heschel declared, "We are not all guilty, but we are all responsible."[3]

In this country, we need not suspend the law to protect human life. We do need, however, to interpret the law, not on a scale of benefits or guilt, but against a measure of responsibility.

The admission of refugees and asylees is a process heavily freighted with the demands of both foreign and domestic policy. The term *political refugee* has come to mean not so much one who has fled political persecution as one who is recognized as a refugee for political purposes. If the Refugee Act is to be administered equitably and fairly, basic changes will be necessary in several areas. The first step in the reform of our refugee policy must be to establish a just, impartial, and fair basis for determining refugee status and for choosing refugees for admission. The Refugee Admission Priority scale described below should satisfy both those criteria. Second, an independent refugee authority should be established that will adjudicate all requests for refugee status or asylum in a disinterested manner. Third, protection should be provided for all legitimate refugees, including those who cannot be resettled in any third country. Fourth, the Office of the Coordinator for Refugee Affairs, at present a position with little real power, should be given stature and permanence by moving the office to the White House. Finally, in resettlement funding, changes should be made that shift the emphasis from the goal of reducing costs to the goal of best assisting refugees.

Refugees today number in the tens of millions; refugee admissions to the United States are calculated in the tens of thousands. Even if one removes from the refugee roster those who are victims of natural disasters and those who await possible repatriation, there remains a greater number of refugees than the United States is willing to resettle. The Refugee Act clearly defines who may be admitted as a political refugee, but offers no guidelines for choosing among the many who qualify. Instead, the act provides that the president each year report to the Congress "the foreseeable number of refugees who will be in need of resettlement . . . and the anticipated allocation of refugee admissions" for the coming year. In practice, the president has transferred that responsibility to the State Department, which allocates refugee numbers so as to reinforce the department's goals—foreign policy goals.

The actual admission of refugees for the six years from 1980 through 1985 demonstrates that the Department of State has allocated refugee admissions most advantageously. For those six years, the United States resettled 517,411 refugees. However, 495,196 of that number came from ten countries: Vietnam, Cambodia, Laos, the U.S.S.R., Poland, Rumania, Afghanistan, Ethiopia, Iran, and Cuba. During that same six-year period, the United States admitted only eighty-one refugees from South Africa, ninety-six from the Philippines, and none from Haiti or Argentina.[4]

The allocations system for refugees, as it is constituted at present, has led to two major inequities. Refugees from large areas of the world—such as most of the Western Hemisphere— are not even eligible for refugee admission. Since no numbers exist for the admission of a Chilean refugee, for example, he may not even apply for resettlement. Conversely, because the numbers are assigned to each country at the beginning of the fiscal year, and because the bureaucracy deplores an unused allocation, in areas of the world where the demand for resettlement may be less than expected, such as Eastern Europe, the U.S. will offer resettlement to people who have left their countries for reasons other than political persecution, so as to meet the allotted numbers.

The same political bias permeates asylum decisions, so that individuals from just three countries—Iran, Poland, and Nicaragua—win three-quarters of all asylum grants. An asylum applicant from a country allied to the United States has virtually no chance of having his claim decided fairly. Then too, since the Refugee Act sets no limit on the number of asylum claims that may be granted, such grants are shadowed by the fear of numbers. Complicating the situation further is that the refugee approved abroad for resettlement in the United States must wait until the allocations permit him to be admitted. When an individual is granted asylum, he is immediately resettled in this country. Because an award of asylum carries a major advantage that the granting of refugee status does not, the elimination of long and difficult periods of waiting, the standards for asylees have been made stricter than those for refugees. Yet most refugees from the Western Hemisphere have been precluded from applying for refugee resettlement in the United States, and have no choice but to enter this country illegally and ask for asylum.

The present system of allocations addresses none of these difficulties. The reform of the system that will be proposed is intended to alleviate the problems. Two simple postulates should govern the admission of refugees and asylees to the United States. First, there must be responsible limits on the number of refugees admitted. Second, those admitted should be persons whose need for protection is greatest.

The adoption of a Refugee Admission Priority (RAP) scale would serve as a kind of preference system for refugees, enabling the United States to choose from among the worldwide pool of applicants those who are most in need of resettlement. The RAP scale would work in the following manner. A refugee anywhere in the world (including an asylum applicant in the United States or at its borders) who wishes to be resettled in this country would have his case carefully considered by a newly created federal refugee authority. (The refugee authority will be discussed below.) The authority would weigh all evidence of past persecution or the threat of persecution, and the potential risk to the refugee if returned, as well as reports of human-rights conditions in the refugee's country of origin, and would then determine how strongly the refugee is in need of protection and possible resettlement. On this basis, the authority would assign the refugee a number from the Refugee Admission Priority scale.

The highest numbers would indicate that a refugee has probably already suffered persecution and that there is little or no chance of his returning to his homeland. Political prisoners, for example, or an individual who has received a death threat might fall into this category. Numbers in the middle of the scale would signify that no persecution had yet occurred, but that such persecution was quite probable. The lowest numbers would go to refugees who are fleeing generalized violence, refugees who might foreseeably be able to return home at some future time. Applicants whose claims of refugee status were found to be totally unsupported would be given no number whatsoever and might be deported.

Allocations, then, would not be based upon the recommendations of the State Department, and would not be assigned geographically, but would be based on the actual needs of refugees worldwide. In any given year, it would be reported to the Congress precisely how many refugees await resettlement from each point of the RAP scale. For example, one such annual report might show that there are thirty thousand refugees around the world with the highest RAP number, another forty thousand with the next highest, and so on down to the lowest numbers.

Congress would thus have a precise picture of the levels of need among the world's refugees and could determine, with greater fairness, how many ought to be resettled in the United States. Resettlement would be offered first to refugees with the highest RAP numbers, those refugees who most need to be resettled. Refugees with lower RAP numbers would continue to receive the protection they require. For the latter, every effort would be made to secure their safe repatriation or, failing that, to enable them to achieve some measure of economic self-sufficiency.

The RAP scale would ensure that we meet our obligations to refugees equitably and with compassion. No legitimate refugee would be denied protection because he could not be given resettlement. (Protection centers will be discussed later.) Furthermore, those who are not legitimate refugees would not gain entry by being swept in under an allocation for a country, a region, or a group. In any refugee group, a certain proportion will meet the standard set forth in the UN Protocol on Refugees; others will have migrated for a variety of reasons. If we were to admit refugees not by groups, but by need, we would have a responsible way to distinguish among them.

Giving preference to a particular refugee is not foreign to our present refugee practice. The INS has already established, in cooperation with the Department of State, a system of priorities for refugees. The problem with the present system is that it is politically biased. The priorities are only awarded in certain countries. The Select Commission on Immigration and Refugee Policy, in its 1981 report, was more catholic. It recommended that in each year's allocation, "specific numbers be provided for political prisoners, victims of torture, and persons under threat of death, regardless of their geographic origin." Among other reasons it gave for the proposed change was that basing an allocation on "refugee characteristics" would "[i]ncrease flexibility and institute greater equity in allocations, following the intent of the Refugee Act of 1980."[5]

Well-intentioned as the scale might be, the question will inevitably arise of whether such a scale is not, by its nature, inequitable. Are not all refugees, by definition, in need of refuge? The answer of course is yes. The RAP scale does not deny the need of any refugee for protection. Every refugee who qualifies, even those with the lowest numbers, will be assured of safe haven. At the same time, we cannot resettle every refugee. Instead, we would assume the obligation of resettling those refugees who most need resettlement.

How does one assess such a need? There are several factors to consider in the awarding of RAP numbers. The most obvious factor is the degree of probable danger that the refugee faces if he is returned. As the Select Commission recognized, political prisoners, both present and former, people who have been tortured, and people who have received death threats are in the greatest danger. Nearly as great is the danger to individuals in outlawed or persecuted groups. There are also the refugees of special interest to the United States, those to whom we have a strong obligation because they fought with or worked for us.

Other factors would include an assessment of the conditions in the refugee's country of asylum. Certain asylum countries, for example in Southeast Asia, are far less hospitable to refugees than others, making resettlement from those countries more urgent. Additionally, whether the individual has close links to another country or the possibility of resettlement or temporary safe haven elsewhere should be determined. These refugees are less in need of resettlement in this country.[6]

Members of persecuted groups—for example, a Jew in the Soviet Union, a Baha'i in Iran, an ethnic Chinese in Vietnam—could begin with a fixed number on the scale. An individual within that group whose persecution was more severe would receive a higher number. Similarly, a member of a group with strong links to the United States, such as the Hmong, would also begin with a fixed minimum number.[7] It is critical, however, that group determinations never be made *against* a group—

as when, for example, Haitians were determined to be economic migrants. To decide against a group is to violate both the Refugee Act and the UN protocol, which are intended to guarantee every individual the opportunity to have his refugee claim heard and decided without prejudice.

Perhaps the most important benefit of the RAP system would obtain in asylum cases. At present, if the government acknowledges that an individual has been persecuted, it must also grant him asylum and at least temporary resettlement. The fear of mass asylum claims, as from countries in the Western Hemisphere, has led the INS and the State Department to reject in wholesale fashion many well-based claims of persecution. Under the Refugee Admission Priority system, an individual with a well-founded fear of persecution, who has requested asylum, would be given an RAP number and protection, but he would not be offered resettlement until such time as the allocations allowed. An individual whose claim of persecution is patently unfounded would, of course, be given no number at all and would be subject to deportation.

There would not be two applicant pools, but only one that would include both refugees and asylees. Since the only difference between the two groups would be where they ask for asylum, they would be treated as a single entity. An asylum applicant would, along with all other refugees, await resettlement. As is true for refugees, however, an asylum applicant with a low number might not be resettled in the United States.

As the difference between applicants for refugee resettlement and for asylum disappear, so would the necessity of applying a stricter standard to asylum seekers. An asylee would not be given immediate resettlement, but would have to wait, just as the refugee does, for an allocation. Making asylees subject to allocations brings the problem of asylum numbers under control, while affording safe haven to every legitimate asylum seeker fulfills our protocol obligations.

In the debate on asylum policy, there is reason on both sides.

The present system is riddled with inequities, it is prejudicial, and it violates our protocol obligations. On the other hand, the present system can be abused by impatient immigrants and the United States has no control over asylum numbers. Adoption of the RAP scale would alleviate both sets of problems. The Refugee Admission Priority scale, however, can be no more effective and no fairer than the agency that administers it. For that reason, we propose further that a new refugee authority be created.

The two functions of the Immigration and Naturalization Service—service and enforcement—are essentially in conflict with each other. The U.S. Commission on Civil Rights recognized this as far back as 1978, when, in its study of the INS, it wrote:

> In addition to its border enforcement role, INS also administers the immigration laws. Thus, at the same time it is expected to judge issues of human rights objectively, it is also expected to deter entry by undocumented aliens. These two roles are often incompatible and have resulted in the past in emphasis on the enforcement function to the detriment of the other administrative law functions.[8]

INS sees itself as an enforcement or police agency because the public and the Congress demand, and reward, strong enforcement, frequently ignoring the service's other obligations. When the performance of the INS is evaluated, the critical questions are: How many attempted illegal entrants did the INS intercept? How many undocumented workers were arrested? How many drug smugglers? When these numbers rise from year to year, the service believes that its performance is improving. Since no rewards (in the form of additional manpower and funding) accompany increased refugee admissions or additional asylum adjudications, the latter functions must frequently defer to the less-difficult and better-rewarded enforcement activities.

Like any enforcement agency, the INS leans toward action, strength, decisiveness, rather than to deliberation, judgment, discernment. The service works best within a set of unequivocal and unvarying rules. To the INS, every non-American who seeks entry to the United States is an alien, either documented or undocumented. Documented aliens have merely to be processed; undocumented aliens must be incarcerated. It is the practice of incarceration, in fact, that most clearly demonstrates the inappropriateness of asking the INS to make refugee and asylum decisions. Under our system of law, we do not ask the jailers to try the defendant; policemen do not sit on the bench.

Nor does the INS itself feel comfortable in the conflicting roles. The service prefers to enforce the law, not to adjudicate it. For this reason, a number of district directors refuse to receive asylum applications, insisting that the decision be made instead by an immigration judge. The immigration judges themselves have come up through the ranks of INS and are evaluated by the numbers of cases they dispose of, not by the complexity of their cases or the fairness of their decisions. Thus the judges, too, are reluctant to devote to asylum decisions the additional time such decisions require.

Since the INS finds itself ill-at-ease with, and often ill-prepared for, the subtle inquiries necessitated by refugee decisions, it turns for guidance to the State Department. The State Department is far better suited to deliberation than is the INS, and it has current information on human-rights conditions around the world. But the Department of State is no better suited to the making of refugee determinations than the INS. The work of the State Department is to advance the interests of the United States, a concern that has no place in refugee work. The relations of the United States with a foreign country do not matter; the relationship of the refugee himself to that country does. Whether a foreign government is friendly or hostile, whether we wish to maintain, improve, or sever relations, has no bearing on the single question that has weight: was the refugee per-

secuted or threatened with persecution? The human-rights reports of the State Department, on which the INS relies so heavily, have been criticized by human-rights organizations as being
less than forthcoming about the abuses of governments that we
wish not to offend. In the same vein, asylum opinions by the
State Department are reviewed first by the department's appropriate country desk before they are sent on to the INS. All
but overlooked in this process is the asylum seeker.

Since the Second World War, the rights of refugees have been
protected by the UNHCR and the voluntary agencies and, within
the United States, to some extent, by the courts. Any administrative reform must begin with the establishment of an independent refugee authority. Like the UNHCR and the voluntary agencies, the refugee authority must assist those who
are without protection. Like the judiciary, its decisions must be
governed not by political considerations, but by the law.

Many analysts of U.S. refugee policy have recommended the
establishment of just such an independent authority. Refugee
expert John A. Scanlan, just after the passage of the Refugee
Act, recommended to the Select Commission on Immigration
and Refugee Policy that asylum was not an immigration matter
and proposed the creation of an independent board.[9]

In one exhaustive study, Christopher L. Avery compared the
refugee status determination systems of ten countries. For each
of the ten countries, Avery analyzed six components of the
process: initial reception at the border, the refugee's first interview, the role of the decision-maker, available sources of information, a review of the decision, and the role of the UNHCR.
In every one of the six areas, he found the system used by the
United States to be "in significant need of improvement."[10]

T. Alexander Aleinikoff, in his comparative study of political
asylum, concluded by recommending that a federal agency to
adjudicate asylum claims be created, and that it be independent
of both the INS and the State Department. He proposed that
even the advisory role of the State Department be limited to

providing information, when asked, on conditions in foreign countries; the department, Aleinikoff concluded, ought not to render advisory opinions on asylum claims.[11]

In Canada, W. Gunther Plaut, himself a refugee from Nazi Germany as well as a rabbi and an attorney, was asked to study Canada's system for determining refugee status. Central to Rabbi Plaut's recommendations for reform was his insistence that "the determination whether or not a person is a refugee must be made by *an independent body*."[12] Totally autonomous, the refugee board proposed by Plaut would incorporate a number of important features, among them the opportunity for the refugee to present his case orally, and not merely in writing, to the board. Oral hearings were indicated, Plaut felt, for two reasons. First, refugees are often not able to provide written documentation of their claims; the decision-maker, therefore, must be able to evaluate the refugee's credibility. Second, the board would be able to clarify confusing or unexplained points, rather than simply dismissing the case for lack of evidence or inconsistency.

Plaut also recommended that decisions be rendered speedily: he argued that delays of two to five years only prolong the unsettled condition of the refugee, while they encourage those who are not genuine refugees to buy time with frivolous claims. Perhaps the most seminal of Plaut's recommendations is that the refugee hearings ought not to be adversarial. Rather, Plaut felt that the refugee hearing should be "a cooperative inquiry in which claimant, counsel, and the [refugee board] member(s) participate."[13]

Such an approach is diametrically opposed to the present American asylum hearing, in which the refugee must appear before an immigration judge for a deportation or exclusion hearing. Ranged against the refugee and his counsel usually are the INS, which wishes to deny him entry, and the State Department, which advises that his claim to asylum is unfounded.

Under the system being proposed for the United States, when

a refugee appears in a country of first asylum (which might be the United States) and asks for resettlement in this country, he would be placed under the aegis of a voluntary agency. The volag would act on the refugee's behalf, helping him to prepare his claim and obtain documentation, assigning him counsel, providing interpreters, and shepherding him through the entire process. The refugee would be scheduled to appear before the refugee authority as soon as possible, and his appearance there would be in the nature of an inquiry, rather than a hearing. The refugee authority would attempt to elicit from the refugee any information that could bear on his case, and the authority could also call upon human-rights organizations, the UNHCR, and academic specialists, as well as the State Department, to cast light on the refugee's history. The refugee himself would be permitted to see his own dossier.

The major benefit of these reforms would be to restore rationality to the system and to build public confidence in it. If the refugee process is just, fair, and expeditious, there will be no basis for the class action suits that have, to date, been the only recourse against illegality and bias. Moreover, careful and proper decisions will reassure the public that those who are admitted as refugees are not impatient immigrants or economic migrants, but individuals in genuine need of the protection of our government.

When the refugee authority had completed its inquiry, it would assign the refugee an RAP number. Every applicant, even one who had been denied refugee status, would be allowed a single appeal. (Scanlan, in his report, recommended the creation of an independent asylum appeals board. Were the refugee authority to be instituted, such an appeals board would be within its agency.) Like the initial hearing, the appeal would be scheduled as soon as possible. A refugee who receives no number at all—one whose claim was entirely unfounded—would be turned over to the INS for deportation, if in the United States, or to the local authorities, if abroad. All others would be placed in protection centers to await resettlement.

At present, a refugee might find himself in one of three types of facilities. In Southeast Asia, in Europe, and in the Sudan, there are United Nations-administered refugee camps from which refugees are selected for resettlement in third countries, among them the United States. In most of Africa and in Latin America, there are United Nations camps that offer assistance to refugees, but from which the United States accepts no refugees for resettlement. In the United States, refugees who ask for asylum are placed in detention for lengthy periods, while they await deportation.

We do not need to build prisons for refugees; we need to build protection. Just as the proposed system of admissions would eliminate geographic distinctions among refugees, as well as the distinction between refugees and asylum seekers, so too should the protection offered be the same for all refugees. No refugee should ever be placed in detention, but should, instead, be taken to a refugee protection center, there to await either resettlement or eventual repatriation. Any refugee, anywhere in the world, who requires protection, would go to a United Nations refugee center. There, if he wishes to be considered for resettlement in the United States, a voluntary agency would begin the process by which the refugee would establish his claim. In each refugee protection center a branch of the United States refugee authority would hear the claim and assign the refugee a Refugee Admission Priority number. Those with the highest numbers would be resettled first and quickly. Those with low numbers might have little chance of resettlement, but would not be denied the protection of the camp.

Asylum seekers within the United States would be handled slightly differently. An asylum seeker who is legally within the country (as, for example, a defector, or one who is politically displaced) would be permitted to remain here while he pursues his claim. A refugee who entered the country illegally, or one who overstayed his visa, would be taken by a volag to the refugee processing center nearest to his country of origin. There he would apply, like every other refugee, for an RAP number.

Applicants for asylum within the United States would have their cases heard by the refugee authority in this country. No one would be kept in detention, either in the United States or elsewhere. For documented entrants, there would be no need of detention. All others would be considered for resettlement only as long as they remained under the auspices of the refugee processing center.

Placing refugees in the area of the world from which they come would have two desirable effects. First, such placement would encourage other refugees to come to the protection center, rather than directly to the U.S. Second, the refugee would be in an environment that is closer to his origins. Should repatriation not be possible, it is probable that the refugee could more easily be integrated into a neighboring country.

The system will work, however, only as well as the centers are made to work. If the centers are not safe, if the refugees are subject to raids and harassment, if no refugee is ever resettled from the camps to a third country, then they will have become no more than detention camps on foreign soil, and the refugees will shun them, preferring, as many do now, to take their chances underground.

In times of war and emergency, refugee camps have become squalid places: unsafe, unhealthy, and inhumane. Even in less stressful times, without constant vigilance, refugee camps can easily sink below the standards acceptable for human existence. The camps, therefore, must assure at a minimum that all residents are secure and protected, not subject to the terrors of the military or the hostility of the host government. Residents of the camps should be able to resume some semblance of a normal existence. Families should be housed together, with provisions for their privacy. Each refugee should be able to work toward self-sufficiency; children should be in school; adults should be able to labor productively. Most of all, the refugees must never be regarded as a client population, but should have a say in their own governance.

The costs of running these refugee protection centers would undoubtedly be higher than our present contribution to the protection budget of the UNHCR, though possibly lower than the present costs of maintaining asylum seekers in detention within the United States. In the end, however, it is not a question of economic trade-offs, but of achieving a humane and lasting solution when lesser solutions have failed.

As the admission of refugees is a national responsibility, so too, is their resettlement. The Refugee Act recognized that refugees arrive with liabilities and that it is a responsibility of the federal government to help them become productive members of their new society through assistance to the states, localities, and the voluntary agencies which are involved in refugee resettlement.

The present refugee-resettlement system, which has a low political priority, suffers from impermanence, fragmentation, and discontinuities in policies, programs, and funding. The federal government's stress on the "economic self-sufficiency" of the refugee is unidimensional and short-sighted, focusing only on short-term costs while it ignores future gains. Moreover, these short-term costs, although an insignificant part of the federal budget, have a significant influence on the numbers of refugees the United States is willing to admit. The cost of resettlement has become the price of admission.

Resettlement can be improved in a number of ways. First, the Office of the Coordinator for Refugee Affairs should be moved from the State Department to the executive office of the president. Second, the educational and cultural orientation activities in the overseas processing centers and the reception and placement grants should be removed from the jurisdiction of the Department of State and given to the Office of Refugee Resettlement. Third, the present system of funding resettlement, and some of its present rules and regulations, should be changed. And finally, there should be an enlarged use of the matching-grants program.

It has been recommended before that the Office of the United States Coordinator for Refugee Affairs be moved from the State Department to the executive office of the president. As far back as 1981, the Select Commission on Immigration and Refugee Policy and other refugee policy analysts made such a recommendation.[14] Four years later, Ambassador H. Eugene Douglas, who was coordinator longer than either of his predecessors, made a similar recommendation.[15] Physically situated in the executive office, the coordinator would have enhanced visibility, greater prestige, and better access to the president. Moving the coordinator's office to the White House has both symbolic and practical value. Symbolically, the move will demonstrate to the international community that the United States affords a high priority to the problem of refugees and that the United States is willing not only to contribute money and commodities, but also to accept those most in need for admission and resettlement. For too long the national government has responded to the world's refugee needs on a foreign-policy and situational basis. The move would demonstrate to the Congress and the public that the United States has given refugee concerns not only a high political priority, but also a permanent commitment.

The coordinator, if he were perceived as an important person in an important position, attacking a permanent problem (and unfortunately the realities of the world guarantee the permanence of the problem) could make some changes in the operation of the resettlement system. Housing the coordinator in the White House would signal that his function transcends the interests of any one department. No longer perceived as an adjunct of the State Department, the coordinator would be above all departments; thought of as the president's person, he would more readily be perceived as a coordinator, one to be responded to more readily and more readily respected.

The educational and cultural orientation programs in the overseas processing centers and the reception and placement grants should be removed from the jurisdiction of the Department of State and placed within the jurisdiction of the Office of Refugee Resettlement in HHS. The educational and orientation programs are now under the control of the State Department's Bureau for Refugee Programs because the programs are given overseas, but the content of the programs is a function of domestic assistance. With the removal of the State Department from the process of admitting refugees, there will no longer be any basis for State to administer the reception and placement grants. Moreover, the State Department has a limited interest in, and limited capacity to monitor, the volags' reception and placement agreements. State's mission is not domestic, and it is not geared to the development and monitoring of performance standards. ORR, by contrast, is comfortable with this task. The reception and placement grants are integral to resettlement; if they were given to ORR, all domestic resettlement efforts would be under the aegis of a single agency. Fragmentation would be reduced and coordination and oversight of resettlement services and programs would be improved.

Certain specific policies on resettlement in the United States need improvement. States should receive block grants to help them relieve the fiscal drains of impactment and to assist refugees in nonimpacted states. ORR and the states could work out formulae based on such data as the state's refugee population, the rate of welfare dependency, the number of refugee children in school, and other agreed-on indices. Giving the states block grants would enable the states to determine best how the money should be spent. If states and localities know how much money they can expect, they will be better able to tailor their programs to specific state and local conditions and requirements.

The ORR regulation that requires states to spend eighty-five percent of their social-service dollars on employment-related services, such as job training, is arbitrary and should be discontinued. The absolute requirement ignores the varying needs among, and within, the different refugee groups, states, and localities. The rule undermines the states' and localities' abilities to determine the mix of services best needed for their refugee populations. It ignores the role nonemployment services, such as language lessons, health care, and other programs, have in promoting economic self-sufficiency. (An ill refugee either cannot work or is less productive.) The rule also ignores the needs of women who must stay at home, of children in school, of the disabled and the elderly.

The present policy of pushing volags to liquidate refugee transportation loans within thirty-six months should be reversed. The refugee should not have to begin repaying his transportation loan until after thirty-six months, unless, in the judgment of his volag sponsor, his earnings enable him to do so earlier. Requiring the refugee who is trying to start anew to immediately repay a loan places an additional burden on him. InterAction's Committee on Migration could work out a common formula by which a volag would determine when payments should begin for each refugee. Such a formula would take into consideration such factors as net income, age of the children, medical needs, and other variables.

And finally, the matching-grant program should be enlarged. Reagan administration proposals to reduce the already very small program make no sense. The MGP has proven to be successful in reducing cash-assistance use and promoting high employment rates. And most importantly, because of its matching component, there is a private sector commitment in dollars and services. The program stretches resettlement dollars and builds bridges between the resident community and the new Americans.

In recent years, American refugee policymakers have focused on restriction, on how best to discourage, deter, deport the alien, how least to disturb the peace and the pocketbooks of receiving communities. Shifting their goals, refugee planners now advise that it is not admission that most benefits refugees, but assistance abroad. Granted that assistance is needed. Granted also that the United States cannot alone alleviate the world's refugee problem. But we ought not to lose sight of the fact that materially, culturally, intellectually, and spiritually, refugees in the end enrich us more fully than we do them. It is time to begin thinking not of how to shut the gate, but of how most justly to regulate its opening, and how best to help our newest entrants.

As a world power we have an obligation to set a moral standard. We must guard the gate; but guard it also against those inside the walls who plead "compassion fatigue," who fear foreigners, who respect costs more than human lives. We must guard the gate so as to permit entry to those who most need haven and refuge. We must not allow policy to subvert the tradition of welcome. Rhetoric and reality can and should be made one.

Acknowledgments

Because the study of United States refugee admissions and re-settlement policies is in its infancy, research for this book relied largely on primary documents and on interviews with the people who were making refugee policy, carrying it out, or responding to it. The assistance and cooperation we received from federal, state, local, and nongovernmental officials were essential and are greatly appreciated. Career personnel in the Departments of State, Justice, and Health and Human Services gave us generous assistance. Voluntary-agency and sanctuary workers across the country did likewise. To name all those who spoke with us at length, suggested other people to see, and gave us access to their files would fill a small telephone book. We thank them all.

A number of officers in the Departments of State and Justice requested anonymity. We cannot, for that reason, thank them by name, but this book is richer for their assistance. At the Office of Refugee Resettlement, we were helped by Oliver Cromwell, William Eckhof, Linda Gordon, David Haines, Philip Holman, and David Howell. Susan Forbes and Dennis Gallagher of the Refugee Policy Group were always willing to share their expertise and their files. Others in Washington, D.C., who assisted us are Nan Borton, Jesse Bunch, David Ford, Joachim

Henkel, Donald G. Hohl, Norman V. Lourie, Juan Mendez, David North, Brenda Pillors, Anselme Remy, Charles Duryea Smith, Robert Stein, Sue Sullivan, Dale F. (Rick) Swartz, John D. Tenhula, Carolyn Waller, and Roger P. Winter.

Throughout the country and abroad, we were helped by Sheppie Abramowitz, Garret G. Ackerson, Jr., María del Socorro de Aguilar, Deborah E. Anker, Hal Boldin, Mark Brahm, Mayor Kathy Buchoz, Clair Cherkasky, Father Antonio Clark, Jim Corbett, Dan Dale, Lou De Sitter, Jack Elder, Mary Kay Espinosa, Dolores Ferguson, Reverend John Fife, Steven Forester, Sharon Fujii, Linda Garrett, Susan R. Giersbach, Patrick Hughes, Beverly Hunter-Curtis, Lynton Joaquin, Eva Kelly, Kathleen Kelly, Wells C. Klein, Ira J. Kurzban, Cleo Lachapelle, Laurie Lemel, Gary MacEoin, Grady Mangham, Stacey Merkt, Sid L. Mohn, Sister Darlene Nicgorski, Peter L. Nimkoff, Jan Papanek, Lauren Pressman, Juan Rascón, Daniel Remine, Mark Rodriguez, Cecilio L. Ruiz, Jr., Lydia Savoyka, Zdenka Seiner, Colleen Shearer, Charles Sternberg, Sidney Talisman, Patrick A. Taran, Ralph Thomas, Mark Tijima, Monsignor Brian Walsh, Ingrid Walter, Marvin Weidner, Vera Weisz, Rabbi Joseph Weizenbaum, Dennis White, and Ellen and Philip Willis-Conger.

We are particularly grateful to Bruce Leimsidor, who shared his knowledge and his hospitality with us in Vienna. Peter I. Rose, on several occasions, brought us together with leading refugee experts from around the world at Smith College conferences, where some of the ideas in this book were first aired. Gilburt Loescher's contributions, although not always credited, were invaluable.

The coterie of scholars studying refugees is small and cooperative. We were permitted to use, prior to publication, the research findings of Robert L. Bach, John Finck, Robert Kahn, Charles B. Keely, Gilburt Loescher and John A. Scanlan, David Martin, Mario Rivera, Barry N. Stein, and Alex Stepick. Our friends James F. Findlay, John A. Scanlan, Ronald Scheinman, and Arthur B. Stein shared the unenviable task of commenting critically on the manuscript.

Paul Anderson provided valuable research assistance. Sharon Woodmansee performed a wide variety of tasks with intelligence and good humor. At the University of Rhode Island Library, Martha Hills and Michael C. Vocino, Jr., of Government Documents, and Vicki M. Burnett, Sylvia C. Krausse, and Marie S. Rudd, of Interlibrary Loan provided extensive help. Jean Gefrich and Joanne Walsh typed and retyped several versions of the manuscript.

Norman L. Zucker is grateful for a variety of support. Martha Derthick provided a congenial atmosphere for his stay as a Visiting Scholar in the Governmental Studies Program at The Brookings Institution. The Rockefeller Foundation awarded him a Humanities Fellowship in Human Rights. The University of Rhode Island granted him a sabbatical; the University Council for Research awarded him a Faculty Summer Fellowship and research grants; and the College of Arts and Sciences awarded him a Faculty Support Grant. He is also grateful to William R. Ferrante and the Academic Affairs Office for providing funds to help defray the cost of delivering a paper at a refugee symposium at Oxford University, England, and to the late Barry A. Marks for several Dean's Office Awards.

The authors also must thank their children: their son, Sam, who was usually one of the first to read and criticize each chapter, and their daughter, Sara, who was usually one of the last.

John Radziewicz, our editor, understood what we were trying to do from the start; he poked, stroked, and red-penciled to make this a better book.

Kingston, Rhode Island
January 1987

Notes

INTRODUCTION
WHO GOES THERE?

1. Elie Wiesel, "The Refugee," in *Sanctuary: A Resource Guide for Understanding and Participating in the Central American Refugees' Struggle*, ed. Gary MacEoin (New York: Harper & Row, Publishers, Inc., 1985), p. 8.

2. Kane, Parsons & Associates, Inc., *A Survey of Public Attitudes Toward Refugees and Immigrants: Report of Findings, Submitted to: United States Committee for Refugees* (New York: American Council for Nationalities Service, April 1984), pp. 3–5.

3. Edwin Harwood, "Alienation: American Attitudes Toward Immigration," *Public Opinion* vol. 6, no. 3 (June/July, 1983): p. 51.

4. *New York Times*, July 1, 1986, p. 1.

5. United States Commission on Civil Rights, *The Tarnished Golden Door: Civil Rights Issues in Immigration* (Washington, D.C.: U.S. Government Printing Office, September 1980), pp. iii, 130.

CHAPTER ONE
IN SEARCH OF ENTRY: THE REFUGEE IN AMERICAN HISTORY

1. Robert A. Pastor, "Caribbean Emigration and U.S. Immigration Policy: Cross Currents," paper prepared for the confer-

ence, International Relations of the Contemporary Caribbean, sponsored by the Caribbean Institute and Study Center for Latin America (CISCLA) of Inter American University of Puerto Rico, held in San German, Puerto Rico, April 22–23, 1983, p. 7.

2. Howard P. Nash, Jr., *Third Parties in American Politics* (Washington, D.C.: Public Affairs Press, 1959), p. 8.

3. Betty Lee Sung, "Polarity in the Makeup of Chinese Immigrants," in *Sourcebook on the New Immigration: Implications for the United States and the International Community*, ed. Roy Simon Bryce-Laporte (New Brunswick: Transaction Books, 1980), p. 37.

4. E. P. Hutchinson, *Legislative History of American Immigration Policy: 1798–1965* (Philadelphia: University of Pennsylvania Press, 1981), pp. 127–28.

5. Robert A. Divine, *American Immigration Policy, 1924–1952* (New Haven: Yale University Press, 1957), p. 4.

6. John Higham, *Strangers in the Land: Patterns of American Nativism 1860–1925* (New Brunswick: Rutgers University Press, 1955), p. 221.

7. John Higham, *Send These to Me: Jews and Other Immigrants in Urban America* (New York: Atheneum, 1975), p. 52.

8. Divine, pp. 11–13. Divine quotes Laughlin's testimony before the House Committee on Immigration and Naturalization on p. 13.

9. Arthur S. Link, *American Epoch: A History of the United States Since the 1890's* (New York: Alfred A. Knopf, 1956), p. 241.

10. Leonard Dinnerstein and David M. Reimers, *Ethnic Americans: A History of Immigration and Assimilation* (New York: Dodd, Mead & Company, 1975), p. 71.

11. Neil James George, "The Interplay of Domestic and Foreign Considerations in United States Immigration Policy" (Ann Arbor, Michigan: University Microfilms International, 1980), p. 120, Ph.D. dissertation, Case Western Reserve University, June 11, 1975.

12. Staff Report of the Select Commission on Immigration and Refugee Policy, *U.S. Immigration Policy and the National Interest* (Washington, D.C.: April 30, 1981), p. 193.

13. For an understanding of the anti-immigration and nativist forces, see Higham, *Strangers.*

14. Hutchinson, pp. 171–72.

15. George, pp. 121–22.

16. George., p. 122.

17. Richard A. Easterlin, David Ward, William S. Bernard, and Reed Ueda, *Immigration* (Cambridge: The Belknap Press of Harvard University Press, 1980), pp. 94–95.

18. Divine, pp. 6–7.

19. Easterlin et al., p. 97.

20. Saul S. Friedman, *No Haven for the Oppressed: United States Policy Toward Jewish Refugees, 1938–1945* (Detroit: Wayne State University Press, 1973), p. 21.

21. George, p. 150.

22. Divine, p. 18.

23. John George Stoessinger, *The Refugee and the World Community* (Minneapolis: The University of Minnesota Press, 1956), pp. 16–17.

24. Stoessinger, p. 16.

25. Stoessinger, pp. 24–25.

26. Stoessinger, pp. 31–32.

27. Divine, p. 48.

28. George, pp. 153–54.

29. Divine, pp. 62–63.

30. A number of excellent books document America's refusal to open the gate to European refugees. See particularly: David S. Wyman, *Paper Walls: America and the Refugee Crisis 1938–1941* (Amherst, Massachusetts: The University of Massachusetts Press, 1968); David S. Wyman, *The Abandonment of the Jews: America and the Holocaust 1941–1945* (New York: Pantheon Books, 1984); Henry L. Feingold, *The Politics of Rescue: The Roosevelt Administration and the Holocaust, 1938–1945* (New Brunswick: Rutgers University Press, 1970); and Friedman, *No Haven.* For Canada's refusal to accept Jewish refugees, see: Irving Abella and Harold Troper, *None Is Too Many, Canada and the Jews of Europe* (Toronto: Lester & Orpen Dennys Ltd., 1982). For Britain's refusal to accept Jewish refugees, see: Bernard Wasserstein, *Britain and the Jews of Europe 1939–1945* (Oxford: Oxford University Press, 1979). Those who found sanctuary in Shanghai held reunions in 1980 and 1985; see *New York Times,* August 4, 1980, p. 8, and September 4, 1985, p. B2.

31. Julian L. Simon, *How Do Immigrants Affect Us Economically?* (Washington, D.C.: Center for Immigration Policy and Refugee Assistance, Georgetown University, 1985). For Simon's conclusions, see pp. 86–91.

32. Wyman, *Abandonment,* pp. 6–9.

33. Divine, p. 93. Wyman, *Paper Walls,* p. 67.

34. Friedman, pp. 91–93.

35. Barbara McDonald Stewart, *United States Government Policy on Refugees From Nazism: 1933–1940* (New York: Garland Publishing, Inc., 1982), p. 531. Feingold, p. 150. Friedman, p. 94. Wyman, *Paper Walls,* p. 85.

36. Feingold, p. 149.

37. Wyman, *Paper Walls*, p. 169.

38. Wyman, *Paper Walls*, p. 174.

39. Feingold, p. 133.

40. Wyman, *Paper Walls*, p. 173.

41. Wyman, *Abandonment*, p. 127.

42. Feingold, p. 149.

43. *New York Times*, November 19, 1978, p. 13.

44. Stewart, p. 442.

45. For the story of the SS *St. Louis*, see Gordon Thomas and Max Morgan Witts, *Voyage of the Damned* (New York: Stein and Day Publishers, 1974).

46. Feingold, p. 127.

47. Friedman, p. 218.

48. Wyman, *Abandonment*, pp. 266–68. For an interesting account of the free-port tokenism, see: Ruth Gruber, *Haven: The Unknown Story of 1000 World War II Refugees* (New York: Coward-McCann, 1983).

49. Leonard Dinnerstein, *America and the Survivors of the Holocaust* (New York: Columbia University Press, 1982), p. 113.

50. *New York Times*, October 27, 1981, p. C12.

51. Divine, pp. 113–16.

52. Dinnerstein, *America*, pp. 174–75. Jacques Vernant, *The Refugee in the Post-War World* (London: George Allen & Unwin Ltd., 1953), pp. 482–83.

53. Dinnerstein, *America*, p. 182.

54. Richard Ferree Smith, "Refugees," in *The New Immigration, The Annals of the American Academy of Political and Social Science*, ed. Edward P. Hutchinson, vol. 367 (September 1966): p. 45.

55. Divine, p. 137.

56. George, p. 187. Select Commission, p. 208.

57. Vernant, p. 53.

58. Marion T. Bennett, *American Immigration Policies: A History* (Washington, D.C.: Public Affairs Press, 1963), pp. 195–96.

59. U.S., Congress, Senate, Committee on the Judiciary, *Review of U.S. Refugee Resettlement Programs and Policies*, Congressional Research Service, 96th Cong., 2d sess. (Washington, D.C.: U.S. Government Printing Office, 1980), p. 9.

60. *Review of U.S. Refugee Resettlement*, pp. 9–10.

61. Smith, p. 47.

62. *Review of U.S. Refugee Resettlement*, pp. 10–11.

63. Robert L. Bach, "Cubans," in *Refugees in the United States: A Reference Handbook*, ed. David W. Haines (Westport: Connecticut: Greenwood Press, 1985), pp. 77–93.

64. U.S. Department of State, "Position Paper: Cuban Refugee Processing," Meeting of the SIG/RP, July 29, 1985, pp. 1–2.

65. Abba P. Schwartz, *The Open Society* (New York: Simon and Schuster, 1969), p. 217.

66. Schwartz, pp. 112–16.

67. *New York Times*, pp. 1, B5.

68. Schwartz, p. 127.

69. Bach, pp. 83–84. Department of State, "Cuban Refugee Processing," pp. 1–2.

70. Bach, p. 84.

71. U.S., Congress, Senate, *Dangerous Stalemate: Superpower Relations in Autumn 1983*, 98th Cong., 1st sess. (Washington, D.C.: U.S. Government Printing Office, 1983), pp. 42–45.

72. *New York Times*, May 25, 1980, p. 6.

73. Language and Orientation Resource Center, *The Armenians* (Washington, D.C.: Center for Applied Linguistics, September 1981), pp. 2–4.

74. Rita J. Simon, "Soviet Jews," in *Refugees in the United States: A Reference Handbook*, ed. David W. Haines (Westport, Connecticut: Greenwood Press, 1985), p. 181. Abraham Karlikow, "Soviet Jewish Emigration: The Closing Gate," in *World Refugee Survey 1983*, ed. Rosemary E. Tripp (Washington, D.C.: U.S. Committee for Refugees, 1983), pp. 32–35.

75. On the Jackson-Vanik Amendment, see: Paula Stern, *Water's Edge: Domestic Politics and the Making of American Foreign Policy* (Westport, Connecticut: Greenwood Press, 1979); Dan Caldwell, "The Jackson-Vanik Amendment," in *Congress, The Presidency and American Foreign Policy*, ed. John Spanier and Joseph Nogee (New York: Pergamon Press, Inc., 1981), pp. 1–21; William W. Orbach, *The American Movement to Aid Soviet Jews* (Amherst: University of Massachusetts Press, 1979), pp. 122–54.

76. Stephen S. Rosenfeld, "From Washington," *Present Tense* vol. 12, no. 3 (Spring 1985): pp. 56–57.

77. Gail Paradise Kelly, *From Vietnam to America: A Chronicle of the Vietnamese Immigration to the United States* (Boulder: Westview Press, 1977), p. 18.

78. *Review of U.S. Refugee Resettlement*, pp. 28–31.

79. For details on the United States acceptance of Indochinese refugees, see: Gil Loescher and John A. Scanlan, *Calculated Kindness: Refugees and the Half-Open Door, 1945 to the Present* (New York: The Free Press, 1986).

80. U.S., Congress, House of Representatives, Committee on the Judiciary, Hearings Before the Subcommittee on Immigration, Citizenship, and International Law, *Admission of Refugees into the United States*, 95th Cong., 1st sess. (Washington, D.C.: U.S. Government Printing Office: 1977), p. 22.

Chapter Two
The Guarded Gate: Refugee Law and Policy

1. "Text of Reagan's Speech Accepting the Republican Nomination," *New York Times*, July 18, 1980, p. 8.

2. U.S. Department of State, *International Security and Development Cooperation Program*, Special Report no. 116 (April 1984), p. 9.

3. Deborah E. Anker and Michael H. Posner, "The Forty Year Crisis: A Legislative History of the Refugee Act of 1980," *San Diego Law Review*, vol. 19, no. 1 (1981): p. 12.

4. See: Guy S. Goodwin-Gill, *The Refugee in International Law* (Oxford: Oxford University Press: 1983); Peter I. Rose, "The Harbor Masters," in *Research in Social Problems and Public Policy*, vol. 3 (Greenwich, Connecticut: JAI Press Inc., 1984), p. 278.

5. Gil Loescher and John A. Scanlan, *Calculated Kindness: Refugees and America's Half-Open Door, 1945 to the Present* (New York: The Free Press, 1986), p. 214.

6. Arnold H. Leibowitz, "The Refugee Act of 1980: Problems and Congressional Concerns," in *The Global Refugee Problem: U.S. and World Response, The Annals of the American Academy of Political and Social Science*, ed. Gilburt D. Loescher and John A. Scanlan, vol. 467 (May 1983): p. 167. See also: David A. Martin, "The Refugee Act of 1980: Its Past and Future," in *Transnational Legal Problems of Refugees: 1982 Michigan Yearbook of International Legal Studies*, ed. D. Levy (New York: Clark Boardman Company, Ltd., 1982), pp. 91–123.

7. See: Kathleen Newland, *Refugees: The New International Politics of Displacement* (Washington, D.C.: Worldwatch Institute, March 1981), p. 9; Gilbert Jaeger, "The Definition of Refugee: Restrictive Versus Expanding Trends," in *World Refugee Survey 1983*, ed. Rosemary E. Tripp (Washington, D.C.: U.S. Committee for Refugees, 1983), pp. 5–9.

8. Leo Cherne, "Economic Migrants," *New York Times*, October 3, 1981, p. 27.

9. U.S., Congress, Senate, Committee on the Judiciary, *Review of U.S. Refugee Resettlement Programs and Policies*, Congressional Research Service, 96th Cong., 2nd sess. (Washington, D.C.: U.S. Government Printing Office, 1980), p. 13.

10. U.S., Congress, Senate: *The Refugee Act of 1979*, Report No. 96-256, 96th Cong., 1st sess. (Washington, D.C.: U.S. Government Printing Office, 1979), pp. 1–2.

11. Leibowitz, p. 166.

12. Leibowitz, p. 166.

13. G. D. Loescher and John Scanlan, " 'Mass Asylum' and U.S. Policy in the Caribbean," in *The World Today* (London: Royal Institute of International Affairs, October 1981), p. 388.

14. Mario Antonio Rivera, "An Evaluative Analysis of the Carter Administration's Policy toward the Mariel Influx of 1980" (Ph.D. dissertation, Notre Dame University, 1982), p. 6.

15. U.S., Congress, Senate, Committee on the Judiciary, *Caribbean Refugee Crisis: Cubans and Haitians: Hearing*, 96 Cong., 2d sess. (Washington, D.C.: U.S. Government Printing Office, May 12, 1980), pp. 23–24.

16. U.S., Congress, House of Representatives, Permanent Select Committee on Intelligence, Subcommittee on Oversight, *Staff Report: The Cuban Emigres, Was There a U.S. Intelligence Failure?* (Washington, D.C.: U.S. Government Printing Office, 1980), p. 2.

17. *Staff Report*, p. 3.

18. *Staff Report*, p. 3.

19. *Washington Post*, April 27, 1980, p. 1; *New York Times*, April 27, 1980, p. 3.

20. *Washington Post*, April 23, 1980, p. A21.

21. *New York Times*, April 25, 1980, p. 11.

22. *Washington Post*, April 27, 1980, p. 1.

23. *Dallas Times Herald*, April 10, 1980, p. 1.

24. Houston Texas, *Post*, April 10, 1980, p. 1.

25. *Washington Post*, May 4, 1980, p. 1.

26. *Washington Post*, May 6, 1980, p. 1.

27. U.S., Department of State, Bureau of Public Affairs, "President Carter: Cubans Seek Asylum in United States, May 14, 1980" (Washington, D.C.: Current Policy No. 183).

28. *Congressional Record—Senate*, June 6, 1980, pp. S6436–38.

29. "Unanswered Questions: Cuban Refugee Crisis May Prompt Introduction of Specific Legislation," in *Congressional Quarterly Weekly Report* (May 31, 1980), pp. 1496 et seq.

30. *Congressional Record*, p. S6437.

31. *Congressional Record*, p. S6437.

32. Statement by Representative Elizabeth Holtzman, May 13, 1980.

33. U.S., Congress, Senate, Committee on the Judiciary, Subcommittee on Immigration and Refugee Policy, Statement of Thomas O. Enders, Assistant Secretary of State for Inter-American Affairs, *Hearing, United States as a Country of Mass First Asylum*, 97th Cong., 1st sess. (Washington, D.C.: U.S. Government Printing Office, July 31, 1981), p. 3.

34. Rivera, pp. 135–36.

35. Rivera, p. 68.

36. *Miami Herald*, December 14, 1980, p. 32A.

37. *Miami Herald*, November 23, 1981, p. 6a.

38. *Miami Herald*, October 7, 1981, p. 6a.

39. *Washington Post,* May 8, 1980, p. 1.

40. U.S., Congress, House of Representatives, Committee on the Judiciary, *Hearing on Refugee Admissions and Resettlement Program—Fiscal Year 1981,* 96th Cong., 2d sess. (Washington, D.C.: U.S. Government Printing Office, September 24, 1980), pp. 32–33.

41. U.S., Congress, House of Representatives, Committee on the Judiciary, *Hearing: Refugee Admissions Program, Fiscal Year 1986,* 99th Cong., 1st sess. (Washington, D.C.: U.S. Government Printing Office, September 19, 1985); the Fish-Rodino letter may be found on pp. 126–27, the Mazzoli letter on pp. 129–31.

42. U.S., Congress, Senate, Committee on the Judiciary, *Hearing: Annual Refugee Consultation for 1982,* 97th Cong., 1st sess. (Washington, D.C.: U.S. Government Printing Office, September 22, 1981), pp. 26–27.

43. U.S., Department of State, Office of the U.S. Coordinator for Refugee Affairs, "Proposed Refugee Admissions and Allocations for Fiscal Year 1986" (Washington, D.C.: September, 1985), p. 9.

44. U.S., Congress, House of Representatives, *The Refugee Act of 1979,* Report No. 96-608, 96th Cong., 1st sess. (Washington, D.C.: U.S. Government Printing Office, 1979), p. 13.

45. Dennis Gallagher, Susan Forbes, and Patricia Weiss Fagen, *Of Special Humanitarian Concern: U.S. Refugee Admissions Since Passage of the Refugee Act* (Washington, D.C.: Refugee Policy Group, September 1985), p. 30; this is an excellent analysis of the workings of the Refugee Act.

46. *Of Special Humanitarian Concern,* p. 32. Department of State, Bureau for Refugee Programs, *World Refugee Report* (September 1986), p. 103.

47. "Proposed Refugee Admissions, 1986," p. 19.

48. "Proposed Refugee Admissions, 1986," pp. 20–21.

49. "Proposed Refugee Admissions, 1986," p. 21.

50. *World Refugee Report*, 1986, p. 38. *New York Times*, August 8, 1986, p. 7.

51. Department of State, Bureau for Refugee Programs, "Report of the Indochinese Refugee Panel," Department of State Publication 9476 (April 1986), pp. 20–21.

52. Department of State, Bureau for Refugee Programs, *World Refugee Report* (September 1985), p. 36.

53. "Indochinese Refugee Panel," p. 22.

54. *Of Special Humanitarian Concern*, p. 49.

55. *Calculated Kindness*, p. 199.

56. Robert P. DeVecchi, "Determining Refugee Status: Towards a Coherent Policy," in *World Refugee Survey 1983*, ed. Rosemary E. Tripp (Washington, D.C.: U.S. Committee for Refugees, 1983), p. 13.

57. U.S., Department of Justice, Immigration and Naturalization Service, *Worldwide Guidelines for Overseas Refugee Processing* (Washington, D.C.: August 1983), p. iii.

58. U.S., Congress, Senate, Committee on Foreign Relations, *United States Processing of Khmer Refugees*, 98th Cong., 2d sess. (Washington, D.C.: U.S. Government Printing Office, 1984), p. 32.

59. *Processing of Khmer Refugees*, p. 28.

60. Stephen Golub, *Looking for Phantoms: Flaws in the Khmer Rouge Screening Process* (Washington, D.C.: United States Committee For Refugees, April 1986), p. 3.

61. U.S., Congress, House of Representatives, Committee on Foreign Affairs, Subcommittee on Asian and Pacific Affairs, *Hearing: Cambodian Refugees in Southeast Asia*, 99th Cong., 1st sess. (Washington, D.C.: U.S. Government Printing Office, July 31, 1985), p. 139. *Refugee Reports*, vol. VIII, no. 4 (April 17, 1987), pp. 5–6.

62. Patricia Weiss Fagen, "U.S. Refugee Admissions: Processing in Europe," *Migration News*, no. 4 (October–December 1985), pp. 3–4, 8–10.

63. *Calculated Kindness*, p. 125.

64. "U.S. Refugee Admissions Ceilings and Actual Arrivals FY 75–86" (Table), *Refugee Reports*, vol. 7, no. 10 (October 10, 1986): p. 3.

65. U.S., Department of State, Office of the U.S. Coordinator for Refugee Affairs, "Proposed Refugee Admissions and Allocations for Fiscal Year 1987" (Washington, D.C: September 1986), p. 7.

66. "Proposed Refugee Admissions, 1987," p. 36. U.S. Department of State, Bureau of Public Affairs, "U.S. Refugee Policy and Programs for FY 1987," Current Policy No. 872, p. 1.

67. U.S. Department of State, Bureau of Public Affairs, Robert Funseth, "Refugee Resettlement in the Heartland of America," Current Policy No. 847, p. 2.

68. "Indochinese Refugee Panel," p. 1.

69. "Indochinese Refugee Panel," p. 18.

70. "Indochinese Refugee Panel," p. 18.

71. U.S., Congress, House of Representatives, Committee on the Judiciary, Subcommittee on Immigration, Refugees, and International Law, *Refugee Assistance Extension Act of 1985*, 99th Cong., 1st sess. (April 17, 1985), p. 39.

72. "Proposed Refugee Admissions, 1987," p. 9.

73. *New York Times*, September 21, 1986, p. E24; September 27, 1986, p. 6.

74. *New York Times*, April 17, 1986, p. 1.

75. *New York Times*, March 30, 1986, p. 1.

76. U.S. Committee for Refugees, *World Refugee Survey: 1985 in Review*, ed. Virginia L. Hamilton (Washington, D.C.: U.S. Committee for Refugees, 1986), p. 40.

77. *New York Times*, March 13, 1985, p. A5.

78. United States General Accounting Office, *Immigration—Marriage Fraud: Control in Most Countries Surveyed Stronger Than in U.S.* GAO/GGD-86-104BR (July 1986), pp. 1–2.

79. *New York Times*, December 2, 1985, p. A1.

CHAPTER THREE
THE STRANGER WITHIN THE GATE: RESETTLEMENT

1. U.S., Department of State, Bureau for Refugee Programs, *World Refugee Report: September 1985* (Washington, D.C.: 1985), pp. 19–33.

2. Barry N. Stein, "Refugee Resettlement Programs and Techniques," in *U.S. Immigration Policy and the National Interest, Appendix C to the Staff Report of the Select Commission on Immigration and Refugee Policy, Papers on Refugees* (Washington, D.C.: 1981), pp. 383–85.

3. Stein, p. 383.

4. *Working with Refugees: Proceedings of the Simon S. Shargo Memorial Conference*, ed. Peter I. Rose (New York: Center for Migration Studies, 1986), p. 63.

5. For the story of HIAS to the mid-1950s see Mark Wischnitzer, *Visas to Freedom: The History of HIAS* (Cleveland and New York: The World Publishing Company, 1956).

6. For a more detailed account of the history, structure, operational modes, interrelationships, and problems of the volags, see the authors' "The Voluntary Agencies and Refugee Resettlement in the United States: A Report to the Select Commission on Immigration and Refugee Policy," in *U.S. Immigration Policy and the National Interest, Appendix C*, pp. 509–96; "Refugee Resettlement in the United States: The Role of

the Voluntary Agencies," in *Transnational Legal Problems of Refugees: 1982 Michigan Yearbook of International Legal Studies*, ed. D. M. Levy (New York: Clark Boardman Company, Ltd., 1982), pp. 155–77.

7. Norman L. Zucker, "Refugee Resettlement in the United States: Policy and Problems," in *The Global Refugee Problem: U.S. and World Response, The Annals of the American Academy of Political and Social Science*, ed. Gilburt D. Loescher and John A. Scanlan, vol. 467 (May 1983): pp. 172–86.

8. For an understanding of the various refugee programs see: Julia Vadala Taft, David S. North, and David A. Ford, *Refugee Resettlement in the U.S.: Time for a New Focus* (Washington, D.C.: New TransCentury Foundation, 1979), pp. 51–64; the quotation may be found on p. 55.

9. "Current Procedures for Refugee Resettlement," Briefing Paper, Miami Regional Hearing, December 4, 1979, no author, prepared for the Select Commission on Immigration and Refugee Policy, p. 4.

10. Thomas D. Boswell, "The Cuban-Americans," in *Ethnicity in Contemporary America: A Geographical Appraisal*, ed. Jesse O. McKee (Dubuque, Iowa: Kendall/Hunt Publishing Company, 1985), p. 95. Taft et al., pp. 65–91. Briefing Paper, Miami.

11. James A. Elgass, "Federal Funding of United States Refugee Resettlement Before and After the Refugee Act of 1980," in *Transnational Legal Problems*, p. 183.

12. For an excellent analysis of the matching-grant program, see: Timothy J. Eckels, Lawrence S. Lewin, David S. North, and Danguole J. Spakevicius, *A Portrait in Diversity: Voluntary Agencies and the Office of Refugee Resettlement Matching Grant Program* (Washington, D.C.: Lewin and Associates, Inc., New TransCentury Foundation, and National Opinion Research Center, September 1982), p. 20 for statistics on funds awarded, and *passim*. U.S. Department of Health and Human Services, Social Security Administration, Office of Refugee Resettle-

ment, *Report to Congress: Refugee Resettlement Program* (Washington, D.C.: January 31, 1986), pp. 49–51.

13. U.S., Congress, Senate, Committee on the Judiciary, *Review of U.S. Refugee Resettlement Programs and Policies*, 96th Cong., 2nd sess. (Washington, D.C.: U.S. Government Printing Office, 1980), pp. 35–36.

14. Refugee Act of 1980, Public Law 96-212, 94 Stat. 102 (1980). *Indochinese Refugee Reports*, vol. 1, no. 23 (March 11, 1980): p. 11.

15. Office of the U.S. Coordinator for Refugee Affairs, *Proposed Refugee Admissions and Allocations for Fiscal Year 1986: Report to the Congress for Fiscal Year 1986* (Washington, D.C.: September 1985), pp. 19–22. U.S., Congress, House of Representatives, Committee on the Judiciary, Hearings before the Subcommittee on Immigration, Refugees, and International Law, *Refugee Assistance Extension Act of 1985*, 99th Cong., 1st sess. (Washington, D.C.: U.S. Government Printing Office, 1985), pp. 186–88.

16. U.S. General Accounting Office, *Report to the Secretary, Department of State: Stricter Enforcement of Refugees' Transportation Loan Repayments Needed* (Washington, D.C.: GAO/NDIAD-85-86, March 8, 1985), p. 2.

17. Newspaper coverage of the conflict between the Vietnamese and the Texans was extensive. One of the best accounts was Ross Milloy, "Vietnam Fallout in a Texas Town," *New York Times Magazine*, April 6, 1980, pp. 39 et seq.

18. *New York Times*, June 11, 1978, p. 26.

19. Boswell, pp. 95, 101–03.

20. Susan Forbes, *Residency Patterns and Secondary Migration of Refugees: A State of the Information Paper* (Washington, D.C.: Refugee Policy Group, April 1984), p. 7.

21. *Refugee Resettlement Program, 1986*, p. 92.

22. Forbes, *Residency Patterns*, p. 26. *Refugee Resettlement Program, 1986*, p. 90. *New York Times*, July 20, 1983, p. C1.

23. Forbes, *Residency Patterns*, p. 23.

24. *New York Times*, February 1, 1981, p. 20.

25. Berkeley Planning Associates, *An Evaluation of the Favorable Alternatives Sites Project: Final Report, Executive Summary* (Washington, D.C.: Department of Health and Human Services, Office of Refugee Resettlement, May 15, 1984), pp. 3, 7.

26. Refugee Policy Group, *The Chicago Project: An Alternative Resettlement Approach* (Washington, D.C.: United States Catholic Conference, n.d.), pp. 40–41.

27. John Finck, "Voting with Their Feet: Secondary Migrations of Indochinese Refugees," unpublished consultant's report to the Rhode Island Office of Refugee Resettlement (Cranston, Rhode Island: February 20, 1982).

28. David W. Haines, ed., *Refugees in the United States: A Reference Handbook* (Westport, Connecticut: Greenwood Press, 1985), p. 39.

29. U.S. General Accounting Office, Report to the Chairman, Committee on the Judiciary United States Senate and Committee of the Judiciary, House of Representatives, *Refugee Program: Initial Reception and Placement of New Arrivals Should Be Improved* (Washington, D.C.: GAO/NSIAD-86-69, April 1986), pp. 3, 72–77.

30. For an interesting analysis of the assumptions on which the volags' resettlement role rests, see: David S. North, Lawrence S. Lewin, Jennifer R. Wagner, *Kaleidoscope: The Resettlement of Refugees in the United States by the Voluntary Agencies* (Washington, D.C.: New TransCentury Foundation, Lewin and Associates, and National Opinion Research Center, February 1982), pp. 21–22.

31. See the authors' *The Voluntary Agencies*.

32. Lewin Associates, Inc., Refugee Policy Group, Berkeley Planning Associates, *Assessment of the MAA Incentive Grant Initiative: Final Report Prepared For Office of Refugee Resettlement* (U.S. Department of Health and Human Services, January 1986), pp. 2–11, 1.1, 6.12–6.14.

33. For Etzioni's point of view, see: Amitai Etzioni, "Refugee Resettlement: the Infighting in Washington," *The Public Interest* vol. 65 (Fall 1981), pp. 15–29; the quotation may be found on p. 20.

34. For Palmieri's rejoinder to Etzioni, see: Victor H. Palmieri, "The Refugees: What 'Infighting'?" *The Public Interest*, vol. 68 (Summer 1982), pp. 88–90; the quotation may be found on p. 89.

35. *Refugee Reports*, vol. III, no. 8 (March 26, 1982): p. 5.

36. U.S., Congress, House of Representatives, Committee on the Judiciary, Hearings, Subcommittee on Immigration, Refugees, and International Law, *Refugee Assistance*, 98th Cong., 1st sess. (Washington, D.C.: U.S. Government Printing Office, 1983), pp. 128–29.

37. U.S. General Accounting Office, "Analysis of Selected Operations of the Office of the U.S. Coordinator for Refugee Affairs," GAO/NSIAD-83-45 (August 1983), pp. 7–8.

38. Dennis Gallagher, Susan Forbes, and Patricia Weiss Fagen, *Of Special Humanitarian Concern: U.S. Refugee Admissions Since Passage of the Refugee Act* (Washington, D.C.: Refugee Policy Group, September 1985), pp. 67–68.

39. *Refugee Reports*, vol. VI, no. 6 (June 21, 1985): p. 9.

40. U.S., Congress, Senate, Committee on the Judiciary, Subcommittee on Immigration and Refugee Policy, *Annual Refugee Consultation*, 99th Cong., 1st sess. (Washington, D.C.: U.S. Government Printing Office), p. 35.

41. Refugee Policy Group, *Refugee Issues: Current Status and Directions for the Future* (Washington, D.C.: Refugee Policy Group,

1983), pp. 23–27. For a discussion of the various state refugee programs, see: Paul J. Strand and Woodrow Jones, Jr., *Indochinese Refugees in America: Problems of Adaptation and Assimilation* (Durham, North Carolina: Duke University Press, 1985), pp. 45–68.

42. Wells C. Klein, "Testimony on Refugee Resettlement," in *U.S. Immigration Policy and the National Interest: Appendix C*, pp. 242–44.

43. Boswell, p. 112.

44. Peter I. Rose, "Asian Americans: From Pariahs to Paragons," in *Clamor At The Gates: The New American Immigration*, ed. Nathan Glazer (San Francisco: Institute for Contemporary Studies Press, 1985), p. 210.

45. Alice C. Andrews and G. Harry Stopp, Jr., "The Indochinese," in *Ethnicity in Contemporary America*, p. 238.

46. *Refugee Reports*, vol. VI, no. 10 (October 11, 1985): pp. 1–3. *New York Times*, July 22, 1985, p. 12.

47. *New York Times*, June 16, 1980, p. B3; April 30, p. C8; March 25, 1986, p. C3; December 8, 1986, p. B20.

48. Rita J. Simon, "Soviet Jews," in *Refugees in the United States*, pp. 190, 192.

49. *Working with Refugees*, p. 96.

50. *Refugee Assistance Extension Act*, p. 134.

51. Strand, p. 68.

52. U.S., Congress, Senate, Committee on the Judiciary, *U.S. Refugee Programs*, 96th Cong., 2d sess. (April 17, 1980), p. 154; the costs given here are less than one-quarter of one percent.

CHAPTER FOUR
BREACHING THE GATE: THE QUESTION OF ASYLUM

1. U.S., Congress, House of Representatives, Committee on Foreign Affairs, Subcommittee on State Department Organization and Foreign Operations, *Attempted Defection by Lithuanian Seaman Simas Kudirka, Hearings*, 91st Cong., 2d sess. (December 3, 1970), p. 2.

2. Press conference, *New York Times*, December 11, 1970, p. 32.

3. 37 *Federal Register* 3447 (1972).

4. U.S., Congress, House of Representatives, Committe on Foreign Affairs, Subcommittee on State Department Organization and Foreign Operations, *Attempted Defection by Lithuanian Seaman Simas Kudirka, Report* (February 4, 1971), p. 5.

5. *Attempted Defection, Hearings*, p. 5.

6. *New York Times*, November 2, 1985, p. 31.

7. *New York Times*, December 13, 1972, p. 4.

8. Letter signed by U.S. Representatives Bella Abzug, Charles Rangel, and eight others, *New York Times*, August 23, 1973, p. 36.

9. David A. Martin, "The Refugee Act of 1980: Its Past and Future," in *Transnational Legal Problems of Refugees: 1982 Michigan Yearbook of International Legal Studies*, ed. D. M. Levy (New York: Clark Boardman Company, Ltd., 1982), p. 109.

10. INS, *Asylum Adjudications: An Evolving Concept for the Immigration and Naturalization Service* (Washington, D.C.: June 1982), p. i.

11. Immigration and Naturalization Service, unpublished tabulations. Figures for 1980–1985 in "Report to the Congress: Refugee Resettlement Program," U.S. Department of Health and Human Services, January 31, 1986, pp. A-12, A-13.

Figures for 1986 in *Refugee Reports*, vol. VII, no. ii, November 14, 1986, p. 20.

12. Immigration and Naturalization Service, p. A-12. *Refugee Reports*, p. 20.

13. Robert Pear, "U.S. Studies Plan to Ease Access to Asylum for Poles and Others," *New York Times*, March 30, 1986, p. 1.

14. *New York Times*, April 17, 1986, p. 1.

15. Interview with Dolores Ferguson, attorney, Father Moriarty Center, San Francisco, California, August 6, 1984.

16. *New York Times*, October 4, 1982, p. 1.

17. *Providence Sunday Journal*, August 14, 1983, p. 3; August 29, 1982, p. 1.

18. Affidavit of Prosper Bayard, submitted in *Haitian Refugee Center v. Civiletti.*

19. See Lawrence H. Fuchs, "What Has Gone Wrong with American Refugee Policy," *Brandeis Review* vol. 3 (Fall 1982): pp. 4–8; Christopher T. Hansen, "Behind the Paper Curtain: Asylum Policy versus Asylum Practice," *New York University Review of Law and Social Change*, vol. VII, no. 1 (Winter 1978): pp. 107–41; G. D. Loescher and John Scanlan, "U.S. Foreign Policy and Its Impact on Refugee Flow from Haiti," Occasional Paper, New York Research Program in InterAmerican Affairs (New York: New York University, April 27, 1984); John A. Scanlan, "Who is a Refugee? Procedures and Burden of Proof under the Refugee Act of 1980," in *In Defense of the Alien V: Refugees and Territorial Asylum* (New York: Center for Migration Studies, 1983), pp. 23–37; John A. Scanlan and Gilburt D. Loescher, "Mass Asylum, Human Rights, and U.S. Foreign Policy," in *Political Science Quarterly* vol. 97 (Spring 1982): pp. 39–56; Association of the Bar of the City of New York, Committee on Immigration and Nationality Law, "The Future of Political Asylum in the United States" (April 1984). For a discussion of the Reagan administration's views on

authoritarian versus totalitarian governments, see: H. Eugene Douglas, "The Problem of Refugees in a Strategic Perspective," *Strategic Review* (Fall 1982): pp. 11–20; Jeane Kirkpatrick, "Dictatorships and Double Standards," *Commentary*, vol. 68, no. 5 (November 1979): pp. 34–35; Ernest W. Lefever, "The Trivialization of Human Rights," *Policy Review*, vol. 3 (Winter 1978), pp. 11–26.

20. President Reagan's address on Central America, reprinted in *New York Times*, May 10, 1984, p. 16.

21. *New York Times*, January 5, 1985, p. 10.

22. *New York Times*, August 15, 1984, p. 3.

23. *New York Times*, November 10, 1985, p. 18; November 15, 1985, p. 18.

24. Telephone interview with former INS attorney, August 11, 1980.

25. U.S., Congress, Senate, Committee on the Judiciary, *Annual Refugee Consultation for 1982, Hearing*, 97th Cong., 1st sess. (September 22, 1981), pp. 26–27.

26. U.S., General Accounting Office, Report to the Congress of the United States, "Central American Refugees: Regional Conditions and Prospects and Potential Impact on the United States" (July 20, 1984), p. 5.

27. *Refugee Reports*, vol. VI, no. 10 (October 11, 1985).

28. GAO, "Central American Refugees."

29. *Refugee Reports*, vol. VII, no. 10 (October 10, 1986), pp. 3–4.

30. Trial testimony of Todd Greentree, in *Nuñez v. Boldin*, reprinted in U.S., Congress, Senate, Committee on the Judiciary, Subcommittee on Immigration and Refugee Policy, *Fiscal Year 1985 Budget Authorization of Immigration and Naturalization Service, Hearing*, 98th Cong., 2d sess. (March 13, 1984), pp. 71–72.

31. *New York Times*, January 28, 1978, p. 22; January 29, 1978, p. 43; February 4, 1978, p. 34; February 18, 1978, p. 12.

32. See *Matter of 29 Afghans*, INS exclusion proceedings, August 10, 1982; *Matter of Salim*, INS exclusion proceedings, September 29, 1982.

33. INS, *Worldwide Guidelines*, p. 11.

34. INS, *Worldwide Guidelines*, p. 11.

35. See Patricia Weiss Fagen, "Applying for Political Asylum in New York: Law, Policy and Administrative Practice," New York Research Program in Inter-American Affairs (New York: New York University, April 27, 1984); Deborah Anker, "Refugees/Asylum," unpublished paper.

36. INS, *Asylum Adjudications*, p. 53.

37. INS, *Worldwide Guidelines*, p. 23.

38. Martin, p. 112.

39. INS, *Asylum Adjudications*, p. 32.

40. Fagen, pp. 12, 13, 16.

41. U.S. Department of State, *Country Reports on the World Refugee Situation, Report to the Congress* (Washington, D.C.: U.S. Government Printing Office, September 1981).

42. U.S. Department of State, *Country Reports on the World Refugee Situation, Report to the Congress for Fiscal Year 1985*, p. 80.

43. Department of State, *Country Reports, 1985*.

44. *New York Times*, August 5, 1983, p. 23.

45. *Miami News*, June 3, 1982, p. 5a.

46. The Refugee Act of 1980, Sec. 101 (b).

47. See HR 2816, the House version of the bill to amend the INA, in which the word *humanitarian* does not appear.

48. Atle Grahl-Madsen, "Refugees in Orbit—Some Constructive Proposals," *AWR Bulletin*, No. 3 (1979), p. 119.

49. See INS, *Asylum Adjudications*; GAO, *Detention Policies Affecting Haitian Nationals* (June 16, 1983).

50. *New York Times*, February 3, 1985, p. 30.

51. Connie Bruck, "Springing the Haitians," *The American Lawyer* (September 1982): p. 39.

52. Reagan Task Force, Issue Paper, p. 1.

53. Reagan Task Force, p. 2.

54. *Miami Herald*, July 20, 1981, p. 1a.

55. Interview with Hal Boldin, district director, Immigration and Naturalization Service, Harlingen, Texas, August 16, 1984.

56. Site visit, Krome Camp, Florida, August 1982.

57. Site visit, Los Fresnos, Texas, August 1984.

58. *New York Times*, November 29, 1981, p. E19:1.

59. Affidavits before Patrick Hughes, attorney, May 1985, Laredo, Texas.

60. *Congressional Record*, February 11, 1982, p. S. 827.

61. *Orantes-Hernandez v. Smith*, 541 F. Supp. 351 (C.D. Cal. 1982).

62. INS statistics reprinted in *Central American Refugee Report* (Dublin, California: St. Raymond's Church, May 1984), p. 3.

63. Gary MacEoin and Nivita Riley, *No Promised Land: American Refugee Policies and the Rule of Law* (Boston: Oxfam, 1982), p. 41.

64. *New York Times*, September 30, 1981, p. 3.

65. Reagan Task Force, p. 5.

66. Reagan Task Force, p. 5.

67. U.S., Congress, House of Representatives, Committee on the Judiciary, Subcommittee on Immigration, Refugees, and International Law, *Immigration Reform, Hearings,* 97th Cong., 1st sess. (October 28, 1981). Statement by Alan C. Nelson, deputy commissioner, INS, p. 580.

68. *New York Times,* October 1, 1981, p. 34.

69. U.S. Department of State, Bureau of Public Affairs, "U.S. Assistance to Haiti," Special Report No. 141 (February, 1986), p. 2.

70. *Haitian Refugee Center v. Civiletti,* Final Order Granting Relief, pp. 13, 25.

71. *Hearings,* October 28, 1981, p. 581.

72. See: INS, *Asylum Adjudications;* Fagen, "Applying for Political Asylum in New York"; Arthur Helton, "Statement on the Refugee Eligibility Standard," before the Subcommittee on Immigration of the Committee on the Judiciary, U.S. House of Representatives, June 7, 1983; T. Alexander Aleinikoff, "Aliens, Due Process and 'Communities Ties': A Response to Martin," *University of Pittsburgh Law Review,* vol. 44, no. 237 (1983): p. 239.

73. INS, *Asylum Adjudications,* p. i.

74. INS, *Asylum Adjudications,* p. 21.

75. INS, *Asylum Adjudications,* p. 22.

76. Fagen, "Applying for Political Asylum in New York," p. 54.

77. INS, *Asylum Adjudications,* p. 26.

78. U.S., Congress, Senate, Subcommittee on Immigration and Refugee Policy, Committee on the Judiciary, *Immigration Reform and Control Act: Hearings,* 98th Cong., 1st sess. (February 24, 1983), p. 11.

79. Aleinikoff, p. 252.

CHAPTER FIVE
THE REJECTED: THE REMEDIES OF LAW

1. *New York Times*, June 15, 1981, p. B6.

2. U.S., Congress, House of Representatives, Subcommittee on International Operations, Committee on Foreign Affairs, *The Refugee Act of 1979, Hearings*, 96th Cong., 1st sess. (September 19, 1979), prepared statement of Leonard M. Britten, deputy superintendent of schools, Dade County Public Schools, Miami, Florida.

3. Select Commission on Immigration and Refugee Policy, Consultation on Refugee-Related Issues, Washington, D.C., June 4, 1980, statement by Peter Nimkoff.

4. *Sannon v. United States*, 631 F. 2d 1247 (5th Cir. 1980).

5. For the text of the agreement, see: *The Haitians in Miami: Current Immigration Practices in the United States*, a joint report of the Lawyers Committee for International Human Rights, the International Human Rights Law Group, and the Washington Committee for Civil Rights Under Law, Alien Rights Law Project (December 1978). For a discussion of Haitian asylum claims, see: Naomi Flink Zucker, "The Haitians Versus the United States: The Courts as Last Resort" in *The Global Refugee Problem: U.S. and World Response, The Annals of the American Academy of Political and Social Science*, ed. Gilburt D. Loescher and John A. Scanlan, vol. 467 (May 1983): p. 151.

6. INS, Internal Memorandum of Conference on Haitian Undocumented Aliens, July 17, 1978.

7. INS, Notes, Meeting with the Deputy Commissioner Mario T. Noto, August 16, 1978.

8. INS, Internal Memorandum, July 17, 1978.

9. INS, Internal Memorandum, July 17, 1978.

10. INS, Notes, Meeting of August 16, 1978.

11. Letter from Mario T. Noto, deputy commissioner, INS, to Michael J. Egan, associate attorney general, Department of Justice, August 25, 1978.

12. INS, Notes, Meeting of August 16, 1978.

13. Peter L. Nimkoff, telephone interview, June 24, 1980.

14. The discussion of the Haitian Program is drawn from a number of sources, particularly: testimony in *Haitian Refugee Center v. Civiletti*, 503 F. Supp. 442 (S.D. Fla. 1980); "The Haitians in Miami: Current Immigration Practices,"; interviews with attorneys in the Justice Department and attorneys for the Haitians.

15. Interview with attorney Steven Forester, September 1, 1981.

16. *Haitian Refugee Center v. Civiletti*, pp. 1726–27.

17. Sworn affidavit of Lucien Calixte, April 18, 1979.

18. See: *Orantes-Hernandez v. Smith*, 541 F. Supp. 351 (C.D. Cal. 1982); *Nuñez v. Boldin*, 537 F. Supp. 578 (S.D. Tex. 1982).

19. Telephone interview with former Justice Department attorney, August 11, 1980.

20. Peter L. Nimkoff, telephone interview, June 24, 1980.

21. Temporary restraining order issued by U.S. District Judge James Lawrence King, January 1979.

22. Evidence introduced by plaintiffs in *Haitian Refugee Center v. Civiletti*.

23. Evidence introduced by plaintiffs in *Haitian Refugee Center v. Civiletti*.

24. *Haitian Refugee Center v. Civiletti*, pp. 2234–44.

25. *Haitian Refugee Center v. Civiletti*, p. 1587.

26. *Haitian Refugee Center v. Civiletti*, p. 1859.

27. Memorandum, State Department Study Team on Haitian Refugees (June 19, 1979), p. 1.

28. Memorandum, State Department Study Team, p. 12.

29. For an excellent and unbiased discussion of life in Haiti, see Brian Weinstein and Aaron Segal, *Haiti: Political Failures, Cultural Successes* (New York: Praeger, 1984; co-published with Hoover Institution Press, Stanford University, Stanford, California). For the period under discussion here, the Organization of American States has published a full report on human rights in Haiti, including conditions in Haiti's prisons. The report was reprinted in U.S., Senate, Committee on the Judiciary, *Caribbean Refugee Crisis; Cubans and Haitians, Hearing*, 96th Cong., 2d sess. (May 12, 1980). The volume also contains a report by the Lawyers Committee for International Human Rights on "Violations of Human Rights in Haiti, 1980."

30. Weinstein and Segal, p. 56.

31. *Haitian Refugee Center v. Civiletti*, p. 90.

32. *Haitian Refugee Center v. Civiletti*, p. 93.

33. *Haitian Refugee Center v. Civiletti*, p. 24.

34. Michelle Bogre, "Haitian Refugees: (Haiti's) Missing Persons," *Migration Today*, vol. VII, no. 4 (September 1979): pp. 9–11.

35. *Haitian Refugee Center v. Civiletti*, Final Order Granting Relief (July 2, 1980), p. 451.

36. *Haitian Refugee Center v. Civiletti*, Final Order, p. 162.

37. *Miami News*, November 13, 1980, p. 2A.

38. *Miami News*, November 10, 1980, p. 1A; *Miami Herald*, November 11, 1980, p. 2B.

39. Steven Forester.

40. U.S., Congress, House of Representatives, Committee on Appropriations, Subcommittee on Commerce, Justice, State, Ju-

diciary, and Related Agencies and the Administration of Justice, Statement by Arthur C. Helton, Lawyers Committee for International Human Rights, on the Haitian Detention Program, July 14, 1982.

41. Ira J. Kurzban, "The Haitian Saga," *Immigration Newsletter*, vol. 11, no. 6 (November-December 1982): p. 15.

42. *Miami News*, July 7, 1981, p. 5A.

43. Steven Forester.

44. Interviews with Steven Forester and Vera Weisz, attorneys with the Haitian Refugee Center, Inc., September 1, 1981.

45. Remarks of Judge Alcee Hastings, Federal District Court, Miami, Florida, September 2, 1981.

46. Connie Bruck, "Springing the Haitians," *The American Lawyer* (September 1982), p. 38.

47. *Louis v. Nelson*, F. Supp. 881, S.D. Fla., 1982.

48. *Miami News*, April 20, 1982, p. 10A.

49. *Miami Herald*, April 27, 1982, p. 2B.

50. *Louis v. Nelson* No. 81-1260-CIV-EPS, S.D. Fla.

51. *Jean v. Nelson*, 711 F. 2d, 11th Cir., 1983.

52. *New York Times*, April 14, 1983, p. 24:1.

53. *Jean v. Nelson*, F 2d, 11th Cir., No. 82-5772, February 28, 1984.

54. Press conference, March 1, 1984, quoted in *Interpreter Releases*, vol. 61, no. 9 (March 5, 1984): pp. 164–65.

55. *New York Times*, April 27, 1984, p. 4:3.

56. *Federal Register*, vol. 47, no. 132 (July 9, 1982): pp. 30044–45.

57. Department of Justice, Immigration and Naturalization Service, Office of Congressional and Public Affairs, information

provided in letter to Education and Public Welfare Division, Congressional Research Service, Library of Congress, n.d.

58. *Nuñez v. Boldin*, 537 F. Supp. 578, S.D. Tex. 1982, quoted in *Interpreter Releases*, vol. 59, no. 33 (August 27, 1982), p. 551.

59. *Nuñez v. Boldin*.

CHAPTER SIX
THE UNPROTECTED: THE REMEDIES OF CONGRESS

1. United Nations, Executive Committee of the High Commissioner's Programme, "Note on International Protection" (A/AC. 96/660), July 23, 1985, p. 10.

2. America's Watch, *Little Hope: Human Rights in Guatemala, January 1984 to January 1985* (New York: Americas Watch Committee, 1985), p. 2.

3. *Little Hope*, p. 2.

4. The Watch Committees, the Lawyers Committee for Human Rights, *The Reagan Administration's Record on Human Rights in 1986* (New York, Washington, D.C.: February 1987), p. 60.

5. See: Alan K. Simpson, "We Can't Allow All Salvadorans to Stay," *Washington Post*, July 10, 1984, p. 13; Richard D. Lamm, "The U.S. Accepts Too Many Refugees," *New York Times*, December 15, 1985, p. E23.

6. U.S., Congress, Senate, Subcommittee on Immigration and Refugee Policy, Committee on the Judiciary, *Annual Refugee Consultation: Hearing*, 98th Cong., 1st sess., September 26, 1983, statement of Edward J. Derwinski, counselor, U.S. Department of State, p. 26.

7. *Annual Refugee Consultation: Hearing*, September 26, 1983, Statement of Attorney General William French Smith, p. 14.

8. Linda S. Peterson, U.S. Bureau of the Census, *Central American Refugee Flows: 1978 to 1983*, mimeo, p. 19.

9. Peterson, p. 22.

10. Peterson, p. 23.

11. Peterson, p. 23.

12. Peterson, p. 24.

13. See: Gil Loescher, *Humanitarianism and Politics in Central America*, The Helen Kellogg Institute for International Studies, University of Notre Dame, Working Paper #86 (November 1986).

14. Letter from Guido Fernandez, *New York Times*, December 8, 1986, p. 26.

15. First introduced in 1983, as H.R. 4447.

16. House of Representatives, Resolution 107, introduced in 1985.

17. U.S., Congress, House of Representatives, Subcommittee on Census and Population, Committee on Post Office and Civil Service, *Central American Refugees: Hearing*, 99th Cong., 1st sess. (June 27, 1985), p. 131.

18. U.S., Congress, House of Representatives, Subcommittee on Immigration, Refugees, and International Law, Committee on the Judiciary, *Temporary Suspension of Deportation of Certain Aliens: Hearing*, 98th Cong., 2d sess. (April 12, 1984), response by Elliott Abrams, p. 109.

19. U.S., Congress, Senate, Committee on the Judiciary, Subcommittee on Immigration and Refugee Policy, *Fiscal Year 1985 Budget Authorization of Immigration and Naturalization Service: Hearing*, 98th Cong., 2d sess. (March 13, 1984), pp. 26–27.

20. Laura J. Dietrich, Deputy Assistant Secretary, U.S. Department of State, "Chronological List of Grants of 'Extended Voluntary Departure,' " November 25, 1985.

21. Dietrich.

22. INS, *Asylum Adjudications: An Evolving Concept and Responsibility for the Immigration and Naturalization Service* (June 1982), pp. 67–68.

23. Dietrich.

24. *Asylum Adjudications.*

25. See, for example, prepared statement of Elliott Abrams, assistant secretary of state for human rights and humanitarian affairs, before the Committee on the Judiciary, Subcommittee on Immigration and Refugee Policy, U.S. Senate, Washington, D.C., April 22, 1985.

26. Prepared statement of Laura J. Dietrich, deputy assistant secretary of state for human rights and humanitarian affairs, before the Committee on the Judiciary and Subcommittee on Immigration, Refugees, and International Law, United States House of Representatives, Washington, D.C., November 7, 1985, p. 8. (Elliott Abrams made an identical statement to the Senate Subcommittee on Immigration and Refugee Policy of the Committee on the Judiciary on April 22, 1985.)

27. Correspondence from Laura Dietrich, November 25, 1985.

28. UNHCR, *Refugees*, no. 23 (November 1985), statement of Duke Austin, INS press officer, p. 29.

29. Linda S. Peterson, U.S. Bureau of the Census, *Central American Refugee Flows: 1978 to 1983*, p. 53.

30. William Stanley, "Economic Migrants or Refugees from Violence? A Time Series Analysis of Salvadoran Migration to the United States" (March 1985).

31. Stanley, pp. 12–13.

32. Stanley, p. 24.

33. Stanley, p. 24.

34. Robert Kahn, *Other People's Blood: Central American Refugees in the United States*, unpublished manuscript.

35. Kahn.

36. Kahn.

37. Kahn.

38. Kahn.

39. See: *New York Times*, December 25, 1985, p. 17; November 29, 1985, p. 26; October 8, 1985, p. B4; November 5, 1985, p. 28.

40. *New York Times*, September 7, 1986, p. 50.

41. UN, "Note on International Protection."

42. *Refugee Reports*, vol. VII, no. 12 (December 12, 1986), p. 14.

43. Leonel Gomez, "The Politics of Salvadoran Refugees," in *In Defense of the Alien, Vol. VII, Immigration Reform and Refugee Policy Developments*, ed. Lydio F. Tomasi (New York: Center for Migration Studies, 1985), pp. 151–55.

44. Affidavit of David Patterson, May 15, 1985, Maricopa City, Arizona; translation by Patterson.

45. Letter from Ruth Ann Myers, INS district director, Phoenix, Arizona, May 20, 1985.

46. Interview with Mark Rodreguez, Centro de Asuntos Migratorios, Los Angeles, California, August 15, 1984.

47. Letter from Elliott Abrams to Representative Barney Frank, January 2, 1985.

48. *Temporary Suspension of Deportation of Certain Aliens*, p. 132.

49. Political Asylum Project of the American Civil Liberties Union, "The Fates of Salvadorans Expelled from the United States" (September 5, 1984), p. 9.

50. "The Fates of Salvadorans," pp 9–10.

51. Yvonne Dilling with Ingrid Rogers, *In Search of Refuge* (Scottsdale, Pennsylvania: Herald Press, 1984), pp. 46–47.

52. U.S., Congress, House of Representatives, Committee on Foreign Affairs, Subcommittee on Inter-American Affairs, *Salvadoran Refugees in Honduras: Hearing*, 97th Cong., 1st sess. (December 17, 1981), p. 5.

53. *New York Times*, July 10, 1986, p. 10.

54. UNHCR, *Refugees*, no. 6 (June 1984), p. 10.

55. See: *New York Times*, September 5, 1985, p. 3; September 7, 1985, p. 4; September 8, 1985, p. E5.

56. Patricia Weiss Fagen, "Refugees and Displaced Persons in Central America" (Washington, D.C.: Refugee Policy Group, March 1984).

57. Comptroller General, Report to the Congress, *Central American Refugees: Regional Conditions and Prospects and Potential Impact on the United States* (Washington, D.C.: GAO: July 20, 1984), pp. 8–10.

58. UNHCR, *Refugees*, no. 20 (August 1985).

59. *Central American Refugees, Regional Conditions and Prospects*, p. 45.

60. *Central American Refugees, Regional Conditions and Prospects*, p. 46.

CHAPTER SEVEN
THE UNPROTECTED: THE REMEDIES OF CONSCIENCE

1. *Washington Post*, July 10, 1980, p. 10.

2. Gary McEoin, "A Brief History of the Sanctuary Movement," in *Sanctuary: A Resource Guide*, ed. Gary McEoin (San Francisco: Harper and Row, 1985), p. 17.

3. McEoin, p. 18.

4. Interview with Jim Corbett, Tucson, Arizona, June 5, 1985.

5. McEoin, pp. 19–20.

6. Interview with John Fife, Tucson, Arizona, June 4, 1985.

7. Interview with Joseph Weizenbaum, Tucson, Arizona, June 5, 1985.

8. *¡Basta!*, October 1985, p. 7.

9. *¡Basta!*, October 1985, p. 8.

10. Letter from Jim Corbett, December 26, 1984 (reprinted in *¡Basta!*, January 1985).

11. Jim Corbett, interview.

12. Renney Golden and Michael McConnell, *Sanctuary: The New Underground Railroad* (Maryknoll, New York: Orbis Books, 1986), p. 52.

13. *¡Basta!*, February 1986, p. 22.

14. Jim Corbett, interview.

15. "The Current Practice of the Tucson Refugee Support Group Concerning Refugee Placements and Relays," May 1, 1985, mimeo.

16. Jim Corbett, interview.

17. Interview with Darlene Nicgorski, June 7, 1985.

18. *El Diario California*, Berkeley, California, May 5, 1986.

19. *Christian Century*, April 27, 1983, p. 387.

20. Speech by A. Bates Butler, III, presented at the annual meeting, Presbytery de Cristo, January 25, 1985.

21. "The Sanctuary Movement: A Time for Reappraisal," *Religion and Democracy*, Newsletter of the Institute for Religion and Democracy, March 1985, p. 1.

22. *Religion and Democracy*, p. 1.

23. Rael Jean Isaacs, "Sanctuary Scoundrels," *The American Spectator*, vol. 19 (April 1986), p. 23.

24. Letter from William H. Ball, III, July 31, 1985.

25. Interview with Jack Elder, San Benito, Texas, August 15, 1984.

26. Interview with Hal Boldin, Harlingen, Texas, August 16, 1984.

27. Statement by Eugene Fitzpatrick, deputy district director INS, Phoenix, Arizona, in *Phoenix Gazette*, August 2, 1983.

28. Interview with Mary Kay Espinoza, Nogales, Arizona, June 6, 1985.

29. Nat Hentoff, "Snoops in the Pews," *The Progressive*, vol. 49, no. 8 (August 1985), p. 26.

30. Ignatius Bau, *This Ground is Holy: Church Sanctuary and Central American Refugees* (New York: Paulist Press, 1985), p. 81.

31. *Migration Today*, vol. XIII, no. 5 (1985), p. 5.

32. *New York Times*, July 13, 1986, p. 7.

33. Letter from Thomas Hammarberg, secretary general, Amnesty International, to Mr. Robert J. Hirsch, June 16, 1986; reprinted in *¡Basta!*, September, 1986.

34. Amnesty International press release, quoted in Rio Grande Defense Committee Newsletter, May 1987, p. 4.

35. Interview with Antonio Clark, Nogales, Arizona, June 6, 1985.

36. *New York Times*, May 27, 1986, p. B2.

37. *New York Times*, July 15, 1986, p. B16.

38. Newsletter of the Central American Refugee Project, Phoenix, Arizona, May and June, 1986.

39. Central American Refugee Defense Fund *Newsletter*, March 1986, p. 6.

CHAPTER EIGHT
REFLECTIONS AND RECOMMENDATIONS

1. Francisco Isgro, "Quo Vadis Asylum," *Migration Today*, vol. XII, no. 3 (1984), p. 39.

2. David Wyman, *Paper Walls: America and the Refugee Crisis 1938–1941* (Amherst: University of Massachusetts Press, 1968), p. 174.

3. Quoted in: Marshall T. Meyer, "The International Struggle for Human Rights," in *Sanctuary: A Resource Guide*, ed. Gary McEoin (San Francisco: Harper & Row, 1985), p. 131.

4. Figures supplied by INS, in: U.S. Department of Health and Human Services, Social Security Administration, Office of Refugee Resettlement, *Report to the Congress: Refugee Resettlement Programs* (Washington, D.C.), January 31, 1986, p. A11.

5. *U.S. Immigration Policy and the National Interest, The Final Report and Recommendations of the Select Commission on Immigration and Refugee Policy*, March 1, 1981, p. 164.

6. See David A. Martin, "The Refugee Act of 1980: Its Past and Future," in *Transnational Legal Problems of Refugees, 1982 Michigan Yearbook of International Legal Studies* ed. D. Levy (New York: Clark Boardman Company, Ltd., 1982), p. 105.

7. For a discussion of group profiles, see: John A. Scanlan, "Who Is a Refugee? Procedures and Burden of Proof under the Refugee Act of 1980," speech delivered at Center for Migration Studies Fifth Annual National Legal Conference on Immigration and Refugee Policy, Washington, D.C., March 25, 1982. See also: Scanlan, "The Refugee Act of 1980," in *U.S. Immigration Policy and the National Interest, Appendix C to the Staff Report of the Select Commission on Immigration and Refugee Policy, Papers on Refugees* (Washington, D.C.: 1981), pp. 60–62, 66–68.

8. U.S. Commission on Civil Rights, *The Tarnished Golden Door: Civil Rights Issues in Immigration* (Washington, D.C.: U.S. Government Printing Office, September 1980).

9. For a full discussion of the asylum board, see Scanlan, "The Refugee Act of 1980."

10. "Refugee Status Decision-Making: The Systems of Ten Countries," *Stanford Journal of International Law*, vol. XIX, no. 2 (Summer 1983), p. 353.

11. "Political Asylum in the Federal Republic of Germany and the Republic of France: Lessons for the United States," *Journal of Law Reform*, vol. 17, no. 2 (Winter 1984), pp. 183–241.

12. *Refugee Determination in Canada*, a Report to the Honourable Flora MacDonald, minister of employment and immigration, April 17, 1985, p. 20.

13. *Refugee Determination in Canada*, p. 123. David Martin has similarly suggested that if it is fair, the asylum process does not have to be adversarial; "Due Process and Membership in the National Community: Political Asylum and Beyond," in *University of Pittsburgh Law Review*, vol. 44, no. 165 (1983), p. 221.

14. *U.S. Immigration Policy and the National Interest: The Final Report and Recommendations of the Select Commission on Immigration and Refugee Policy to the Congress and the President of the United States.* (Washington, D.C., March 1, 1981), p. 197. Norman L. Zucker and Naomi F. Zucker, *The Voluntary Agencies and Refugee Resettlement in the United States: A Report to the Select Commission on Immigration and Refugee Policy in U.S. Immigration Policy and the National Interest Appendix C to the Staff Report*, p. 572.

15. U.S., Congress, House of Representatives, Committee on the Judiciary, Subcommittee on Immigration, Refugees, and International Law, Hearings, *Refugee Assistance Extension Act of 1985*, 99th Cong., 1st sess. (Washington, D.C.: U.S. Government Printing Office, 1985), p. 28.

Index